CHINA'S GALAXY EMPIRE

WEALTH, POWER, WAR, AND PEACE IN THE NEW CHINESE CENTURY

John Keane and Baogang He

OXFORD
UNIVERSITY PRESS

Oxford University Press is a department of the University of Oxford. It furthers the University's objective of excellence in research, scholarship, and education by publishing worldwide. Oxford is a registered trade mark of Oxford University Press in the UK and certain other countries.

Published in the United States of America by Oxford University Press
198 Madison Avenue, New York, NY 10016, United States of America.

© Oxford University Press 2024

All rights reserved. No part of this publication may be reproduced, stored in a retrieval system, or transmitted, in any form or by any means, without the prior permission in writing of Oxford University Press, or as expressly permitted by law, by license, or under terms agreed with the appropriate reproduction rights organization. Inquiries concerning reproduction outside the scope of the above should be sent to the Rights Department, Oxford University Press, at the address above.

You must not circulate this work in any other form
and you must impose this same condition on any acquirer.

Library of Congress Cataloging-in-Publication Data
Names: Keane, John, 1949– author. | He, Baogang, author.
Title: China's galaxy empire : wealth, power, war, and peace in the new Chinese century / John Keane and Baogang He.
Description: New York, NY : Oxford University Press, [2024] | Includes bibliographical references and index. |
Contents: The idea of empire—Belt and Road—A galaxy empire—Land and sea—Maritime and air power?—Empire and communications—Tencent—State capitalism—Middle classes—Building across borders—Finance matters—A ruling ideology? The poetics of power—Chairman of everything?—Abusive power—Phantom democracy—Domestic troubles—Faraway troubles—Borderlands—Ecological civilisation—Cold peace, hot war.
Identifiers: LCCN 2023058803 | ISBN 9780197629116 (hardback) | ISBN 9780197629130 (epub) | ISBN 9780197629147 (ebook)
Subjects: LCSH: China—Foreign relations—21st century. | China—Foreign economic relations. | Yi dai yi lu (Initiative : China)
Classification: LCC DS779.47 .K43 2024 | DDC 327.51—dc23/eng/20240126
LC record available at https://lccn.loc.gov/2023058803

DOI: 10.1093/oso/9780197629116.001.0001

Printed by Sheridan Books, Inc., United States of America

Contents

Acknowledgements vii

China's New Empire Defined 1
    The Idea of Empire 9
    Belt and Road 20
    A Galaxy Empire 29
    Land and Sea 35
    Maritime and Air Power? 41
    Empire and Communications 47
    Tencent 55
    State Capitalism 58
    Middle Classes 64
    Building across Borders 75
    Finance Matters 85

Resilience, Resistance 95
    A Ruling Ideology? 96
    Chairman of Everything? 106
    Abusive Power 115
    Phantom Democracy 122
    Domestic Troubles 131
    Faraway Troubles 135
    Borderlands 152
    Ecological Civilization 160
    Cold Peace, Hot War 178

Further Reading 205
Index 209

Acknowledgements

Warmest thanks to David McBride, Executive Editor at Oxford University Press, for his unwavering support, wise advice, and skilful interventions in guiding this book towards production. Special thanks as well to project editor Mary Funchion and project manager Kavitha Yuvaraj for their invaluable and always generous professional support. Richard Isomaki expertly copy edited the manuscript. Baogang He contributed raw materials to five sections of this book: 'Belt and Road', 'Building across Borders', 'Finance Matters', 'Chairman of Everything?', and 'Cold Peace, Hot War'. I acknowledge his assistance. For their help with locating references and sharing their views about the significance of this book's unorthodox interpretation of what's conventionally called 'the rise of China', I offer my thanks to Tom Barber, Jude Guan, Kai He, Jorge Heine, Weiyi Hu, Ling Li, Christian Mueller, Wolfgang Petritsch, Stuart Rollo, Hans Dietmar Schweisgut, Ivan Vejvoda, Xuanzi Xu, Keping Yu, Yancheng Zhang, Shaofeng Zhao, and two anonymous readers.

John Keane
Sydney
October 2023

China's New Empire Defined

When the winds of change blow, Chinese people say, some people build walls while others build windmills. The wisdom is ancient but its fresh significance is daily confirmed by an epochal shift of global importance: a transition from faltering attempts to maintain America's greatness to China's return, after two centuries of subjugation, to global prominence.

The spinning shadows of windmills are everywhere on the world's walls. China is now the largest trading country and owner of half the world's patents. It has outflanked bodies such as the International Monetary Fund and the World Bank to become the largest global creditor. Measured by total assets, the four biggest banks in the world are Chinese. China is the EU's main trading partner in goods. It is the principal investor and trader in the world's most sizeable free trade zone in Africa, where a million Chinese employees are engaged in 'cross-border workforce cooperation' in many thousands of infrastructure projects. In Latin America, for the first time in two centuries of independence from the Spanish Empire and de facto economic and military dependence upon the United States, countries such as Chile, Peru, Ecuador, Uruguay, and Colombia are actively drawing closer to China. China-backed trade agreements, tariff reductions, and import-export deals are the new fashion. Investments, extraction of mineral resources, and trade in agricultural products jumped tenfold in the first two decades of this century. China is now the largest buyer of the region's iron, lithium, copper, oil, and soybeans.

In the Pacific Islands region, China's Belt and Road Initiative financing of wharves, roads and airports, and other strategically important infrastructure projects has set the pace and fuelled geostrategic rivalries with a host of countries scrambling to match Chinese efforts with belated initiatives sporting names such as the 'Pacific Pledge' (United States), 'Pacific Reset' (New Zealand), 'Pacific Uplift' (United Kingdom), and 'Pacific Elevation' (Indonesia). Shanghai has meanwhile overtaken Hong Kong, Tokyo, and Singapore to become the most important financial hub of the Asian region. For millions of 'sea turtles', students and professionals studying abroad, and for the country's four-hundred-million-strong middle classes more generally, global expansion became a way of life during recent decades. Burgeoning state investment in higher education—a nearly tenfold increase during the past two decades—has produced more STEM (science, technology, engineering, and mathematics) graduates than India, the United States, Japan, Germany, France, Italy, the UK, and Canada combined. After experiencing low levels of life expectancy like those in the West a century ago, life expectancy in China (77.1 years in 2022 compared with 51 in 1962, according to World Bank data)[1] has surged beyond levels in the United States, where healthy life expectancy at birth is declining.

China is home to the Alibaba Group, China Telecom, and several other of the world's largest telecommunications and e-commerce companies. Despite US-led efforts to 'decouple' from China by applying tariff penalties and boycotting its products and services, the country continues to attract upstream investment from major foreign companies such as Airbus SE, Tesla, and German chemicals giant BASF. The People's Liberation Army is now the globe's largest standing army, with two million troops backed by an expanding nuclear arsenal, more submarines than any other power, sophisticated military hardware, and a commitment to a new model of hybrid warfare bent on confusing, wearing down, or frightening enemies without firing a single shot. Little wonder that outside politicians and diplomats wax eloquent about China as 'an extraordinarily important country' (former Chilean foreign minister Roberto Ampuero), see it

---

1. 'Life Expectancy at Birth, Total (Years)—China', *World Bank* (2022), https://data.worldbank.org/indicator/SP.DYN.LE00.IN?locations=CN (accessed September 21, 2023).

as 'a pillar of international cooperation and multilateralism' (UN secretary general António Guterres) and as a 'gigantic fact in our lives' (former prime minister Boris Johnson), or predict that China 'will define this century' (Ursula von der Leyen, president of the European Commission). And little surprise that more nervous politicians and many journalists, diplomats, and military leaders express growing concerns about the 'rise' and 'expansion' of China and its role as an 'existential threat' to the West; or that a president of the United States draws the conclusion that his country must 'grow and expand' in order to stop China from becoming 'the leading country in the world, the wealthiest country in the world, and the most powerful country in the world'.[2]

The global trends are unmistakably clear, and they may be thought to confirm another old Chinese saying, that east winds break up frosts, but the reality is that strange prejudices, bitter disputes, and conflicting predictions are clouding recognition of their long-term significance. The gigantic fact of China is proving controversial. There are Western observers who endorse China's superior 'strength, resilience and dynamism' and praise its 'remarkable ability to reinvent itself in a manner that no other country or civilization has succeeded in doing'.[3] By contrast, other observers are already sure that China's rise to global prominence is unsustainable, or that forecasts of its global triumph are grossly exaggerated. With the fate of the Soviet Union in mind, still others are sure it's a 'peaking power' heading inevitably for economic and political collapse. There are China watchers who claim that the CCP regime is turning its back on the world, or who instead forecast that a troubled real estate sector, youth unemployment, an aging population, and general economic stagnation are symptoms of the country's imminent downfall. Several have been

---

2. 'Remarks by President Biden in Press Conference', *The White House*, March 25, 2021, https://www.whitehouse.gov/briefing-room/speeches-remarks/2021/03/25/remarks-by-briden-in-press-conference/.
3. Martin Jacques, 'Why [the] Chinese System Can Offer More Choices Than Western Democracy', *Global Times*, May 10, 2021.

saying that for decades.[4] At the opposite end of the political spectrum are pundits who consider China a durable and dangerous global juggernaut. There are plenty of warnings reminiscent of the old caution attributed to Napoleon: 'There sleeps China! God pity us if she wakes. Let her sleep!'[5] Or the similar counsel of the Silesian-born, nineteenth-century scientist, geographer, and traveller Ferdinand von Richthofen, who denounced the 'suicidal attempt to modernise China' because 'with its massive force of labour China would crush the rest of the world'.[6] In their ranks are military-intellectual complex warriors convinced of the need for 'force multiplication' and 'integrated deterrence' against an awakening 'totalitarian' China. The priority, they say, is to get tough with an uppity Beijing through trade wars, hardline diplomacy, and military brinkmanship in the Taiwan Strait or elsewhere in the South China Sea. The lead architect of the United States' National Defense Strategy (2018) recommends blocking the spread of Chinese power in the Asia Pacific region by means of a Washington-backed 'antihegemonic coalition' committed to strategies of 'denial' and possible engagement in 'a systemic regional war'.[7] Still others believe that a lengthy period of fraught rivalry—a new Cold War peppered with leaked intelligence scandals, rising military tensions, and spy balloon dramas—is upon us. Not to be overlooked are the ironists who think that things are going to end badly for the opponents of China. They predict that rough-tongued and cack-handed efforts to rejuvenate a militarily overstretched, fiscally overburdened, and socially fractious America will unintentionally make China great again.

---

4. See, for example, Minxin Pei, *From Reform to Revolution: The Demise of Communism in China and the Soviet Union* (Cambridge, MA, 1994); *China's Trapped Transition: The Limits of Developmental Autocracy* (Cambridge, MA, 2006); and *China's Crony Capitalism: The Dynamics of Regime Decay* (Cambridge, MA, 2016).
5. William T. Ellis, 'China in Revolution', *The Outlook*, October 28, 1911, p. 458.
6. Ferdinand von Richthofen, *Tagebücher aus China* (Berlin, 1907), vol. 1, p. 144. Special thanks to Dr. Christian Mueller for this reference.
7. Elbridge A. Colby, *The Strategy of Denial: American Defense in an Age of Great Power Conflict* (New Haven, 2021).

Like bellows to a fire, outsider misrepresentations of China are everywhere inflaming public controversies and stoking political divisions. The cause of cool, calm, and clarity—championed by this book—is not helped by some views currently circulating inside China. When asked about their country's emergent global role, scholars, journalists, diplomats, and Party officials often reply by noting that Deng Xiaoping's era of 'crossing rivers by feeling for stones' has been replaced by Xi Jinping's fearless 'crossings of oceans'. They say that China is no longer a fearful or bashful power. At home and abroad, it is becoming a self-confident force for economic growth, good governance, and moral improvement. The same observers pay tribute to China's global role as an engine of poverty reduction and environmental protection. Some scholars give things a twist and take things further. They calculate that China's new-found global role is to foster peaceful cooperation among the states and peoples of our planet in harmony with the ancient Confucian principle of 'all under one heaven' (*tiān xià*).[8] Central to this commitment, they say, is that China is an expanding power, potentially a big power (*dà guó*), whose rulers are the latter-day sons of heaven and fathers of the people, upon whom heaven has bestowed the right and duty to rule, and to rule wisely. The inference is that China's leaders don't indulge their own interests at the expense of the needs and interests of the peoples of the world. Otherwise, they know they will be punished: failing to behave benevolently on the world stage by stirring up political disorder or war will jeopardize their 'mandate of heaven' (*tiān míng*). That is why, say some international relations scholars, China is a force for global stability and peace. 'The old order is rapidly disintegrating, and strongman politics is once again popular among the world's major powers', writes a prominent scholar who is well connected to high circles of government. He adds: 'Behind the collapse or reestablishment of any international order is blood and fire, violence and war'.

8. Zhao Tingyang, *The System of All-under-Heaven: A Philosophical Introduction to a World Institution* (Nanjing, 2005); in Chinese.

That is why China refuses to bring wolves into the house of global arrangements. 'The reason why a great power is a great power, or is regarded as a great power, lies not in its ability to challenge the old order, much less in its ability to wage war, but in its responsibility for promoting and maintaining international peace'.[9] Other international relations scholars say that their country is proving to be an example of 'humane authority to improve the world'. It shows that true political leadership is founded not on force but morality, the ability of a government to improve the lives of its people at home while building its global reputation for strategic integrity and effectiveness. China is also described as a 'civilizational state' (*wén míng guó jiā*). By that phrase is meant that China does more than combine the key features of its five-thousand-year-old civilization (*wén míng*: literally the self-improvement of people through seeing the light) with a huge modern state. By acknowledging and warmly embracing the diversity of the world's cultures, it is a beneficent force, not 'a source of global conflict'. The rise of China signals a shift from a 'vertical world order' dominated by Western wealth and ideas towards a more equal 'horizontal order' of states. China is 'an engine driving the advance of human civilizations'—a civilizing state that displays respect for other states and refrains from interfering in their affairs.[10]

Note the silence of these Chinese scholars about empire (more about this shortly) and its flip side: their acquired taste for state-centred, so-called realist interpretations of world affairs. These scholars view international relations as a jungle of differently sized territorial states independently pursuing their national interests defined by their leaders' sense of morality. They say that China is exceptional. It is a 'sovereign' state that at home and abroad is capable of standing by the codes of what's called 'moral realism': strong but humane leadership committed

---

9. Zheng Yongnian, 'Ukraine and the New World Order', February 25, 2022, https://www.readingthechinadream.com/zheng-yongnian-ukraine-and-the-new-world-order.html.
10. Yan Xuetong, *Leadership and the Rise of Great Powers* (Princeton, NJ, 2019); and Zhang Weiwei, *The China Wave: Rise of a Civilizational State* (Hackensack, NJ, 2011), pp. 2–3.

to universal standards of peace and justice for all other 'sovereign' territorial states and their peoples.[11] China's commitment to 'sovereignty and territorial integrity' is also the predominant terminology used by its governing officials when describing and justifying their country's growing global power. Talk of 'sovereignty' is a constant theme of Party statements and documents, and has been so since April 1954, when the Five Principles of Peaceful Coexistence were proclaimed by Chinese premier Zhou Enlai and Indian prime minister Jawaharlal Nehru. Designed to reassure India and other regional non-communist governments that the Maoist revolution would not be carried abroad, the five-spice principles included sovereignty and territorial integrity of states; mutual non-aggression; non-interference in each other's internal affairs; the importance of respect, equality, and mutual benefit in international relations; and peaceful coexistence among sovereign states.

In diplomatic and high Party circles, the language of sovereignty still reigns. 'No one should underestimate the strong determination, firm will and strong ability of the Chinese people to safeguard national sovereignty and territorial integrity', said Xi Jinping during his hour-long speech marking the one hundredth anniversary of the founding of the Chinese Communist Party in Beijing. 'The Chinese people have never bullied, oppressed or enslaved the people of other countries. It has never done so in the past, does not do so now and will never do so in the future. At the same time, the Chinese people will never allow any outside forces to bully, oppress or enslave us. Anyone who tries to do so will be crushed to death before the Great Wall of steel built with the flesh and blood of over 1.4 billion Chinese people'.[12] Sovereignty is treated as sacrosanct: no state has the right to meddle with the internal affairs of other states, runs the reasoning. Those who try to interfere with China's sovereignty will be punished.

---

11. The phrase 'moral realism' first appears in Feng Zhang, 'The Tsinghua Approach and the Inception of Chinese Theories of International Relations', *Chinese Journal of International Politics*, 5.1 (2012), pp. 73–102; it is developed in Yan, *Leadership*.
12. C.K. Tan, 'Xi vows to crush meddling forces and Taiwan independence attempts', *Nikkei Asia*, July 1, 2021.

'China is sure to fight', officials warn. Entitled to reclaim its lost territories (Taiwan) and to put right the country's humiliation by past defeats, China's own sovereignty is simply not negotiable.[13]

The regime's use of state sovereignty language offers several strategic advantages. Since sovereignty extends to all activities within the territory of China, it pops up often in official pronouncements about the need for the state to regulate institutions such as banks, tech companies, television stations, and places of spiritual worship and in plans to blaze trails in quantum computing, military equipment, artificial intelligence, and other fields. The state sovereignty principle serves other handy purposes, most obviously to fortify the spirits of Chinese citizens by showing them that the tides of history are flowing in their favour, and by reminding the United States that since it is no longer master of the world, its governments and corporations must respect the inviolable dignity of the Chinese people. American-led allegations of human rights violations in Hong Kong, Tibet, and Xinjiang are roundly condemned as unwarranted violations of sovereignty and insults to the dignity of the Chinese people. 'The problem is that the United States has exercised long-arm jurisdiction and suppression and overstretched its national security using force or financial hegemony', said Yang Jiechi, China's director of the Office of the Central Commission for Foreign Affairs at the US-China Alaska summit (March 2021). 'What is needed is to abandon this Cold War mentality and zero-sum game approach. We must change the way we think and make sure that in this century . . . countries big or small, particularly the big countries, should come united together to contribute to the future of humanity and build a community with a shared future for humankind'. In Africa, Asia, Latin America, and the Middle East, the sovereignty doctrine signals China's willingness to work indiscriminately and pragmatically with all governments,

---

13. See the Chinese-language platform *Wenweipo*, '中國未來50年裡必打的六場戰爭' [Six wars China is sure to fight in the next fifty years], July 8, 2013, discussed by Indian military analysts at http://www.indiandefencereview.com/news/six-wars-china-is-sure-to-fight-in-the-next-50-years/.

whatever their political complexion. In these continents' hot-spot zones, the discourse of sovereignty equally serves to justify China's non-intervention—to reaffirm its commitment to peaceful negotiations and to caution other big powers not to meddle with local states at the expense of Chinese interests. The refusal to take sides in the Ukraine-Russia war that erupted in early 2022 is a well-documented example. Often called 'principled neutrality', China's stance was based on the calculation that it was not in its interest to strengthen relations with Russia at the expense of relations with Ukraine, Europe, and the United States, and on the belief that a negotiated peaceful settlement of the war required not only offers of 'normal and friendly' relations and humanitarian assistance to Ukraine but also the rejection of a NATO-driven Cold War mentality that promotes acrimony and conflict among states. The language of sovereignty and territorial integrity also has a global twist, linked into lots of talk of 'building a community of shared future for mankind'. This is intended to mean that all countries—whatever the size of their territory or wealth—are entitled to cooperate as equals to tackle common problems democratically, rather than taking their cues from, or bowing down before, the most powerful states. Talk of sovereignty and territorial integrity joins hands with declarations of 'win-win cooperation' and commitments to 'build a world of common prosperity' and 'peace'.

The Idea of Empire

A notable feature of these official Chinese viewpoints and statements is the absence of a little word—empire—to describe the country's burgeoning global role. This silence about empire comes as no surprise because great powers that turn themselves into empires are prone to act in denial of their imperial status. It is as if immodesty, shame, guilt, and conscience are unbearable. Their defenders have been known to say (as the British historian John R. Seeley once famously remarked) that empires can be born quite by accident, 'in a fit of absence of mind', rather than through calculation and contrivance.[14] But even when that happens, so that imperial conquests of territory, resources, and people are products of unintended consequence rather than design, their rulers often stay silent or speak in euphemisms about their power to shape and reshape the world. Think of the way the word 'empire' triggers embarrassed silence in the United States. Americans today commonly regard themselves as a benign global power, as a democratic force that stands against 'autocracy' in support of a rules-based international order. Things were once different. The founders of the republic knew what it meant to confront an empire. A revolution against the British Empire yielded hard-fought victory. The new republic's constitution writers were intimately familiar with writings on the ancient Greek and Roman empires. Thomas Jefferson later spoke of the birth of the American 'empire of liberty', a phrase often repeated by those who helped build and expand the commercial and political power of the republic during the nineteenth and early twentieth centuries. There were moments of exceptional high-minded praise for America's 'wonderful ... democratic empire'[15] counterbalanced by other periods when military aggression caused discomfort and division and denunciations of empire, as during the conquest of northern Mexico (1845–48) and the ruthless destruction of the Philippines independence movement (1898–1904). But then came the moment when American statesmen dropped the word 'empire' and instead began to sing in unison about the material benefits of unlimited expansion of the realm of freedom and commerce and the historic role of the United States as the City on the Hill to Guide the Whole of Humanity. 'There are many kinds of Americans', President Franklin D. Roosevelt told White House dinner guests in 1942, 'but as a people, as a country, we're opposed to imperialism—we can't

---

14. John Robert Seeley, *The Expansion of England* (London, 1883), p. 8; on this point more generally, see David Armitage, *The Ideological Origins of the British Empire* (Cambridge, 2000), pp. 16–17.
15. Franklin Henry Giddings, *Democracy and Empire: With Studies of Their Psychological, Economic, and Moral Foundations* (London, 1900), p. 11.

stomach it'.[16] In the decades that followed, the United States in reality established cross-border rules in vital matters ranging from financial regulations, trade agreements, and styles of consumption to military interventions in the name of 'human rights' and 'liberal democracy'. It unleashed military operations in over two hundred countries and territories and these days (2023) spends more on its armed forces than the next ten countries combined, with troops stationed in 750 military bases in at least eighty countries. The United States became the world's most powerful empire ever: an empire priding itself on being empire's opposite, an 'indispensable nation' (former secretary of state Madeleine Albright) whose massive economic, cultural, and military power functions as both an aphrodisiac and an opioid. International relations scholars have noted the paradox, sometimes in awkward language: 'The United States today is not an empire', writes one scholar, 'but it does exert substantial authority over other states in a range of hierarchical relationships'. The defense secretary under George W. Bush, Donald J. Rumsfeld, put things more candidly. 'We don't seek empires, we're not imperialistic', he replied to a question from an Al Jazeera reporter shortly after the 2003 US-led military invasion of Iraq. 'We never have been. I can't imagine why you'd even ask the question'.[17]

The tart words could just as easily have come from the lips of the current Chinese leadership. In a case of unexpected symmetry, they have an aversion to the word 'empire' (*dì guó*). Empire is treated as a pejorative signifier. It applies only to others. All Chinese people know

---

16. Cited in Robert Dallek, *Franklin D. Roosevelt and American Foreign Policy, 1932–1945* (New York, 1979), p. 324.
17. David A. Lake, 'The New American Empire?', *International Studies Perspectives* 9.3 (August 2008), p. 281; Donald Rumsfeld interview with Al Jazeera (April 2003); more generally on the American denial of empire see William Appleman Williams, *Empire as a Way of Life* (New York, 1980); Gore Vidal, *The Decline and Fall of the American Empire* (Berkeley, 1992); and 'The Last Empire', *Vanity Fair*, November 1997; Daniel Immerwahr, *How to Hide an Empire: A History of the Greater United States* (New York, 2019); and Stuart Rollo, *Terminus: Westward Expansion, China, and the End of American Empire* (Baltimore, 2023).

this well, runs the reasoning of this 'humiliation narrative'.[18] China suffered insult and degradation for over a century at the hands of Western empires. Empire is a bad word. It does not apply to China itself. China stands against empire.

Readers with only a cursory understanding of Chinese history will raise their eyebrows, for the historical fact is that the territory and peoples of what is today the People's Republic of China is the product of the imperial statecraft of the Yuan (1271–1368 CE) dynasty and the Qing Empire (1636–1912 CE), whose powerful eighteenth-century rulers extended China's reach into the western Eurasian landmass, to control Xinjiang and Tibet.[19] Fascinated television audiences are daily and nightly reminded of the powerful grip of these past empires in blockbuster, award-winning series such as *Empresses in the Palace: The Legend of Zhen Huan* (2011) and *Ruyi's Royal Love in the Palace* (2018). In defiance of the official silence about empire, Wang Hui and other leading Chinese scholars have also begun to debate the history of these empires and to ask whether, or to what extent, the notion of empire is truly applicable to present-day China, or its past.[20] Whatever is thought of this debate, the plain fact is that parts of the territory marked as China on world maps during the republican and post-1949 communist periods were ruled on an imperial basis for over two millennia. Government officials nowadays like to speak of a five-thousand-year-old Chinese civilization. They sometimes record

---

18. Shi Zhan, 'What Is China?', lecture delivered at the Institute of International and Strategic Studies, Peking University, April 9, 2021, available at: http://en.iiss.pku.edu.cn/dynamic/lh/4448.html.
19. Peter C. Perdue, *China Marches West: The Qing Conquest of Central Eurasia* (Cambridge, MA, 2005).
20. Compare Mu Ch'ien, *Merits and Demerits of Political Systems in Dynastic China* (Beijing, 2019), pp. 127–129: 'The term imperialism originated in the West. There was no such a thing in China. From the Qin down to the Ming dynasty, China was never an imperialist country. An imperialist country must have conquered territory over which the government does not rule on equal terms, such as Hong Kong under British rule and India under British rule in the past'; Wang Hui, *The Rise of Modern Chinese Thought*, ed. Michael Gibbs Hill (Cambridge, MA, 2023), chap. 7; and Yu Keping, 'A New Theory of Empire', *Tsinghua University Journal of Philosophy and Social Sciences*, issue 2 (February 2022).

that the Shang (1766–1045 BCE) and their successors the Zhou (1045–256 BCE) were the first imperial dynasties, but most archaeologists and historians tell us that throughout this early period ancient China comprised many different groups of peoples, including non-speakers of Chinese (some with indecipherable scripts in Sichuan and Jiangxi provinces) and forest-dwellers and nomads living quite different lives. Rivalries and infighting were commonplace. The invention of China as a unified political space took many centuries and only happened later, at the end of the Warring States period in 221 BCE under the leadership of the short-lived Qin dynasty. Consolidated by the Han dynasty that ruled during the next four centuries, Chinese-speaking peoples governed by Chinese-speaking dynasties together imposed imperial unity on a vast landmass roughly two-thirds the size of contemporary China. The rise and triumph and decline and collapse of empires enjoying suzerainty over neighbouring vassal states that paid tribute to the Middle Kingdom thereafter became the prevailing pattern—until the early years of the twentieth century, when the Qing dynasty collapsed (in 1912) and a new politics of awakening and mass revolutionary politics of national self-determination began to flourish.[21]

The key point here is that the official embrace of 'sovereignty and territorial integrity' is a comparatively recent historical development, with roots principally in the last decades of European colonial domination. That period witnessed flourishing talk of the nation, nationalism, sovereign statehood, and the need for the Chinese people to awake and rise in unison to throw off their chains. Rejuvenation of the nation was the thing. 'When China was strongest', said Sun Yat-sen during his famous 1924 Canton public lectures, 'her political power inspired awe on all sides, and not a nation south and west of China

---

21. Valerie Hansen, *The Open Empire: A History of China to 1600* (New York, 2000); John Fitzgerald, *Awakening China: Politics, Culture, and Class in the Nationalist Revolution* (Stanford, CA, 1996); Jonathan Spence, *The Search for Modern China* (New York, 1990), especially chap. 6; and Rebecca E. Karl, *Staging the World: Chinese Nationalism at the Turn of the Twentieth Century* (Durham, NC, 2002).

but considered it an honor to bring her tribute. At that time European imperialism had not invaded Asia, and the only country of Asia that deserved to be called imperialistic was China'. China had more recently become 'a colony of the Powers'. The remedy: China must regain her lost 'national spirit' by reviving 'nationalism' and building a sovereign state capable of protecting the nation (*mín zú*) against the 'political and economic domination' and 'long-range aggression' of Western imperial powers.[22] This political language of nation, nationalism, and sovereignty—ironically—was a colonial import now blessed with Chinese characteristics. For the next century, until today, the rhetoric of defending the sovereignty of China against outside powers and the rest of the world became the orthodoxy. Hence the reigning official silence about empire.

But what is an empire? It's a tricky term that is today overused in vulgar form as an epithet of abuse, to discredit any military, economic, or cultural interference by a state in the lives of others as 'imperialist' or a malevolent instance of 'colonialism'. Unfortunately, the name-calling does damage to its older and much richer connotations. The English word has deep roots (from the Latin *imperium*: rule, command, from *imperare*, to command, requisition) and for several centuries its meanings have been heavily contested. In a fit of imprecision, the first English dictionary (1604) defines it as 'gouernement [*sic*]: or kingdome' but it came to have much sharper and clearer connotations. According to later usages, an empire is a large polity that holds sway, using money, cultural resources, force, and other means, over peoples who live at a great distance from its command centres. Empire is long-armed rule defiant of state borders and geographic limits. Unlike territorial states defined by strictly demarcated borders, empires typically have fuzzy edges, indistinct margins marked by gradations of control, complex chains of command, power contests, and general wheeling and dealing among those loyal or opposed to imperial

---

22. Sun Yat-sen, *San Min Chu I: The Three Principles of The People* (Shanghai, 1927), pp. 35, 53–54, 79.

controls. Whereas modern states formally recognize their neighbours as equals, even when they are manifestly unequal in such matters as economic capital and armed force, empires act as power brokers entitled to decide things for others. Those who govern empires often proclaim that they are sovereign (nation) states, but in practice they have a habit of intervening in the affairs of other peoples and states, and they do so because in power terms they consider them to be manipulable, or inferior. Empires are in this sense much more than 'hegemonic powers'.[23] They not only affect the behaviour of other states from the outside; they also meddle with their economies, governing institutions, and the everyday lives of their peoples. Empires are carriers of a superiority complex. Those who rule empires—an emperor (from the Latin: *imperator*) or imperial group—cling to their privileges by projecting onto their subjects ideological claims to moral superiority based on religion, or money, law, race, history, or refined manners. Empire is unbounded control over vast swathes of territory based on the control of the means of communication, investment and trade, law and governmental regulations, usually with the help of political monkey business, patronage, graft, and bullying. Empire building is typically nasty business: it has often involved the conquest and humiliation of people through force, threatened or actual. Empires are dominant powers whose rulers measure their strength against all their rivals combined. Empire is occupation and possession, the will to succeed, the enforced submission of the subjugated. But empires are based not only on economic power and military force and not just marked by continual 'brooding over advantages'[24] the rulers fear they do not comprehensively enjoy. Empires seek to routinize their authority by persuading the losers and winning over doubters. They cut deeply into the psychology and everyday habits of their subjects. Empires yearn to get under the skin of their subjects by

23. Michael W. Doyle, *Empires* (Ithaca, NY, 1986), pp. 12, 38–40.
24. Alexis de Tocqueville, 'Pourquoi les Américains se montrent si inquiets au milieu de leur bien-être', in *De la democratie en Amérique* (Paris, 1981 [1835]), vol. 2, part 2, chap. 13, p. 171.

making empire a whole way of life—thereby proving the legitimacy of rule by the superior over the inferior.

Seen in the looking glass of this admittedly simplified but well-established and workable definition, the Chinese objections to using the word 'empire' are remarkable. They are arguably disabling as well: to the extent that Chinese government officials carry on talking as if their country is only a country, they risk blinding and fooling themselves about the historic opportunities but also the grave dangers confronting a fledgling empire now spreading its worldly wings. The realities are more obvious. If 'empire' means a jumbo-sized state that exercises political, economic, and cultural power over millions of people at great distances from its own heartland, without much regard or respect for the niceties of territorial sovereignty, then, technically, China is rapidly becoming one. It is not true that 'the last true empires disappeared in the twentieth century' or that 'empire does not pay in today's world'.[25] And contrary to local Chinese scholars who say that 'the era of empires is gone forever',[26] the word 'empire' is the most accurate signifier to describe—without knee-jerk rejection or gushing approval—China's growing global role in capital formation, technology innovation, logistics, and diplomatic, military, and cultural power. The headline statistics are widely circulated inside and outside China, but the true scale of what's happening can be grasped only by delving deeply into the big trends. They make clear that China is much more than a 'sovereign state' or a 'big power'—that it is an emergent empire of a kind never before seen in world history.

25. Dominic Lieven, *In the Shadow of the Gods: The Emperor in World History* (London, 2022), p. 1; and *Empire: The Russian Empire and Its Rivals* (New Haven, 2000), p. 410.
26. Yu, 'New Theory of Empire': 'After the Second World War, as national independence movements swept the world, empires not only withdrew from the stage of history, but were cast aside.... The era of human empires officially ended with the disintegration of the British Empire, and the era of empires will never return.... Humanity officially bid farewell to imperial systems that lasted for thousands of years, and entered the "post-imperial era" in which the nation-state has become a major player.... Since in this post-imperial age, empire and democracy are structurally incompatible with each other, and since there is democracy, there is no empire. Democratization means the collapse of empire' (in Chinese).

Consider one trend: the half-century history of China's growing involvement in international governing institutions. There was a time, during the Cold War years, when the fledgling People's Republic of China boycotted the United Nations and other global governing institutions. They were denounced as imperialist plots and paper tiger challenges to revolutionary socialism. China played the role of champion of the Third World. It abstained or voted against the rich and powerful states; with some reticence softened by realism it joined bodies such as the World Meteorological Organization, UNESCO, and the Food and Agriculture Organisation. Following the Nixon-Kissinger-Mao accord in the early 1970s, the death of the Great Helmsman and the rise to power of Deng Xiaoping, China softened its Third World criticisms of the West and the United States, stepped up its anti-Soviet rhetoric, and joined the Asian Development Bank and the principal Bretton Woods institutions of the World Bank, the International Monetary Fund, and the General Agreement on Tariffs and Trade.[27] For government officials and diplomats and state-owned enterprises, membership in these bodies provided both administrative experience and access to intergovernmental resources. Towards the end of the past century, China quickly became the largest recipient of loans and grants from bodies such as the Asian Development Bank and the World Bank. It signed on to international treaties and conventions such as the Convention against Torture and Other Cruel Inhuman or Degrading Treatment or Punishment (1988), the Convention on the Rights of the Child (1992), the Nuclear Terrorism Convention (2005), and the Convention on the Rights of Persons with Disabilities (2007). In 1998 it also signed, but never ratified, the International Covenant on Civil and Political Rights.

As the country grew more active in regional and global governing bodies, Chinese leaders and officials became more vocal when commenting on world affairs. In bodies such as the UN General Assembly, they often still sided with the poorer and less powerful

---

27. Harold K. Jacobsen and Michael C. Oksenberg, *China's Participation in the IMF, World Bank, and GATT: Toward a Global Economic Order* (Ann Arbor, MI, 1990).

countries. Frequently voicing doubts about US dominance, Chinese leaders argued the need for a less Western and more multipolar global order, bolder global solutions for global problems, and respect for the territorial sovereignty of states. Striking was their air of growing confidence. Within multilateral institutions, Chinese diplomats, negotiators, and other officials began to impress outsiders with their well-prepared knowledge of technical details and procedural rules, and their tough negotiating skills. 'China is thorough, exceedingly well-prepared and well organized about executing its responsibilities as an institutional member', noted a 2011 US congressional report. 'It does its "homework" and raises detailed, substantive questions about matters which not only affect China's interests, but also on issues of purely institutional relevance'.[28] Chinese negotiators displayed tactical prowess and full acceptance of binding legal decisions within such bodies as the World Trade Organisation Dispute Settlement Body. Surprises grew in frequency. When the Trump administration moved to paralyse its operations, China partnered with the European Union, Canada, Australia, Singapore, Brazil, Chile, and a dozen other countries to form an interim appeal arbitration body (known as the Multi-Party Interim Appeal Arbitration Arrangement [MPIA]) comprising a pool of ten judges selected by the World Trade Organization's country members.[29]

During the past two decades, spurred on by Xi Jinping's 2018 call for China to 'lead the reform of the global governance system with the concepts of fairness and justice', China has invested much energy in building new multilateral institutions and actively partnering with its fourteen neighbouring states. It plays a high-profile role in regional

---

28. Stephen Olson and Clyde Prestowitz, *The Evolving Role of China in International Institutions* (Washington, DC, January 1, 2011), p. 11, https://www.uscc.gov/sites/default/files/Research/TheEvolvingRoleofChinainInternationalInstitutions.pdf.
29. Li Xiaojun, 'Learning and Socialization in International Institutions: China's Experience with the WTO Dispute Settlement System', in Mingjiang Li, ed., *China Joins Global Governance* (Lanham, MD, 2012), pp. 75–94; Xiaojun Li, 'Understanding China's Behavioral Change in the WTO Dispute Settlement System,' *Asian Survey* 52.6 (December 2012), pp. 1111–37.

bodies such as the Asia-Pacific Economic Cooperation, the Shanghai Cooperation Organization, the Chiang Mai Initiative currency-swap arrangement, and the Regional Comprehensive Economic Partnership. Institutional restructuring and soliciting leadership roles within global bodies is equally high on its agenda. Chinese negotiators and diplomats are busily working to reshape the spirit and policymaking structures of the United Nations; and by mastering the arts of winning heavily contested elections abroad, China now heads four of the fifteen UN's Specialized Agencies.[30] In recent years, it has also helped build, and now leads, multilateral institutions such as BRICS and the China-Arab States Cooperation Forum, which are founded on meetings and summits, policy coordination, and pragmatic consent, not formal treaty alliances.

Such developments suggest that China is no longer mainly preoccupied with negotiating the byzantine rules and clumsy procedures of multilateral governing institutions, and that instead it has grown in confidence to the point where it is altering the topography of more than a few global governing bodies. The trends contradict earlier assessments by scholars that China displays deep ambivalence about its involvement in global affairs, that it lacks allies and is best described as a friendless lonely power that is nowhere near capable of becoming a genuine world power. 'China is, in essence, a very narrow-minded, self-interested, realist state, seeking only to maximize its own national interests and power', it was said. Except for its vigorous defence of the principles of non-intervention and state sovereignty, it 'cares little for global governance and enforcing global standards of behavior'. China was judged to be 'a lonely strategic power, with *no allies* and experiencing distrust and strained relations with much of the world', an insecure state that 'relies explicitly on coercion' and 'displays periodic evidence of being a dissatisfied, frustrated, aggrieved, and angry

---

30. Thomas William Barrett, *China & the United Nations Specialised Agencies: The Establishment of a World Power* (Honours dissertation, University of Sydney, 2021).

nation that seeks redress against those that have wronged it in the past or with which it has disagreements at present'.[31]

Belt and Road

Doubts about the accuracy of such descriptions of China's emerging planetary role—and the urgent need to update them using the keyword 'empire'—are compounded by considering China's most prominent global initiative: the so-named Belt and Road Initiative (BRI), launched a decade ago.

Its scale and complexity are astonishing. It is sometimes compared to the original Silk Road launched during the Han dynasty period (206 BCE–220 CE). Powering an early phase of globalization, its trade networks stretched west through central Asia, down to the Indian subcontinent, and all the way to Europe. The BRI boldly updates this old vision. Launched in 2013, the mega-project construction of railways, roads, deep-sea ports, bridges, power grids, and other infrastructure works is set to cost more than a trillion dollars, seven times as much (when adjusted for inflation) as the US investment in western Europe after the Second World War. Fifty special economic zones, modelled on the Shenzhen Special Economic Zone that Deng Xiaoping opened in 1980, are planned. Dozens of industrial parks and free trade zones—such as the Suez Canal Economic Zone in Egypt and the China-Belarus Industrial Park—have already been built. Seen in terms of investment opportunities, export markets, and domestic policies designed to boost income and consumption, the BRI is clearly China's alternative to the United States' 'pivot to Asia'. The renminbi, China's official currency, is naturally being promoted among Belt and Road partners as a serious alternative to the greenback.

---

31. David Shambaugh, *China Goes Global: The Partial Power* (Oxford, 2013), pp. 3, 6–7, 310–311; Elizabeth Economy, 'Xi Jinping's New World Order: Can China Remake the International System?', *Foreign Affairs*, January–February 2022, https://www.foreignaffairs.com/articles/china/2021-12-09/xi-jinpings-new-world-order.

Funded by China's massive foreign reserves ($3.128 trillion in US bonds, notes, and bills in December 2022), BRI is developing hundreds of projects to link more than sixty-five countries. Many of these projects—a $5.8 billion hydropower dam in Nigeria and a high-speed railway linking Kunming to Singapore, for instance—are still under construction, but the contours of the linkages are already clear. Going far beyond an earlier Ministry of Foreign Affairs plan to promote infrastructure diplomacy in Asia and Africa—a 'China goes west' strategy on the scale of the Marshall Plan—Beijing-financed infrastructure projects are reordering the lives of millions, from South Africa, Nigeria, Hungary, Greece, Iran, and Sri Lanka to Cambodia, Papua New Guinea, Jamaica, Mexico, and Argentina. Every continent is touched by the investments, including Antarctica, where Chinese government investments in research and development are outpacing those of Britain, the United States, and Australia. After signing the Antarctic Treaty (in 1983), China quickly built the Great Wall station (*chángchéng zhàn*) on King George Island. Three more stations were subsequently built. A year-round base for researchers working in such fields as marine biology and glaciology, a fifth station located on Inexpressible Island near the Ross Sea became operable in 2022.

Chinese officials wax eloquent about the broad aims of the BRI. They speak of its enhancement of an 'orderly and free flow of economic factors, highly efficient allocation of resources and deep integration of markets', its support for 'an open, inclusive and balanced regional economic cooperation architecture that benefits all'. They praise the ways in which its regional production and supply chains supported by maritime networks, industrial zones, and related infrastructure are positive contributions to 'new models of international cooperation and global governance' and 'world peace and development'.[32] Fine general words, but in reality the initiative is designed to serve a far wider range of functionally specific purposes. More a visionary framework with 'omnibus' qualities than a rigidly defined

---

32. National Development Reform Commission, 'Vision and Actions on Jointly Building Silk Road Economic Belt and 21st-Century Maritime Silk Road' (2015).

juggernaut hamstrung by a 'brewing BRI debt crisis' that is putting China on 'the road to ruin', BRI programmes are proving to be a mix of things to many different countries, organisations, and people.[33]

We shouldn't be surprised. Unlike the idealized inner harmony of states—one bounded territory, one people, one polity—empires typically have a cluttered, kaleidoscope quality. The complex architecture and multiple functions of the BRI—a key driver of the emerging Chinese empire—shows that China is no exception to this old rule.[34]

When probing the contours of the BRI, it becomes clear, amidst the great complexity, that the grand vision has an economic rationale. Designed to boost investment, production, and consumption by unlocking additional markets well beyond the country's borders, BRI is seen by state officials as a functional solution to China's 'new normal' of single-digit economic growth and a remedy for the overcapacity and outdated technology problems in several 'smokestack industries' linked to the pre-1979 growth model.[35] The search for profitable new markets and new resources through new capital flows—what's locally called the 'Going Out' policy—is a new normal. Consider megadam construction, a market field in which China is now the world leader. Since the 1950s, spurred on by Mao's call to 'conquer nature' and backed by government assurances of the vital role of dams in generating electricity, reducing pollution, preventing droughts and

33. Michael Bennon and Francis Fukuyama, '"China's Road to Ruin:" The Real Toll of Beijing's Belt and Road', *Foreign Affairs*, September/October, 2023; Tim Summers, 'China's "New Silk Roads": Sub-national Regions and Networks of Global Political Economy', *Third World Quarterly* 37.9 (2016), p. 1639; and Adrian Raftery, 'Many Belts, Many Roads: How China's Provinces Will Tweak a Global Project', *The Diplomat*, February 4, 2017, http://thediplomat.com/2017/02/many-belts-many-roads-how-chinas-provinces-will-tweak-a-global-project/.
34. The distinction between state ('kingdom') and empire is noted in John Trusler, *The Difference, Between Words, Esteemed Synonymous, in the English Language* (London, 1766), vol. 2, p. 15: 'The word, *empire*, conveys an idea of a vast territory, composed of various people; whereas that of *kingdom*, implies, one more bounded; and intimates the unity of that nation, of which it is formed'.
35. Alvin Cheng-Hin Lim, 'Africa and China's 21st Century Maritime Silk Road', *Asia-Pacific Journal* 13(10).1 (2015), p. 3; Gabriel Wildau, 'China's State-Owned Zombie Economy', *Financial Times*, March 1, 2016, https://www.ft.com/content/253d7eb0-ca6c-11e5-84df-70594b99fc47 (accessed September 1, 2017).

floods, providing irrigation for farms and drinking water for cities, and generally enhancing human well-being, more than twenty-two thousand large-scale dams have been built in China, roughly half the world's total.[36] Partly due to the overseas search for new profits and local fears of safety, environmental damage, and protests, the trend has more recently slowed. Many aging hydroelectric dams are earmarked for closure. But with the launch of the BRI, foreign dam building has boomed. In a Beijing private seminar in 2019, a manager of a major dam-building state-owned enterprise (SOE) reported that the company had 'surplus capital, sophisticated modern technology, and a strong labour force of three hundred thousand workers who have already built most dams in China during the past 30 years. But now that domestic demand has decreased, our workers need new work to survive'. Such expectations have fuelled China's drive to build over three hundred dams across Southeast Asia and throughout Central Asia, South America, and Africa. Led by giant state-owned companies such as the China Three Gorges Corporation and Sinohydro, China now dominates the global hydropower market in terms of capital investment, the size and number of dams built, and design and sales of power generation equipment. The modus operandi of its giant companies differs from other countries' dam builders. Not only are they backed by generous state funding and loan offers. Defined as they are by a pragmatic willingness to work with host governments of all persuasions and to set aside environmental assessments—a practice earlier displayed during the construction of the Three Gorges dam, which involved flooding thirteen cities, 140 towns, and 1,350 villages; the relocation of 1.3 million inhabitants, many from rural areas to cities; and the destruction of numerous sites of cultural, historic, and religious heritage—their profit-seeking investment projects are often tied to aid and trade deals. Not infrequently, the dam-building frenzy has been bound up with China's own need for access to energy

---

36. Charlton Lewis, 'China's Great Dam Boom: A Major Assault on Its Rivers', *YaleEnvironment360*, November 4, 2013, https://e360.yale.edu/features/chinas_great_dam_boom_an_assault_on_its_river_systems.

and mineral resources.[37] Myanmar, Cambodia, Vietnam, Thailand, and Laos are cases in point: operating as large-scale job creation machines for Chinese workers, they are also exporters of huge quantities of cheap, low-carbon electricity from Chinese dams back to China. Laos has even named itself the 'battery of Asia'.

Dam building is just one layer in the intricate architecture of the BRI, which is moulded for many other purposes, and by the labyrinthine policy dynamics through which projects are activated. The complexity of the Belt and Road adventure is easily misunderstood. Simple thinking abounds, for instance among observers who suppose that the BRI is Xi Jinping's pet project, that he plays the role of a free-handed 'autocrat' and master dramaturge of an ambitiously expansionist vision that aggregates investment, industry, consumption, aid, trade, military security, and foreign policy. The reality is more serpentine.

The Party leadership indeed formulated the big vision—the largest project in human history—for which Xi will no doubt be remembered, and his legacy judged.[38] He first officially announced the BRI during trips to Kazakhstan and Indonesia in 2013. Under his leadership, the National Leading Group for Promoting the Construction of the Belt and Road was created in 2015. Located in the National Development and Reform Commission, its role is to oversee, coordinate, and implement BRI projects, to win support for its bold accomplishments at home and abroad, and to ensure against regime instability.[39] But the

---

37. Frauke Urban and Johan Nordensvard, 'China Dams the World: The Environmental and Social Impacts of Chinese Dams', *E-International Relations*, January 30, 2014, https://www.e-ir.info/pdf/46146; Andrea K. Gerlak, Marcelo Saguier, Megan Mills-Novoa, Philip M. Fearnside, and Tamee R. Albrecht, 'Dams, Chinese Investments, and EIAs: A Race to the Bottom in South America?', *Ambio* 49.1 (January 2020), pp. 156–164.
38. Christopher K. Johnson, *President Xi Jinping's 'Belt and Road' Initiative*, Centre for Strategic and International Studies, March 28, 2016, p. 3, https://www.csis.org/analysis/president-xi-jinpings-belt-and-road-initiative; Matt Ferchen, 'How New and Crafty Is China's "New Economic Statecraft?"', *Carnegie-Tsinghua Center for Global Policy*, March 22, 2016.
39. Hong Yu, 'Motivation behind China's One Belt, One Road Initiatives and Establishment of the Asian Infrastructure Investment Bank', *Journal of Contemporary China* 26.105 (2017), p. 363.

body chaired by Xi is constrained—unsurprisingly—by the complex, often topsy-turvy dynamics of the overall project. Scholars regularly point out that China's domestic polity has multilayered and 'fractured' qualities chronically fuelled by intense bargaining among government ministries.[40] These dynamics are on display within the BRI, which is not understandable as the unified outcome of a monolithic grand strategy decided by the Politburo or its leader. It is rather shaped by power struggles and self-interested bargaining among 'poligarchs': corporate executives, SOE bureaucrats, ministry officials, Party cadres, and other bodies at all levels of the political system.[41] The policy bargaining mechanisms often seem obscure, and public accountability checks and balances are in short supply. There's no Chinese equivalent of US congressional hearings and approvals—the kind of soliciting of congressional support required of President Truman when the Marshall Plan was enacted.[42] Yet transparency shortages aren't equivalent to the absence of consultation, policy coordination, or careful forward planning. In the new Chinese empire, in high matters of political economy, the neo-Confucian spirit of consultation and deliberation, or what is going to be called 'phantom democracy', lives on.[43] Behind-the-scenes dialogue, negotiation, and bargaining are routine, as evidenced by the passing of a full year between the official launch of the BRI (in the autumn of 2013) and the announced details of its myriad project investments.

Government departments such as the Ministry of Foreign Affairs and the Ministry of Commerce play an important role in these byzantine

---

40. Pierre Landry, *Decentralised Authoritarianism in China* (Cambridge, 2008); and Lee Jones and Shahar Hameiri, *Fractured China: How State Transformation is Shaping China's Rise* (Cambridge, 2021).
41. The term 'poligarch' is defined at length in John Keane, *The New Despotism* (London, 2020).
42. Diane B. Kunz, 'The Marshall Plan Reconsidered: A Complex of Motives', *Foreign Affairs* 76.3 (1997), pp. 166–167.
43. On the old tradition of Confucian consultation and its impact on contemporary Chinese politics, see Baogang He, 'Deliberative Culture and Politics: The Persistence of Authoritarian Deliberation in China', *Political Theory* 42.1 (2014), pp. 58–81.

bargaining processes.[44] Each ministry has an action plan tailored to its own specific objectives. The Ministry of Culture promotes the Belt and Road as a cultural 'brand' and champions cultural industries and exchanges along its routes.[45] The Ministry of Education's 2016 action plan included support for hundreds of overseas think tanks and research institutes and scholarships for fifty thousand BRI-partner students to study in China.[46] Local governments and provincial universities have since chipped in, offering scholarships for developing countries such as Pakistan, where on the streets of Lahore scholarships to study free of charge in China are openly advertised. Countless protocols, agreements, memoranda of understanding, and other documents have meanwhile been signed between Chinese ministries and foreign partners.[47] In 2017, the International Liaison Department of the Chinese Communist Party even hosted a World Political Parties Dialogue Summit in Beijing attended by some three hundred political party representatives from Belt and Road and other countries; in 2021, five hundred political parties from 160 countries attended the follow-up meeting.

SOEs are also active within the high-level bargaining and among the most important contributors to Belt and Road projects. They confirm that state institutions are key drivers of the new Chinese empire and that this empire is not driven by money and markets alone. In 1995, there were only 3 SOEs, growing to 10 in 2000, 16 in 2005,

44. Ministry of Foreign Affairs of the People's Republic of China, 'Vision and Actions on Jointly Building Silk Road Economic Belt and 21st-Century Maritime Silk Road', March 28, 2015, http://2017.beltandroadforum.org/english/n100/2017/0410/c22-45.html.
45. 'Ministry of Culture's Action Plan for Belt and Road Cultural Development (2016–2020)', *HKDTC Research*, December 28, 2016, http://china-trade-research.hktdc.com/business-news/article/The-Belt-and-Road-Initiative/Ministry-of-Cultures-Action-Plan-for-Belt-and-Road-Cultural-Development-2016-2020/obor/en/1/1X000000/1X0A9K2A.htm.
46. 'China's New Scholarship to Sponsor Students from Belt and Road Initiative Nations', *Xinhua News*, August 11, 2017, http://news.xinhuanet.com/english/2016-08/11/c_135587410.htm.
47. See the details summarized in 'List of Deliverables of the Belt and Road Forum for International Cooperation', *China Daily Europe*, May 16, 2017, http://europe.chinadaily.com.cn/china/2017-05/16/content_29359530.htm.

46 in 2010, 98 in 2015, and 116 in 2019. By 2021, the Fortune Global 500 list included 136 Chinese firms, compared to 124 American companies, answerable to state ministries, and in many cases to the highest echelons of the Party. These state-backed firms have a *political utility* in that they can be leveraged by government in pursuit of local political objectives and geopolitical calculations. The strategic value of SOEs such as the China Export-Import Bank is that they are politically controllable entities that can be relied upon to toe the Party-state line—and to be deployed overseas to implement China's 'global pork-barreling'.[48]

These Party-state dynamics shaped by numerous ministries and other bodies help explain why the BRI is marked by polycentric dynamism. Its contours are strongly contested at all levels of the system, including in sub-national domains. Official documents speak of the need to transform provinces such as Xinjiang and Fujian into new engines of economic growth capable of driving the next phase of Chinese development. Just as the heartlands of the British Empire were differentiated—London was its financial hub, and Belfast's famous shipyards built the *Titanic*—so China's emergent empire designates certain provinces as strategic hubs of BRI activity. In practice, fierce rivalries among provinces for a share of the huge sums of available funding are common. Yunnan's and Guangxi's competing claims to be China's gateway to Southeast Asia are an example.[49] Provinces inevitably have different needs and objectives, and the tensions (in accordance with the well-known advantages of polycentric

---

48. Scott Cendrowski, 'Inside China's Global Spending Spree', *Fortune*, December 12, 2016, http://fortune.com/china-belt-road-investment/; Vivien Foster, William Butterfield, Chuan Chen, and Nataliya Pushak, *Building Bridges: China's Growing Role as Infrastructure Financier for Sub-Saharan Africa* (Washington, DC: International Bank for Reconstruction and Development, 2009), p. 55.
49. Tim Summers, 'China's "New Silk Roads": Sub-national Regions and Networks of Global Political Economy', *Third World Quarterly* 37.9 (2016), p. 1639; Shashi Tharoor, 'China's Silk Road Revival—and the Fears It Stirs—Are Deeply Rooted in the Country's History', *New Perspectives Quarterly* 32.1 (2015), p. 19; Ministry of Foreign Affairs of the People's Republic of China, 'Vision and Actions'.

governance)[50] may well in the long run boost the overall chances of Belt and Road success. One thing is already certain: these rivalries are yielding a BRI *distinct* from that originally envisaged by the central government leadership. The case of Guangdong Province is illustrative: after its Party standing committee won official central approval (by the Leading Small Group in June 2015) for its BRI plans, a think tank director explained to us, Guangdong became the BRI vanguard, ranking first in its provincial participation index by hosting international forums, establishing city-to-country links with Pacific Island states, and embracing a Singaporean training scheme for officials and professionals from Silk Road countries.

China has so far signed memoranda of understanding with more than 140 countries, spread across all continents. Nearly a third (43) are in sub-Saharan Africa; the remaining partnerships are spread through Central Asia and Europe (35 countries, including 18 member states of the European Union), East Asia and the Pacific (25 countries), Southeast Asia (6 partners), and Latin America and the Caribbean (21 countries). The BRI partnerships comprise a truly global kaleidoscope of business and diplomatic negotiations, big investments, small and large projects, and countless numbers of dams, highways, trains, ports, and air freight routes befitting a 'powerful transportation country'[51] that aspires to connect most of the world according to its own designs. The BRI has strong regional aspirations as well. In the East Asian region, the BRI's investment initiatives and infrastructure projects aim to break China's dependence on Japanese and Korean technology, for instance by pioneering its own brand of high-speed railways and tightening diplomatic and economic relations with other neighbours. While the Trump administration (2016–2020) talked of

50. Elinor Ostrom, 'Beyond Markets and States: Polycentric Governance of Complex Economic Systems', *American Economic Review* 100.3 (June 2010), pp. 641–672; see also Wiebke Rabe, *China's Provinces Go Global: Internationalization under Guided Autonomy* (London, 2023).
51. Bin Wang and Jing Liu, 'Comprehensive Evaluation and Analysis of Maritime Soft Power Based on the Entropy Weight Method (EWM)', *Journal of Physics: Conference Series* 1168 (2019), pp. 1–8.

building a wall to separate the United States from Mexico, the Belt and Road committed China to the establishment of what officials call a new 'borderland civilization' featuring more cross-border flexibility and special economic zones along the open borders between China, Laos, Vietnam, and Myanmar. The Belt and Road has other regional ambitions. In South Asia, amidst Sino-Indian rivalries, it aims to pry countries from India's strategic orbit. In 2016, China invested $62 billion in China-Pakistan Economic Corridor projects—22 per cent of the total GPD of Pakistan in that year. Bangladesh and Sri Lanka have meanwhile signed partnership agreements with China; these countries' trade with China now exceeds their levels of trade with India, while the partnerships feature large-scale Chinese infrastructure projects, such as ports in Hambantota and Chittagong and a Chinese-built solar power plant that supplies electricity to Bangladesh's national grid. And the Bangladeshi armed forces have been equipped with Chinese tanks, frigates, and fighter jets.

A Galaxy Empire

How do we best make sense of this vast, dizzying portfolio of Belt and Road activities and institutions within the country and interconnected regions, and on the global stage? It has already been suggested that China is fast becoming an empire, but this begs the question of what kind of empire it is. This book proposes to call it a galaxy empire (*yín hé di guó*). The phrase is unfamiliar. It is unorthodox. It takes aim at the conventional clichés, prejudices, and dog-tired formulas used by politicians, diplomats, journalists, academics and citizens when trying to make sense of China and its 'rise'. Supposing that corrupt language corrupts thinking, the idea of a galaxy empire offers a fresh beginning, a new way of classifying and thinking more imaginatively about China's growing importance in global affairs. The galaxy empire phrase draws upon a celestial simile—celestial refers to stars or heavens—but it is intended to be much more than a pun that recalls the fact that during the nineteenth century, in countries such as the United States, Canada, and Australia, 'celestials' was the nickname used by white people to describe, sometimes with hostility, Chinese diasporas in their midst. For Chinese writers and poets, by contrast, the phrase 'celestial empire' or 'heavenly dynasty' (*tiān cháo*) was used with pride to refer to Qing dynasty China. Talk of celestials and a celestial empire later fell into disuse, although more recently netizens in China have used it to praise its emergence as a global power, or to satirize the existing regime, as in sentences such as 'the celestial empire goes to pot' (*tiān cháo shàng guō*) that double as near-homonyms for 'celestial empire above all other nations'.

The experimental use of the celestial simile is altogether more serious, and more directly linked to the sciences of astrophysics and astronomy, where researchers commonly refer to a galaxy as a vast gravitational system comprising dust, dark matter, gas, and thousands of dispersed but interconnected stars arranged in spiral or elliptical or irregularly shaped clusters. Everybody knows that the inner complexity of any given galaxy (there are an estimated one hundred billion of them in our observable universe) is astonishing. That is why mapping their constantly changing contours induces giddiness. Stars burning blue, red, and yellow. Gaseous dust clouds. Comets with tails stretching across the heavens. Red and green aurora shimmering in night skies. Massive exploding stars called supernovas that outshine the galaxy before quickly disappearing into oblivion. Fast-spinning pulsars radiating intense magnetic waves. Super-bright quasars emitting ferocious heat, beams of parallel matter called jets and measurable electromagnetic waves. Black holes that elude distant observation because their fields of gravity are so strong that nothing, not even light, escapes their grip. Pole stars whose location appears to be so fixed that the whole sky appears to rotate around them, as if they are the hub of a giant wheel. Stellar winds and solar flares. Gravitational waves. Differently coloured planets, small and large, dim and bright, hot and cold. Moons. Shooting star showers of small-body meteorites and rock and ice clusters called planetesimals. Diminutive building-block objects such as positrons, protons, and neutrons. Minuscule elementary particles called quarks.

This much is clear to scientists of the crowded heavens. But why seek help from the word 'galaxy' to make sense of the spread of Chinese power throughout the world? The first of several reasons ought to be the most obvious. Put very briefly: to speak of China as an emergent galaxy empire is an appeal to sharpen our sense of *the great spatial complexity of its contours* and to pay attention to its *dynamic—constantly evolving and shapeshifting—features*.[52] Previous descriptions of contemporary China as a rigid and repressive empire, a monolithic 'autocracy' and 'imperial Leninist dictatorship' based on premodern Chinese imperial traditions and Western Marxism are both outdated and much too simple.[53] It is equally mistaken to describe China in Western realpolitik terms as a bordered 'sovereign state' or a hegemonic 'big power' or monolithic 'autocracy'. The new Chinese empire has protean, shapeshifting, galactic qualities. Descriptively speaking, we could say that it comprises a massive galaxy of dynamically entangled institutions and activities gravitationally centred on its Beijing-led heartland. The empire's spatial mega-complexity—mirrored for analytic purposes in the galactic style of this chapterless book of interconnected essays—is among its significant features. To put things metaphorically, the galaxy empire comprises untold numbers of quasars, burning stars, stellar winds, black holes, planets and moons, clusters and super-clusters of plans, projects, and personnel. Its spatial heterogeneity is remarkable. So are the attraction-repulsion dynamics of its institutions. Its thoroughly twenty-first-century dynamism is without precedent—we are going to see it bears only a limited resemblance to previous Chinese and Atlantic-region empires—and its gravitational push/pull effects are being felt everywhere, even beyond

---

52. The phrase 'galaxy empire' owes something to the prior work of anthropologists on 'galactic polities', as in the pioneering work of Stanley Jeyaraja Tambiah, 'The Galactic Polity in Southeast Asia', *Hau: Journal of Ethnographic Theory* 3.3 (2013), pp. 503–534.
53. Ross Terrill, *The New Chinese Empire: Beijing's Political Dilemma and What It Means for the United States* (Sydney, 2003).

Earth's bounds. Here the word 'galaxy' has a second significance: it alerts us to the way *China's leaders are showing signs of intense strategic interest in the world beyond our planet.* Past partisans of empire dreamed of annexing the heavens, 'these vast worlds which we can never reach ... so clear and yet so far'.[54] The galaxy empire is actually making this old dream come true. It is reaching for the stars. It aims to become the world's leading spacefaring power, principally not for military and espionage reasons, or nuclear deterrence, but actually because of designs to strengthen the prestige and power of hundreds of state-owned and state-protected private enterprises such as the China Great Wall Industry Corporation; and to develop space-based solar power, undertake lunar and asteroid mining, and establish a permanent space station—perhaps the only station remaining in the inner solar system after the projected shutdown of the US/Russia International Space Station by 2031.[55]

Space exploration began during the 1950s, but it was only in 1970, supported by the Chinese Academy of Space Technology, that the country launched its first rocket into outer space, with the song 'East Is Red' broadcast from orbit. China's first manned *Shenzhou V* space probe happened in 2003, culminating in the safe return of a Chinese astronaut named Yang Liwei. Since then, despite the debarring of China by the United States in its space programmes, Chinese governments have begun to think big, plan long term, and work hard. A rover landed on our moon in 2008. An anti-satellite missile capable of

---

54. The words of the British diamond magnate and imperialist politician Cecil Rhodes, in *The Last Will and Testament of Cecil John Rhodes* (London, 1902), quoted in Emanuele Saccarelli and Latha Varadarajan, *Imperialism Past and Present* (Oxford, 2015), p. 15.
55. The following section draws upon Namrata Goswami, 'China in Space: Ambitions and Possible Conflict', *Strategic Studies Quarterly* 12.1 (Spring 2018), pp. 74–97 and 'Star Wars: From Space-Based Solar Power to Mining Asteroids for Resources: China's Plans for the Final Frontier', *Policy Forum*, September 7, 2016, https://www.policyforum.net/star-wars/; State Council, People's Republic of China, 'Full Text of White Paper on China's Space Activities in 2016', December 28, 2016, http://english.www.gov.cn/archive/white_paper/2016/12/28/content_281475527159496.htm; and Liu Jia, 'Riding an Asteroid: China's Next Goal in Space', *Chinese Academy of Sciences*, March 1, 2017, http://english.cas.cn/newsroom/archive/china_archive/cn2017/201703/t20170301_174455.shtml.

jamming, ramming, and destroying US and other satellites was tested successfully (in 2015); sophisticated cyber weapons capable of mimicking, tricking, and confounding the signal systems of enemy satellites are reportedly in development. Commercial plans have been drawn up to rocket tourists into suborbital space. Work was completed on the global navigation system Beidou ('Big Dipper'), a rival to the US Global Positioning System named after the seven brightest stars of the Ursa Major constellation. Autonomous cargo ship delivery and on-orbit refuelling systems followed. In 2018, China for the first time launched more satellites into orbit than any other country. The following year, China became the first to land a spacecraft on the far side of the moon. The world's largest filled-aperture radio telescope, a five-hundred-metre dish known as 'the eye of heaven', was completed. *Tianwen-1*, an interplanetary mission launched in July 2020, entered Martian orbit in February 2021. Three months later, its *Zhurong* rover touched down on Mars, making China the second country (after the United States) to land on the Red Planet. There has since been much official talk of more probes to sample the surface of Mars, flights to Venus and Jupiter, and the building of orbiting solar power stations equipped with giant solar panels capable of trapping the sun's rays and generating electricity beamed back to all parts of the globe using red laser beams and microwaves. The galaxy empire has plans to search robotically for titanium, helium 3, and water on the dark side of the moon. Feasibility studies have begun to consider mining platinum and titanium and other minerals on asteroids such as 1996FG3, for instance by nudging them into Earth's orbit.

Then came a landmark moment: in mid-June 2021 China docked three astronauts ('taikonauts') at the twenty-ton *Tianhe* (Harmony in Heaven) core module of the space station Tiangong (Heavenly Palace), the second space station to achieve permanently occupied status, after the International Space Station. Perhaps with tongues tucked in their cheeks, Xinhua and other sources reported that the space station doubled as the first Communist Party branch founded in outer space. Xi Jinping sent a letter to the mission team congratulating them for progressing 'the spirit of the "two bombs and one satellite"' (he was referring to China's early commitments to producing nuclear weapons and intercontinental ballistic missiles and artificial satellites) and helping to strengthen 'a modern socialist country'. Rhetoric aside, the successful mission had long-term significance. On board the *Tianhe*, the largest Chinese spacecraft to date, the crew began preparations to link and attach two auxiliary laboratories known as Wentian (Quest for the Heavens) and Mengtian (Dreaming of Heavens). The T-shaped multi-modular complex will have the capacity for 3D printing in support of in-orbit manufacturing and communicating and docking Xuntian (Survey of the Heavens), a giant modular telescope with a field of vision three hundred times larger than the Hubble telescope. The station has other plans, including onboard purification of water, electrolytic oxygen generation, testing embryonic stem cells under weak gravity conditions, and the growing and harvesting of fruit and vegetables.

It may seem trite to describe at length the galactic qualities of the new Chinese empire, but doing so minimally has the advantage of underscoring the rarity of empires on this scale. Although China isn't the first genuinely global empire—the United States and the Soviet Union were the post-1945 pioneers—the galaxy empire is the first global power to be born of its entanglement with the United States, and to expand with its help. The grand irony of this wholly unexpected outcome should be noted. Empires with a truly global footprint are rare. Whatever their stated visions of world conquest, the Mongols, Muslims, Ottomans, Ming dynasty, the British and other European empires had geographically limited territorial reaches. For the first time, during the years of bipolarity (1945–89), two economically and militarily detached global empires vied for world dominance. Following the collapse of the Soviet Union, a breakdown uncontested by China, the United States tried to do something no empire had ever done: to exercise complete hegemony alone. It failed. So now it is confronted with the realities of a Chinese empire it helped to empower in the early 1970s following the 'table tennis' played by

President Nixon and Chairman Mao Zedong.[56] For the first time in human history, two entangled empires marked by competing intentions and practices shadow the globe. To paraphrase Otto von Bismarck, we are living in wondrous times in which the strong grow weaker and the weak grow stronger. For the foreseeable future, the competition and rivalry—some observers speak of 'coopetition'—of these two empires will be a fact of life. After all, it is the rule rather than the exception that modern empires typically come in pairs. Just as the Spanish and English, Portuguese and Dutch, British and American, Russian and Japanese empires locked horns, so China and the United States now find themselves energized by deepening competitive rivalries.

Land and Sea

But what more can be said about the mechanics of the new galaxy empire? When diagnosing its contours and inner workings, it's important to understand the ways in which it defies some classic distinctions, most obviously between land and maritime empires. Wei Yuan (1794–1857), a geographer and historian, urged Qing dynasty officials to think of their empire as both a land and maritime power. He championed the simultaneous strengthening of the empire's frontier territories and maritime perimeters, for instance through large-scale emigration of Han Chinese people to Xinjiang and an increased reliance upon sea transportation of grain to the imperial capital.[57] Land and sea metaphors strongly gripped Western political thinking about power, politics, states, and empires, too. Understood as ways of seeing the world in terms of representative symbols, maritime metaphors

56. The expression used by Mao Zedong during a meeting with President Richard Nixon: 'Mao Zedong Meets Richard Nixon, February 21, 1972', USC US-China Institute, https://china.usc.edu/mao-zedong-meets-richard-nixon-february-21-1972 (accessed September 21, 2023).
57. Jane Kate Leonard, *Wei Yuan and China's Rediscovery of the Maritime World* (Cambridge, MA, 1984).

with practical consequences stretch all the way from Plato's damning comparison of democracy to a rudderless ship lost at sea to interpretations of politics as the precautionary art of navigating 'a boundless and bottomless sea' where there is neither 'harbour for shelter nor floor for anchorage' nor 'starting place nor appointed destination. The enterprise is to keep afloat on an even keel'.[58] When power and politics and the human condition are thought of this way, maritime metaphors often emphasize the need for caution and modesty, respect for the complexity and fluidity of things, and recognition of the dangers posed by matters unknown, storms unforeseen, and being trapped in a 'big boat that has been hit by fierce wind and huge waves' (the words used during the global economic crisis by a top Chinese official, Dai Bingguo, at the US-China Strategic and Economic Dialogue held in Washington in July 2009). By contrast, land metaphors emphasize the centrality of property, bounded territory, partition, and conquest. Land metaphors encourage the association of politics with overcoming challenges—building bridges and roads, taking highways, climbing mountains, stringing lights on the hill—and resolving serious tensions and bitter conflicts, if necessary by using military force, as when observers refer to 'fighting' electoral campaigns on 'battlegrounds', the celebration of 'victories' in 'safe areas', and 'setbacks' and 'heavy losses' in 'strongholds'.

When it comes to the general subject of empires, and how in particular to classify and make sense of the galaxy empire, Carl Schmitt's *Land und Meer: Eine weltgeschichtliche Betrachtung* (1942) is surely the classic analysis of the role played by land and sea in the rise and decline of empires. 'World history is a history of the battle of sea powers against land powers and of land powers against sea powers', he wrote.[59] While humans are 'land beings and land dwellers', past empires centred on Athens, Venice, Spain, and Portugal proved that the

---

58. Michael Oakeshott, *Rationalism in Politics and Other Essays* (Indianapolis, 1991 [1962]), p. 127.
59. This and the following quotations are from Carl Schmitt, *Land and Sea: A World-Historical Meditation* (Candor, NY, 2015), pp. 11, 5, 31, 46–47, 91, 83.

oceans could be harnessed to extract great wealth and wield enormous power over subjects living at great distances from the imperial heartlands. Beginning with the Dutch, who by 1600 had become the 'uncontested masters of shipbuilding', Europeans perfected the use of rigging and mounted guns, maps and compasses, and other methods of ocean sailing to effect what Schmitt called a 'spatial revolution'. This was more than the opening of a great divide between land and sea powers and their bloody battles. The human fear of emptiness and unknown vacuums and crossing the equator was conquered. 'For the first time in its history, the human held the whole terrestrial orb like a ball in its hand.' The British Empire eventually became the highwater mark of the trend towards 'world domination erected upon the domination of the oceans.' No longer thinking of itself as an island whose destiny was 'bound up with that of Europe', the 'lady of the sea' acted as if it was a 'maritime world empire' destined forever to enjoy 'uncontested rule of the sea'.

Schmitt was aware that the advent of radio and jet-propelled aircraft complicated his preoccupation with land and maritime powers: the air, symbolized by 'a great bird', was probably becoming 'a new elementary domain of human existence', he said. His remarks on air power did more than register the fact of long-distance aerial bombardment as a new and terrible feature of war. They tabled unanswered questions about whether the dichotomy of land and sea, symbolized by the monsters of Behemoth and Leviathan, was still 'the basic law of the planet',[60] or whether it was fast becoming an obsolete template for categorizing empires. China's galaxy empire compounds these doubts. Grasping its unusual dynamics in fact requires jettisoning the land-sea dichotomy.

For a start, despite portrayals of the People's Republic of China as an expansionist and territorially aggressive power, the galaxy empire is

---

60. Ibid, p. 81. Schmitt predicted that this 'basic law' would be confirmed by the rise of an American empire: 'America is the great island out of which the British appropriation of the seas shall be eternalized and advanced in grander style as Anglo-American sea dominion over the world' (p. 87).

not mainly preoccupied with grabbing land and redefining territorial boundaries. The Chinese scholar Ho-fung Hung speaks of China as an emergent 'informal empire'—a 'state with the ambition and capability to project its political and military power beyond its sovereign space' that has no need of 'formal colonies as the old British and French empires had'.[61] He has a point. Topography was the obsession of Europe's imperialists when they met in Berlin (in the winter of 1884–85). In the absence of African voices, representatives of a dozen European states, together with the Ottoman Empire and the United States, decided to carve up the African continent as if it was low-hanging fruit to be picked by the rich and powerful and served freely on their high tables. Prior to the Berlin meeting, 80 per cent of Africa was unencumbered by colonial rule; three decades later, 90 per cent of the continent was controlled by European empires. They took decisions based on latitude and longitude, rivers and mountains, and drew straight lines with rulers to demarcate territorial possession that ignored the realities of existing trade and migration routes and ethnolinguistic communities. Their decisions left a long-term legacy of community tensions, destitution, military dictatorship, crimes against humanity, and uncivil war. The American empire grabbed territory, too. Under the flags of 'liberty', 'self-determination', and 'democracy' and rich talk of 'American principles' as 'the principles of mankind' (Woodrow Wilson), the United States—confirming Edmund Burke's famous remark that revolutions are preludes to building empires—also built a vast global empire by deploying diplomacy, money, and guns to seize territories such as Louisiana, Mexico, and a chain of strategically significant Pacific islands.[62] China is different.

---

61. Hong Zhang, 'Clash of Empires: A Conversation with Ho-fung Hung', *Global China Pulse* 1.1 (2022), p. 178.
62. John Keane, 'Empire of Innocence', in *The Life and Death of Democracy* (London, 2009), pp. 359–373; Edmund Burke, 'Speech in Opening the Impeachment [Saturday February 16, 1788]', *The Works of the Right Honourable Edmund Burke* (London 1887), vol. 9, p. 387.

Previous Chinese empires were indeed preoccupied with territory. They were continental land polities whose defence strategies focused on military threats from the north and northwest. The Han dynasty (206 BCE–220 CE) fought a series of military battles against the nomadic Xiongnu confederation; during the seventh century CE, the Tang dynasty rulers launched campaigns against the Western Turks. The galaxy empire similarly guards its own borders, and pushes to consolidate them militarily, as in Hong Kong. It rattles sabres over Taiwan and announces plans to connect it to the mainland via a giant bridge. China's troops are engaged in skirmishes in the high-altitude border zone with India. To curb the smuggling of goods, drugs, and people, the Chinese government builds steel border walls topped with barbed wire, for instance along the Beilun River shared with Vietnam. At many points on the planet, especially where American influence is limited or waning, Chinese state-owned enterprises and private businesses are also exercising control over territories that double as spaces of investment, technology transfers, the extraction of resources, import destinations, and export platforms. Take the example of Myanmar, where an estimated eight hundred Chinese corporations have invested heavily in farming land and industrial estates—prime examples include banana plantations in Kachin state and several hundred textile and clothing factories in Yangon that control half the local industry and employ an estimated four hundred thousand workers. There is as well substantial state-level investment in multi-million-dollar infrastructure projects, including the eleven-hundred-kilometre oil and gas pipeline from Kyaukphyu to Kunming in Yunnan Province co-funded by the China Development Bank; and the Kyaukphyu Special Economic Zone and deep-sea port on the Bay of Bengal tipped to become the terminus of the China-Myanmar Economic Corridor linking China to the Indian Ocean.

If Myanmar is an example of the business colonization of territory, it's important to see as well that there are growing numbers of places where China has already staked out in effect what international lawyers call 'leases', patches of territory the Chinese government or state-owned enterprises control for a specified time with the approval of local owner-states or municipalities.[63] Consider the example of Sihanoukville: it's a southern Cambodian deep-water port and resort city that functions as a tax-free economic zone and hosts a large diaspora of mainland Chinese workers (an estimated eighty thousand, or 90 per cent of the city's expat population). The city has attracted more than one hundred Chinese-owned factories and features skyscrapers and casinos, restaurants and cinemas, and criminal syndicates in the business of drugs and prostitution. There is a four-lane highway linking Sihanoukville to Phnom Penh; and there's a joint venture by China's AMC International and Malaysian company SV International to build a Wisney World located on a sixty-five-hectare plot that includes hotels, water parks, shopping malls, casinos, gardens, and churches.[64]

Nearly nine thousand kilometres to the north-west, the landlocked Republic of Serbia is becoming a territorial hub for large-scale Chinese credit and investment and showcasing cultural activities in what is locally described as a bilateral friendship 'made of steel' and a regional partnership—the originally named 16 + 1 mechanism (it now includes Greece and excludes Latvia and Lithuania)—established by China to facilitate cooperation with the countries of central and eastern Europe, including Serbia. The Chinese government has funded a new arts and culture centre built on the site in central Belgrade where NATO fighter planes bombed the Chinese embassy in 1999. Chinese corporations RTB and Zijin Mining, one of the largest gold miners in China, jointly operate a huge copper mine in the eastern city of Bor; in 2016, China's Hesteel Group acquired from the Serbian government a steel mill in the city of Smederevo once owned by U.S. Steel; while a Chinese company Linglong is building a $1 billion tire

---

63. 'Lease, International', in John P. Grant and J. Craig Barker, eds., *Encyclopaedic Dictionary of International Law*, 3rd ed. (Oxford, 2009), p. 132.
64. Hin Pisei, 'We're Going to Wisney World!', *Phnompenh Post*, June 21, 2018, https://www.phnompenhpost.com/business/were-going-wisney-world.

factory in Zrenjanin and is the leading sponsor of Serbia's premier football league. The Chinese government is also funding Confucius Institutes in Novi Sad and Belgrade. Several Serbian universities—in Nis, Novi Sad, and Belgrade—have signed cooperation agreements with Shanghai's Jiao Tong University. The Chinese conglomerate CEFC China Energy helps fund the foreign policy think tank the Center for International Relations and Sustainable Development; and the Chinese video-surveillance technology company Dahua Technology has a partnership with the University of Kragujevac, a city in central Serbia. The Export-Import Bank of China financed the construction by the state-owned enterprise China Road and Bridge Corporation of the Pupin bridge across the Danube River in Belgrade; and for use in over eight hundred locations in Belgrade, the Serbian Interior Ministry contracted Huawei to provide cameras and facial recognition software for its 'Safe City' project. When pestilence struck the country in early 2020, China supplied (for the first time anywhere in Europe) over a million doses of Sinopharm vaccine. After declaring earlier that 'European solidarity does not exist. That was a fairy tale on paper ... the only country that will help us is China',[65] the Serbian president, Aleksandar Vučič, publicly blessed the arrival of a team of Chinese medics at Belgrade's airport by ceremoniously kissing the five-golden-starred red flag of an 'old friend'.

Maritime and Air Power?

These sample illustrations of Chinese activities outside the heartlands of the galaxy empire need to be interpreted carefully. We are going

---

65. For the various remarks of President Vučić, including the 'made of steel' relationship between Serbia and China, see 'Vucic: Serbia-China Friendship Made of Steel', *b92*, March 12, 2019, https://www.b92.net/eng/news/politics.php?yyyy=2018&mm=03&dd=12&nav_id=103685; and Sofija Popović, '"Steel Friendship" between Serbia and China Criticised by European Commentators', *European Western Balkans*, March 30, 2020, https://europeanwesternbalkans.com/2020/03/30/steel-friendship-between-serbia-and-china-criticised-by-european-commentators/.

to see that China, unlike earlier European empires, is not a land-based and land-hungry empire. Some Western scholars, politicians, and journalists are unconvinced. They point out that although China may not have territorial designs on its neighbours, or elsewhere in the world, a form of 'internal colonialism' is practised in the so-called autonomous provinces of Tibet and Xinjiang, whose peoples have at different moments laid claim to their own homelands.[66] Although fiercely contested in official statements by Chinese officials, who insist that the People's Republic of China does not tolerate outside interference in its domestic affairs, these interpretations rightly expose and condemn the heavy-handed clampdowns taking place in these territories. But still the general point holds: those who rule the galaxy empire aren't principally interested in seizing and controlling swathes of territory beyond the existing borders of the country. In the name of protecting its own sovereignty and backed by claims that it honours the sovereignty of other states, including those in its neighbourhood, the empire operates differently. It has post-territorial qualities.

So where does this analysis lead? Are we to say that the galaxy empire is better understood (in the language of Carl Schmitt) as an emergent sea power polity? In recent years, extensive media coverage of China's maritime claims in the South China Sea sows the seeds of that impression. China stands accused of ignoring the United Nations Convention on the Law of the Sea (which the United States has neither signed nor ratified); inciting dangerous encounters among commercial and naval vessels and violating rights of innocent passage; brushing aside a Hague tribunal ruling (favouring the Philippines against China) that there was no legal basis for Beijing to claim

---

66. Dru C. Gladney, 'Internal Colonialism and the Uyghur Nationality: Chinese Nationalism and its Subaltern Subjects', *Cahiers d'études sur la Méditerranée orientale et le monde turco-iranien* 25 (1998), http://journals.openedition.org/cemoti/48; Dibyesh Anand, 'Colonization with Chinese Characteristics: Politics of (In)security in Xinjiang and Tibet', *Central Asian Survey* 38.1 (2019), pp. 129–147; and Murat Yilmaz, *China's Development Model as Internal Colonialism: The Case of the Uyghurs* (PhD dissertation, University of Cincinnati, June 2021). The idea of internal colonialism is developed in Michael Hechter, *Internal Colonialism: The Celtic Fringe in British National Development, 1536–1966* (London, 1975).

'historic rights' to the sea and its resources; and promoting 'artificial island building, continued militarisation, and activities which pose risks to freedom of navigation and overflight'.[67]

The intensive media coverage of its maritime claims and manoeuvres in the South China Sea reveal that China is indeed a sea power of expanding importance. The vigorous purchasing and development of port facilities by Chinese corporations reinforces the point. Headed by Shanghai, seven of the world's ten largest cargo ports are Chinese owned. And consider for a moment the much-discussed example of the acquisition of the port of Piraeus, in Greece, by the global conglomerate China COSCO Shipping. It tells quite a tale—a story not only about the galaxy empire's embrace of sea power, but the way its maritime operations are tightly integrated with land-based projects and the vigorous commitment to renting and buying overseas land and ports.[68]

Headquartered in Shanghai, the state-owned COSCO enterprise is among the world's biggest port operators and shipping lines. It is also a global leader in state-of-the-art 'smart port' and 'smart shipping' technologies. During 2020, the company reached agreement with Alibaba and its affiliate Ant Group to develop data-secure, blockchain shipping; in partnership with China Mobile, the company for the first time also successfully used 5G technology to move a shipping container at Xiamen Ocean Gate port. COSCO has one of the largest fleets in the world: over thirteen hundred vessels, including more than four hundred container ships as well as oil tankers, passenger ships, car carriers, and cargo-carrying tramps. In 2017, in support of the Belt and Road Initiative, the company was awarded US$26.1 billion by the China Development Bank.[69] The conglomerate earlier took advantage of the

67. Rt. Hon Jacinda Ardern, 'Prime Minister's Speech to NZIIA Annual Conference', July 14, 2021, https://www.beehive.govt.nz/release/prime-ministers-speech-nziia-annual-conference
68. J. Chen et al., 'Overseas Port Investment Policy for China's Central and Local Governments in the Belt and Road Initiative', *Journal of Contemporary China* 28.116 (October 2018), pp. 196–215.
69. Dustin Braden, 'China Cosco Gets $26B for Belt and Road Initiatives', *joc.com*, January 13, 2017, https://www.joc.com/international-trade-news/infrastructure-news/china-cosco-gets-26b-belt-and-road-initiatives_20170113.html.

2008 global financial crisis to negotiate with the Greek government to invest heavily in Piraeus. The majority owner (51 per cent) of the port facilities and the sole owner of the Piraeus terminal, COSCO's business model is to integrate its global liner and port business operations with feeder services that carry smaller cargoes to and from Piraeus within the wider European region. The business aim is to link the Greek port with other European ports, some of which are part-owned by COSCO. COSCO has a majority interest in a port terminal at Valencia, Spain, as well as substantial stakes in terminals in Rotterdam, Antwerp, and Zeebrugge. COSCO's broader aim is to connect these European hubs with its intercontinental shipping services in Asia and beyond, for instance to its new port terminals in Chancay, Peru, and Abu Dhabi's flagship Khalifa deep-water port. COSCO is planning to bring cruise ships to Piraeus and to expand its portfolio of services to include shipbuilding and repairs. The company has meanwhile bought into a rail freight terminal in Budapest and owns a majority share in Piraeus Europe Asia Rail Logistics. This enables the company to channel shipments between central and eastern Europe and Piraeus and, ultimately, to use its port facilities and the company's large global shipping fleet to change the way goods from the rest of the world are transported into and out of the whole of Europe.

The case of COSCO is significant for several reasons. It's a leading example of the global synergies produced by the integration of land and sea—and proof that the division drawn by Carl Schmitt makes no sense when describing and analysing the galaxy empire. The COSCO dynamics also cast doubt on the more recent proposition that the Chinese government is mainly preoccupied with the secret construction of a chain of naval bases—a 'string of pearls'—in order to become a seafaring great power bent on militarily controlling the world's oceans.[70] The claim is that China is essentially a maritime power—a big power bent on expanding its naval presence and

70. The string-of-pearls interpretation was first developed in an internal report prepared by the American consulting firm Booz Allen Hamilton for the US Department of Defense, *Energy Futures in Asia: Final Report* (McLean, VA, 2004).

electronic eavesdropping posts on the sly by building civilian maritime infrastructure stretching from the Chinese coast to the south via Singapore then through the Indian Ocean—Myanmar, Bangladesh, Sri Lanka, Pakistan, the Maldives, and Djibouti—and the Suez Canal to the Middle East and the Mediterranean, via ports such as Haifa, Istanbul, Piraeus, Trieste, and Valencia.

The Chinese People's Liberation Army is no doubt building up its naval forces. Its fleet of submarines, when measured in numbers, is now the largest in the world. A third aircraft carrier was completed in 2022 (the United States has eleven). It has been suggested that Beijing's current geopolitical calculations, particularly its maritime goals, are repeating the strategy recommended at the end of the nineteenth century by the naval historian Alfred Thayer Mahan, who urged the United States to copy the British Empire by radically strengthening its navy in order to strengthen its overseas markets.[71] There's no doubt that the galaxy empire's long-term flourishing depends upon the control of the South China Sea, which would give it the upper hand over Taiwan, wider access to the Pacific Ocean, and a good chance of breaking the grip of the United States on the whole Pacific region. Since 2016, China has meanwhile been operating a naval support base in Djibouti. Its blue-water capabilities include participation in international anti-piracy operations off the coast of Somalia and (no doubt) intelligence collection, non-combat evacuation exercises, and peacekeeping operations. Energy security ranks at the top of its anti-piracy efforts—China is the world's largest trader and largest oil importer—but what's clear from our analysis so far is that its larger maritime objectives are for the moment linked primarily to its land-based commercial interests, not military supremacy, as is claimed by outside observers. More than that: just as Carl Schmitt predicted, China's burgeoning naval strategy is part of

---

71. James Holmes and Toshi Yoshihara, 'The Influence of Mahan upon China's Maritime Strategy', *Comparative Strategy*, 24.1 (2005), pp. 23–51; the key works are Alfred Thayer Mahan, *The Influence of Sea Power upon History, 1660–1783* (London, 1890) and *The Influence of Sea Power upon the French Revolution and Empire, 1793–1812* (London, 1892).

a wider portfolio of land-based activities that are tightly linked to air power as well.

The galaxy empire is rapidly becoming a major air power. We've seen already that China figures prominently in outer space colonization. Expenditure on ground, sea, and air forces is also mushrooming (the PLA has just enjoyed two decades of double-digit budgetary growth). The growing use of air freight by its state-owned enterprises is worth noting, too. By 2021, Hong Kong became the largest cargo airport in the world with Shanghai Pudong International airport ranked third busiest. Serviced by over one hundred forwarding companies, such as Air China Cargo, DHL Aviation, and Lufthansa Cargo, China is now the world's second largest air freight market (after the United States). Air cargo transportation costs are often five or six times higher than for goods transported by sea, but since every single day counts when cargo comprises time-sensitive products that rapidly suffer from obsolescence, or when goods such as foodstuffs have a short shelf life, air power comes into its own. Air cargo is the especially favoured mode of transport for China's high value-to-weight manufactured goods such as pharmaceuticals, medical devices, aerospace components, and microelectronics. Around 40 per cent of the world's air cargo industry is tied to the production and distribution of electronic products, a field in which China is fast becoming a world leader.

Note in all these various examples, drawn from places as far-flung as Belgrade, Sihanoukville, Hong Kong, and Djibouti, the striking interdependence of land, sea, and air power. It is untrue to say, as did a former Australian prime minister, that in contrast to the United States ('a naval power') China is 'a continental power' and 'commander and occupant of the largest landmass in Asia'.[72] The multidimensionality of the galaxy empire is among its most striking structural features.

---

72. From 'Comments by P.J. Keating on the Announced Agreement between the United States, Britain and Australia' (Canberra), *Daily Mail*, September 16, 2021, https://www.dailymail.co.uk/news/article-9995919/Read-ex-PMs-blistering-200-word-rant-American-nuclear-submarines.html.

The combination of land, sea, and air power helps to explain why its leaders deem boundaries for the sake of uniformity and administrative control relatively unimportant. They understand the pitfalls of penetrating territory deeply, as Chinese diplomats did by refusing the call of Bangladesh opposition leaders for China (its largest trading partner and big Belt and Road supporter) to get directly involved in a heavily contested general election in December 2018. We could say that China's state-owned corporations and governing institutions, even its tourist wanderers—the highest number in the world before the global Covid-19 pestilence—prefer unbounded flows, corridor opportunities, and open borders. Outside the heartlands of their empire, the rulers stand for open borders and long-distance transactions. They favour the rapid and unrestricted movement of capital, goods, and services. The contrast with early modern European empires is striking. Those empires drew boundaries and built and functionally depended upon capital cities at home, and in their colonies. China, by contrast, is an empire preoccupied with flows of capital, the spread of new information technologies, and global markets for its competitively priced goods and services. It connects cities and hinterlands with high-speed railways, airports, and shipping lanes. It is building logistics hubs—hundreds of them, all designed to link together airports, rail and road routes, and cargo ports using information and robotics technologies to boost the efficiency and effectiveness of parcel delivery systems; high-speed rail, sea, and air transport; and cold chain capacity for delivering foods, medicines, and vaccines worldwide. Buoyed by its deep dependence on webbed networks of digital communications, fluid mobility is the currency of China's galaxy empire.

Empire and Communications

Here we come to a point of basic importance when trying to make sense of the historic distinctiveness of the galaxy empire. Communication systems, which shrink space and time barriers and enable power to be exercised over great distances, have always been the lifeblood of empires. The Western Han dynasty scholar Sima Qian said as much two thousand years ago in his *Records of the Grand Historian* (also known as *Shǐjì*, completed in 94 BCE). In the first grand history of the world as it was known by ancient Chinese scholars, he proposed that no empire could be ruled by horseback. The vast Mongol empire that later stretched from the Pacific Ocean to Hungary disproved the scholar's conviction, but what he did get right was the foundational importance of modes of communication in the functioning of empires.

We owe the fullest version of this insight to the Canadian scholar Harold Innis, who famously noted the transformative time- and distance-shrinking effects of such communications media as the wheel and the printing press, writing, parchment, papyrus, and radio. Empires are large-scale and long-distance polities and so their ability to exercise power durably always makes them functionally dependent on what Innis called 'efficiency of communication'. We need not dwell on his suspicion of imperial power (he favoured localized oral cultures and had serious doubts about the grip of what he called 'American imperialism' on Canadian media industries) or rehearse the details of his complex historical account of different empires and their corresponding systems of communication. To understand the novelty of how the galaxy empire operates, we need only note his observation that some past empires relied upon time-biased and durable means of communication—clay, parchment, and stone—while others drew strength from space-shaping media such as papyrus and paper. Innis further explained that media that privilege memory and durability—stone sculptures and monuments, parchment texts—favour empires run by religious dynasties bent on controlling their subjects' shared sense of time-bound tradition. Religious empires of the past were decentralized sets of hierarchical institutions. By contrast, empires more reliant on less durable but 'lighter' means of communication, such as printed official bulletins and gazettes, magazines, newspapers, and letters, were better able to operate through less hierarchical systems of government exercising control over vast distances.

Innis was aware that these distinctions were simplifications of much more complex historical realities, but he was persuaded that they helped to explain the resilience and the collapse of empires. No empire lasts forever. Excess leading to blindness and decadence and eventual disintegration has been every empire's fate. But he pointed out that in the past, long-lasting empires were those that managed to strike a balance between time-biased and space-stretching media, so that 'the bias of one medium towards decentralization is offset by the bias of another medium towards centralization'.[73] He offered the prime example of the Byzantine Empire, which after the collapse of the western Roman Empire flourished in the region stretching from northern Mesopotamia to southern Italy for a thousand years thanks to a working functional partnership between a 'Caesaropapist', emperor-led governing bureaucracy in Constantinople using papyrus to rule over a vast territory and a church hierarchy deploying parchment to maintain a grip on religious teaching and tradition and a polycentric network of Orthodox churches.

Innis was surely right: the historical record confirms that empires owe much of their longevity to their rulers' proficiency in inventing and harnessing communications media. The success stories include the Khmer empire, the largest empire ever known in Southeast Asia. Founded in the early ninth century CE and centred on its glorious capital Angkor, it lasted six centuries, held together, like the Roman and Inca empires, by expansive networks of roads and laterite stone bridges.[74] The sprawling Ottoman Empire is further confirmation of the point. For several centuries, its rulers relied on a horse-run network of several hundred land-based

---

73. Harold A. Innis, *Empire and Communications* (Toronto, 1986), pp. 5, 112. Innis repeatedly warned of the dangers of Canada becoming a dependent colony of the United States. 'We are indeed fighting for our lives', he wrote when examining the 'pernicious influence' of American advertising and corporate media power. 'We can only survive by taking persistent action at strategic points against American imperialism in all its attractive guises' (*Changing Concepts of Time* [Toronto, 2004], pp. 13–14).
74. Michael D. Coe, 'The Khmer Empire', in Peter Fibiger Bang, C.A. Bayly, and Walter Scheidel, eds., *The Oxford World History of Empire* (New York, 2021), vol. 2, pp. 430–449.

postal stations to facilitate linked communication between the imperial centre and the distant provinces that ran from Crimea to Cairo and Belgrade to Baghdad. The linked stations were operated by postmasters (*menzilci*) charged with the job of ensuring the smooth circulation and delivery of imperial decrees and orders, official reports, and appointment letters.[75] The Dutch seaborne empire similarly relied upon cutting-edge communications. We have seen already that by the mid-seventeenth century Dutch trading ships, using state-of-the-art sails, compasses, and sea charts, encircled the globe. For a time, in not much more than fifty years, the Dutch seaborne empire became the world's largest seafaring trader. Dutch vessels shipped goods from the eastern Mediterranean to the Baltic regions, sailed across the Atlantic, established bases in the New Netherlands (New York) and the Caribbean islands. They carried slaves from Angola and Ghana to Guyana and Brazil. After the founding of the Dutch East India Company, Dutch ships used the Cape of Good Hope to trade throughout the Indian Ocean, all the way to the Indonesian archipelago and the China Seas.[76] By the early years of the nineteenth century, the Dutch empire had been outmanoeuvred by the rising British Empire in Asia (Malacca, India, Ceylon), South America (Guyana), and Africa (the Cape of Good Hope). Britannia was to rule the waves and dominate world trade thanks to its pioneering development of coal-fired steam engine technology. The steam engine invented by Watt fed upon its own successes. It brought greater reliability and cost efficiencies in mining and manufacturing—cheaper locally produced coal, and access to plentiful sources of coal globally made possible by iron smelting and ships of steel—and much greater mobility in the field of transportation. In place of wooden hulls, sails, and paddles, steam

---

75. Choon Hwee Koh, 'The Ottoman Postmaster: Contractors, Communication and Early Modern State Formation', *Past and Present*, no. 251 (May, 2021), pp. 113–152.
76. Leonard Blussé, 'The Dutch Seaborne Empire: Qua Patet Orbis', in Peter Fibiger Bang, C.A. Bayly, and Walter Scheidel, eds., *The Oxford World History of Empire* (New York, 2021), vol. 2, pp. 862–883.

turbines powered the empire's free-ranging commercial vessels and the propeller-driven fleets of the almighty Royal Navy.[77]

Historians teach us that during this same period America's young empire pushed westwards with the indispensable help of the time- and space-shrinking media of the railroad and the telegraph. China's emergent galaxy empire similarly depends upon state-of-the-art communications media used by its government bureaucracies, armed forces, state-protected corporations, universities, news-gathering platforms, and other bodies operating on a global scale. But the galaxy empire is different. A reason—the key reason—why this phrase is used is that the vast global and outer space reach of Chinese power draws strength not from steam turbines, iron horses, copper wire and telegraph poles, but from a global galaxy of networked, digital communications media. *The new Chinese empire is the first global empire to be born of the age of digital abundance.* It takes advantage of a media revolution that began during the 1960s and is today unfinished—a major upheaval and transformation of the methods and tools of communication shaped by information networks that for the first time in history, thanks to built-in cheap microprocessors, integrate texts, sounds, and images in digitally compact and easily storable, portable, and reproducible form. This new mode of communications has galactic qualities. In striking contrast to both the limited reach of the 'Gutenberg Galaxy' (Marshall McLuhan)[78] of the printing press and the centralized electronic mass broadcasting systems of radio and television, it is flatter and more decentralized and less amenable to monopoly control. From multiple user points, the new mode of communications enables vast webs of information to be produced, sent, received, interpreted, and recycled, in chosen time, either real or delayed, within a vast galaxy of distributed global networks that are affordable and accessible to billions of users scattered across the planet.

77. Steven Gray, *Steam Power and Sea Power: Coal, the Royal Navy, and the British Empire, c. 1870–1914* (Cambridge, 2017).
78. Marshall McLuhan, *The Gutenberg Galaxy: The Making of Typographic Man* (London, 1962).

Here we encounter an obvious elective affinity—as the European sociologist Max Weber would have said, something of a reciprocal attraction, vigorous convergence, and mutual reinforcement—between the new globally interconnected mode of webbed communications and the meshed, reticulate, multi-nodal, and globalized galaxy empire. *China's galaxy empire and the digital galaxy are twins.* But lurking within their elective affinity is a complication, to do with the way that the galaxy empire is reshaping the unfinished digital communications revolution in its own image, for its own purposes. The earliest analyses of the digital communication revolution could not have foreseen this complication. They were marked by widespread fascination mixed with excitement about the liberating effects of digital networks. There was bold talk of the end of the television age, the disappearance of printed newspapers and the printed book, even anticipations of the end of literacy as the world had known it in modern times. Many observers predicted the replacement of spectrum scarcity, mass broadcasting, and predictable prime-time national audiences by information abundance, fragmented narrowcasting, and less predictable 'long tail' audiences. Others praised the growth of networked globe-girdling media whose time- and space-conquering effects were said to be of epochal significance. There were even claims that computer-linked networks were creating a 'global social space', a borderless 'global conversation of bits', a new world 'that all may enter without privilege or prejudice accorded by race, economic power, military force, or station of birth'.[79]

Despite their far-sighted boldness, many of these predictions turned out to be mistaken, especially the expectation that rapidly expanding global media linkages would rid our world of intergovernmental and corporate barriers to communication. The new communications revolution has indeed fostered a genuinely global galaxy of communication systems as never before. What our world is witnessing is

---

79. John Perry Barlow, 'A Declaration of the Independence of Cyberspace', February 8, 1996, Electronic Frontier Foundation,, http://www.eff.org (accessed September 22, 2023); the mistakes of these interpretations are analysed in John Keane, *Democracy and Media Decadence* (Cambridge, 2013).

a leap well beyond nineteenth-century inventions such as overland and underwater telegraphy and the first development of international news agencies, such as Reuters.[80] Global communication networks are doing what the world maps and globes of Gerardus Mercator (1512–1594) manifestly failed to do: to strengthen the intuition of millions of people that our world is 'one world' and that this worldly interdependence beckons humans to share some responsibility for its fate. But what was missing in almost all these early assessments of the advent of communicative abundance was the way the Chinese government and its state-owned and state-protected businesses have decisively shaped the global ecology of information production, distribution, and reception. Often portrayed as a digital laggard, or as a digital thief, there was little outside appreciation of the historic role played by Chinese networked communications systems fashioned by giant state-protected corporations—giants such as the e-commerce and technology behemoths Alibaba, China Unicom, ZTE, and Tencent. These digital behemoths aren't 'homespun' (to use J. M. Keynes's term for describing territorially bound, state-regulated markets). Bursting the bounds of time and space, language and custom, these media big businesses are better described as players within complex global commodity chains and global flows of information, staff, money, components, and products. These state-backed media giants are a serious rival to Silicon Valley, but they aren't just rivals and alternatives to mega-firms like Time Warner, News International, the BBC, Al Jazeera, Disney, Bertelsmann, Microsoft, Sony, and Google. They are also key stakeholders in the communications grids the galaxy empire is casting over spaces well beyond China's borders.

Harold Innis's much-vaunted distinction between militaristic empires fixated on space and religious empires preoccupied with time is not meaningful in relation to China. Its realm isn't a gunpowder or dreadnought battleship or an American-style B-52 bomber, M1

---

80. Peter J. Hugill, *Global Communications since 1844: Geopolitics and Technology* (Baltimore, 1999)

Abrams tank, and drone empire. In matters of power, China rather resembles a digital information empire, the first-ever empire born of the unfinished digital communications revolution. Its communications systems are shaped not only by Party-dominated government agencies. Communication is big business. The empire sells its digital techniques and tools abroad, as in South Africa, the first African country to buy a Huawei-powered 5G network to support smart healthcare and to develop its ports, mining, and manufacturing infrastructure. Digital innovations such as the Beidou (Big Dipper) global satellite navigation system are playing a prominent role in shaping the galaxy empire. So is the empire's surging foreign press corps. Journalists at China Global Television Network, the *China Daily* newspaper, and other agencies are more than reporters filing real-time stories from abroad: in effect, they double as advertising agents and providers of intelligence for the ruling party-state. The combined effect of these various forces is to ensure that the galaxy empire employs high-speed broadband flows of information to promote government policies, corporate investment projects, banking and finance operations, military manoeuvres, news and entertainment, and other cultural products well beyond China's borders. Government talk of 'cyber-sovereignty' is in this respect—as with official statements about sovereignty more generally—a misdescription of things. China is harnessing the unfinished communications revolution on a global scale—replete with digital surveillance systems and official warnings about the need for winning hearts and minds at home and abroad through the 'civilized development of the Internet' and the building of 'international exchange platforms' to promote an 'online civilisation'.[81]

---

81. The General Office of the Communist Party of China Central Committee and the General Office of the State Council joint statement 'Opinion on Strengthening the Construction of the Online Civilization', Beijing, September 14, 2021, http://www.news.cn/politics/zywj/2021-09/14/c_1127861062.htm.

Tencent

Among the key players in this visionary scenario is Tencent, a corporate giant in China's burgeoning digital media industry—an industry that is not simply pushed and dragged along by the world of the global internet but reshaping its time-space contours.[82] Co-founded by Ma Huateng (his English moniker is 'Pony') and launched in 1998, Tencent is neither a state-owned enterprise nor a home-grown corporation. Backed initially by Boston-based venture capital firm IDG Capital and the Hong Kong–based telecommunications giant PCCW, Tencent's principal shareholder is Naspers, an investment firm whose parent company is the South Africa–based media corporation MIH. With this foreign backing, public listing on the Hong Kong Stock Exchange arranged by Goldman Sachs, and the establishment of research academies in Beijing, Shenzhen, and Shanghai, Tencent quickly took advantage of Chinese government efforts to transform an infant telecommunications sector into the backbone of the domestic economy and a force to be reckoned with on the global stage. State funding of science and technology research already began in the late 1980s, around the time that the first email message—'Across the Great Wall, we can reach every corner of the world'—was sent across China's borders; it was followed by government efforts to embed digital networks into universities, research institutes, and other government bodies, all in preparation for a major push (between 1996 and 2010) to go digital within the whole system of state capitalism. Following the 2008 global financial crisis, Tencent took advantage of the government's Twelfth Five-Year Plan, which highlighted the role of digital technologies in boosting domestic production and consumption, and

---

82. Jun Lin and Yuezhou Zhang, *Ma Huateng de Tengxun Diguo* 马化腾的腾讯 帝国 [Ma Huateng's Tencent empire] (Beijing, 2009); Min Tang, 'Dissecting the Tencent Empire', in *Tencent: The Political Economy of China's Surging Internet Giant* (New York, 2019), pp. 40ff.; and Lulu Chen, *Influence Empire: The Story of Tencent and China's Tech Ambition* (London, 2022).

championed state plans to build a network of banks, financial services, e-commerce, entertainment, and other daily services around mobile internet, big data technologies, and cloud computing.

The combination of foreign capital and Chinese government backing enabled Tencent to craft an aggressive business strategy of mergers, acquisitions, and strategic partnerships (with Korean and German game companies, San Francisco–based Glu Mobile and Elon Musk's Tesla, for instance) to become what's been called a 'synergetic empire'.[83] It is now the country's largest publicly listed conglomerate in the fields of video entertainment, artificial intelligence, and other internet-based products and services. Touting itself as an 'online lifestyle services provider', the company is a major stakeholder in tech companies and products including Spotify, Snapchat, and Reddit, the world's biggest maker and vendor of *Fortnite*, *League of Legends*, and *Clash of Clans* video games, the operator of children's online gaming (it launched *Roco Kingdom* in 2010), instant messenger systems (the first was QQ, developed with the help of Israeli technology), and the huge entertainment, fashion, sports, shopping, and news web portal QQ.com.

Its Tencent Music platform controls the lion's share of China's vast music service industry, with over 700 million active users and 120 million paying subscribers. With stakes in over six hundred companies, and a robust strategy of investment in overseas start-ups (during the first year of the global pestilence investments jumped sevenfold), Tencent is now among the world's top technology conglomerates and China's most valuable publicly traded company—and massive shaper of cultural identity in its heartlands and facilitator of information flows throughout the empire.

Tencent's WeChat is among its most valuable assets and a platform vital for the functioning of the whole empire.[84] WeChat serves as the galaxy empire's steamship, railroad, semaphore, telegraph, postal

---

83. Tang, *Tencent*, p. 45.
84. Haoqi Dang, "A Communication Approach to Understand the Weixin Model', 从传播学角度解构微信的信息传播模式, *Southeast Communication* 7 (2012), pp. 71–78 (in Chinese).

service, radio, telephone, and television combined. Launched in 2011 under the name of 'Wēixìn' and used (by early 2022) by 1.26 billion people worldwide, WeChat is the most popular social network in China. Nearly 80 per cent of sixteen- to sixty-four-year-old people use its services. WeChat's footprint transcends borders. Despite opposition from some Western governments who continue to object to Chinese government data theft and censorship, an estimated one hundred to two hundred million people regularly use WeChat outside the country. In the United States, nineteen million people daily use WeChat services. The take-up rate there is highest among young people (over 20 per cent) as it is in the United Kingdom; for reasons to do with digital divides, WeChat usage decreases progressively with increasing age. Before the 2020 global pestilence, Chinese overseas tourist spending exceeded all others, in consequence of which tourist hubs such as New York, Las Vegas, Sydney, Rome, and London offered WeChat services. Throughout the empire, Chinese diaspora communities and businesses, as well as foreigners wanting to do business with Chinese companies and agencies, including universities, also heavily rely on WeChat platforms.

WeChat is often described as the world's largest multipurpose messaging app, but in practice it is much more influential than that. Combining text, sound, and image in at least seventeen languages, the 'app for everything' (as it is sometimes called) offers a wide variety of services at home and abroad, in over one hundred countries, including Indonesia, Spain, Japan, Germany, and Malaysia (but not in Russia and India). Promoted through advertisements featuring such world-renowned stars as Selena Gomez, Lionel Messi, Liu Tao, and the Backstreet Boys, WeChat users can get news feeds, watch television and full-length movies, translate foreign languages, play games, and send birthday greetings and 'red packet' (*hóng bāo*) gifts to friends. WeChat provides text and broadcast (one-to-many and group) messaging, video calls and video conferencing, videos, and photograph and video sharing. It also offers automatic translation and enables users to exchange contacts with people nearby via Bluetooth; and its services are integrated with Facebook, Tencent QQ, and other social networking platforms. Built on the principle of 'My friend's friend is not my friend', WeChat 'Moments' is an interactive platform that allows users to post text, images, and short videos, and to share music clips and articles and to build mutual friend groups.

WeChat's social bridging and bonding ('social civility') functions spill out well beyond China's geographic borders. So does the pattern of officially approved 'public' accounts for pre-registered users who push information to subscribers, interact with them, and provide business services such as credit card usage, sending and tracking parcels, reservations and appointments, and visa renewals. WeChat also offers 'mini programmes', over three million installable apps within an app that can be used, say, by neighbourhood grocery stores looking for customers, parent-teacher groups, or consumers wanting to buy cinema tickets or pay their bills in supermarkets. Then there is WeBank, which provides loans to small- and medium-sized businesses; and WeChat Pay, an important component of Tencent's move to monetize its products and to become a big player in the field of financial services. With over nine hundred million users of thirteen different currencies spread across twenty-five countries, including South Africa, Italy and the UK, it functions as a digital wallet: with vendors receiving payments in their local currencies, WeChat users with pre-registered bank account details can pay bills, make mobile phone payments for goods and services, buy takeaway food, order a Didi taxi, provide online tips, and transfer money to other users, even across borders.

State Capitalism

In both the heartlands and peripheries of the galaxy empire big businesses like state-owned COSCO and global market player Tencent play a large role, which naturally raises tricky questions about how best to describe its political economy. Whatever is said by its rulers, we can say with certainty that the galaxy empire defies the old nineteenth-century distinction between 'capitalism' and 'socialism'. More than three decades ago, in the aftermath of the dramatic collapse of the Soviet empire, scores of Western observers and leaders predicted that economic reforms in China would do more than bring capitalist prosperity to its people. Market reforms would reduce global tensions by encouraging the country to champion free trade and to 'play a more constructive role in the world'. Capitalism would be the midwife of liberal democracy.[85] It was a wish with an ancient heritage. Earlier in the century, with most European empires on the verge of collapse, it was fashionable to claim that when markets are freed from state control, empire thinking fades and imperial conquests tail off. The boldest version of this claim was crafted by the renowned Austro-American economist Joseph Schumpeter. His reasoning was that 'anti-imperialist tendencies will show themselves wherever capitalism penetrates the economy'. Empires based on political aggression and war were hangovers from premodern times. Imperialism was not the 'highest stage' of capitalism (as Lenin had supposed) but the last gasp of dying monarchies wanting to prop up monopolies by means of protective tariffs, cartels, rigged prices, and bellicose passions. 'In a purely capitalist world', he concluded, 'what was once energy for war becomes simply energy for labour of every kind'.[86] Free market capitalism would put an end to political expansionism. As global market competition gained traction, the atavistic mentality and practice of empire would gradually disappear from the world.

Schumpeter's analysis was flawed—seriously flawed. It ignored the historical fact that 'free trade imperialism' was a defining feature of both the dominant British Empire and the rising American empire.[87]

85. 'Remarks by the President in Address on China and the National Interest', Washington, DC, October 24, 1997, https://clintonwhitehouse4.archives.gov/WH/New/html/19971024-3863.html
86. Joseph A. Schumpeter, *Imperialism and Social Classes* (New York 1951), pp. 90–91 and 70–82.
87. Bernard Semmel, *The Rise of Free-Trade Imperialism: Classical Political Economy, the Empire of Free Trade and Imperialism, 1750–1850* (Cambridge, 1970); and Rollo, *Terminus*.

More seriously, it failed to anticipate the rise of a strange new species of state capitalism in which markets are neither 'competitive' nor 'free' because *government and politics are always the deciding factor when it comes to investment, production, exchange, and consumption.* The galaxy empire is not only today's most powerful instance of state capitalism. It is showing in practice that *this new form of capitalism has expansionary ambitions marked by imperial qualities.*

Chinese scholars and officials aren't especially comfortable with talking this way. We've seen already that they like to say that their country has successfully made a transition from a Soviet-style planned economy to a 'mixed market economy' and 'socialist system' shaped by such Chinese characteristics as pragmatism, respect for social order, and the embrace of Confucian virtues such as meritocratic rule.[88] In reality, state-led capitalism is a more accurate shorthand way of describing the same transition. Inside the galaxy empire, there are pockets of fierce market competition among small- and medium-sized enterprises, for instance in restaurants and street food trading as well as in local agriculture and tourism. Yet small businesses are generally marginal and parasitic upon a political economy dominated by big business entangled with big government.

The galaxy empire is founded on a new form of state-regulated capitalism that practically blurs the boundaries between market and state, economy, and politics. The means of investment, production, and exchange are heavily controlled by state officials who are themselves closely connected with big business circles. Business and government are twins. Poligarchy is the norm. This is to say that the state is the reliable buddy partner of big business: it champions economic growth and is the principal distributor of its fruits and its social and environmental effects. Government bureaucracies underwrite the functional requirements of big business, for instance by means of cheap loans

---

88. Yao Yang, 'The Challenges Facing the Chinese Communist Party and the Reconstruction of Political Philosophy', trans. David Ownby, *Reading the China Dream*, https://www.readingthechinadream.com/yao-yang-on-rebuilding-chinas-political-philosophy.html.

by giant state banks such as the Industrial and Commercial Bank of China (ICBC), the largest Chinese bank by total assets and total numbers of employees and customers. State banking loans are in effect subsidies for companies and whole industries, granting them a competitive edge. The executives of foreign companies such as AT&T and Samsung know—and understandably complain—that the government also places heavy restrictions on outside investment. It pressures foreign companies to share locally their technologies and production methods. The state levies taxes, reinvests profits from state-owned enterprises, applies tariffs and subsidies on traded goods and services, and negotiates international loans, remittances, and various forms of foreign aid. The state is heavily involved in local and global stock markets and generally promotes BRI-style global investment and trade.

Worth noting is the way the galaxy empire's state capitalism isn't a closed economy, as was the former Soviet Union, where within an imperial setting the one-party state owned and controlled the means of investment, production, and exchange and defended the whole political economy against outside 'capitalist' forces. The galaxy empire is different. It doesn't practise autarky in this sense. Its heavily regulated system of state capitalism certainly discriminates against foreign investment in such locally sensitive fields as telecommunications, AI, and the handling of big data. But the whole political economy is on balance open to the world. The term commonly used to describe this regulated openness is *dual circulation*: in the heartlands of the empire, government applies foreign ownership restrictions, administrative reviews, and licensing rules and provides generous tax breaks and cheap financing and resources in order to strengthen the hand of local businesses and reduce their dependence on foreign technologies and products. The larger aim is to promote 'national champions' and 'asymmetrical dependencies abroad'[89] so that Chinese businesses, leveraging their local dominance, display their prowess in regional and global markets. China's dominance of the global lithium-ion battery

---

89. *Strategy on China of the Government of the Federal Republic of Germany* (Berlin, 2023), p. 38.

market—its outflanking of Western automakers who made the mistake of betting heavily on more expensive nickel-based batteries—is a case in point. Huawei, a company that does business in over 170 countries, is another example. Founded in 1987 by Ren Zhengfei, a former deputy regimental chief in the People's Liberation Army, the Shenzhen-based company, whose name was originally drawn from the slogan 'Greater China [including Hong Kong, Macau, and Taiwan] has promise' (*zhōnghua yǒu wéi*), is today a world leader in the design, development, and sales of telecommunications equipment, consumer electronics, and solar power technology. In mid-2020, it surpassed Samsung and Apple to become the world's top-selling smartphone brand.

It is sometimes said that China's one-party state has been kidnapped by business, but it's the opposite: armed with financial sticks and policy carrots, the state specializes in business capture. The distinction between 'economy' and 'state' is difficult to make, for the state makes property rights thoroughly conditional upon government policy decisions and political favours. Government-controlled companies are strategically important players, and leading businesses must be on good terms and well connected with powerful politicians and officials. High-ranking officials sit on the boards of large state-run and 'private' companies. Business oligarchs bent on doing business stay close to state officials, who themselves help run state-owned companies for gain, so amassing enormous personal wealth. It's true that bitter tensions sometimes erupt when state officials are tempted to squeeze companies such as Didi Chuxing and Alibaba. These tensions reveal a deep distrust of private entrepreneurs by the CCP, but the government generally refrains from issuing decrees covering who should produce what, when, and how. There are even moments, as in the live-streamed re-trial (in 2019) of the poligarch Gu Chujun by the Shenzhen Supreme People's Court, when the state strives hard to be seen as the legal defender of property rights.[90]

90. Cui Jia, 'Verdict Called Reassuring to Businesses', *China Daily*, April 11, 2019.

The upshot is that under conditions of state capitalism there is no genuinely independent business community, no bourgeoisie in the sense described and analysed by Karl Marx and other European political economists.[91] Government officials and business tycoons mingle, intermarry, and dine at the same tables. The poligarchs live behind tall walls and in gated communities, and they mix within narrow social circles. They enjoy privileged power positions in state-controlled investment portfolios (sovereign wealth funds), state-owned enterprises, and privately owned corporations operating in such fields as renewable energy, military weaponry, robotics, and telecommunications. The galaxy empire is run by poligarchs. Little wonder that wealth and income patterns are so skewed in their favour. In the heartlands of the galaxy empire patterns of property ownership, wealth, and income are lopsided. Gini coefficients run high (official figures are typically unreliable because of incomplete and doctored data). The rich care first and foremost for manipulating the machinery of the state and doing deals that serve the growth of their business interests, wealth holdings, and political power. The wheeling and dealing are for the most part hidden from the public eye. It goes on behind closed doors, with investigative journalists nowhere to be seen. Officials peddle words and phrases such as 'socialism' (*shè huì zhǔ yì*), 'China dream', 'ancient Chinese civilisation', and 'harmonious society'. There's no end to the talk of 'serving the people' and 'democracy'. But none of this stylized language bears much relationship to the realities of the way institutions and connections and everyday life are marked by great gaps between the rich and the rest. Every week in China, on average, sees the minting of 2 new billionaires, whose total numbers (by 2021) reached 878 billionaires, more than one-fifth of the worldwide total. In 1999, there were no billionaires in China. Its rich list nowadays has a combined wealth of around US$4 trillion, equivalent to the annual

---

91. Anders Åslund, *How Capitalism Was Built: The Transformation of Central and Eastern Europe, Russia, and Central Asia* (Cambridge, 2007), pp. 47–53; Minxin Pei, *China's Crony Capitalism: The Dynamics of Regime Decay* (Cambridge, MA, 2016).

GDP of Germany.[92] Now that China has overtaken the United States as the country where wealth is created in the greatest volumes, often at the fastest rate, it comes as no surprise just how super rich are the members of the three-thousand-strong legislative body known as the National People's Congress. Amidst much media fanfare, the Party-appointed body meets annually for around two weeks in the Great Hall of the People. By global standards, its hand-picked representatives are rich men who live fancy lives at fancy prices. Nearly three-quarters of them are Party members drawn from the ranks of CCP bosses, government officials, military commanders, and company executives. Selected to represent the interests of China's 1.4 billion people, more than one in seven of these delegates hails from the ranks of the 1,271 richest Chinese citizens. The combined net worth of these Chinese delegates is estimated at $463.8 billion, more than the annual economic output of Austria. Their top fifty richest delegates are collectively sixty times wealthier than the top fifty richest members of the US Congress.[93]

Middle Classes

To speak of state capitalism and its currency and finance underpinnings is to raise questions about the Chinese middle classes and the role they play in the young galaxy empire. All long-lasting empires in modern times fostered the political support of a middle class, whose growth and consolidation were linked to imperial expansion. The

---

92. See the UBC and PWC report, *New Visionaries and the Chinese Century: Billionaires Insights* (2018), at https://www.pwc.com.au/financial-services/pdf/ubs-billionaires-2018.pdf (accessed September 22, 2023); and Jane Li, 'A Rich Man's World: China Is Rapidly Producing New Billionaires Despite Covid-19', *Quartz*, October 20, 2020, https://qz.com/1919974/china-created-a-record-number-of-billionaires-despite-covid-19/.
93. Details are drawn from the Shanghai-based Hurun Report 2015 and the Washington-based Center for Responsive Politics, as reported in Michael Forsythe, 'Billionaire Lawmakers Ensure the Rich Are Represented in China's Legislature,' *New York Times*, March 2, 2015; further details are provided in John Keane, *When Trees Fall, Monkeys Scatter* (London, 2017).

late nineteenth- and early twentieth-century rise to global dominance of the American empire coincided with the growth of a middle-class 'consumers' imperium'.[94] European researchers have meanwhile shown that during the so-named golden age of the nineteenth-century bourgeoisie, local middle classes were very much the product of international connections and entanglements.[95] The same pattern was evident in the early modern empires located outside or at the margins of Europe, such as the Ottoman Empire and the Qing dynasty empire, which witnessed the growth of a class of merchants and traders during the massive expansion of commercial activity linked to a vast continental market that stretched across provincial boundaries and into various parts of Southeast Asia and westwards all the way to Europe.[96] In all cases, what is today loosely called a middle class was hatched of local-foreign exchanges. The middle classes of the modern world were not home-grown products. They were typically born of cross-border encounters in an age of globalizing communications shaped by wind-driven clippers, canal boats, coal-fired steamships, railways, and telegraphed messages.

The close functional connection between imperial expansion and the growth of middle classes was spotted by numerous contemporary observers, among them the French traveller and writer Alexis de Tocqueville. He noted that in the new republic of the United States, the middle classes, citizens who were 'not exactly rich nor yet quite poor', were the pioneers and prime movers of westwards expansion, a restless class 'on the march', plunging ahead, aggressively cutting

---

94. Kristin L. Hoganson, *Consumers' Imperium: The Global Production of American Domesticity, 1865–1920* (Chapel Hill, NC, 2007).
95. David Motadel, Christof Dejung, and Jürgen Osterhammel, *The Global Bourgeoisie: The Rise of the Middle Classes in the Age of Empire* (Princeton, NJ, 2019).
96. For the role of the office-holding and property-holding wings of the Ottoman middle classes see Carter Vaughn Findley, *Turkey, Islam, Nationalism, and Modernity: A History, 1789–2007* (New Haven, 2010) and 'Did the Late Ottoman Empire Have a Muslim Middle Class?', https://www.ayk.gov.tr/wp-content/uploads/2015/01/findley-Carter-Vaughn-did-the-late-ottoman-empire-have-a-muslim-middle-class.pdf (accessed September 22, 2023); and Toufoul Abou-Hodeib, *A Taste for Home: The Modern Middle Class in Ottoman Beirut* (Stanford, CA, 2017).

down trees, ploughing virgin soils, conquering newly discovered plains. 'Every year they cross the Mississippi in strength and seize new expanses of wilderness', he wrote. 'They make way for white men in America's wilderness, forming the vanguard of the civilization that will follow, pushing back the Indian, destroying big game, probing the forests'.[97] Tocqueville contrasted the expansionist energy of this class with the 'wholly undistinguished' behaviour of the middle class in his native France. Its monopoly of government, he wrote, infused domestic affairs and foreign policy with a spirit of selfish materialism 'shorn of both virtue and greatness'. He urged the rejuvenation and salvation of the French nation through 'the extension of France itself across the Mediterranean', into Algeria, where the establishment of colony run by an educated middle class would be 'a great monument to the glory of our country' and the envy of all Europe.[98]

The indispensable role of a middle class in building a durable empire was underscored by Tocqueville in an imaginary tale of France ruled by an army led by a Chinese emperor (though he didn't say, perhaps he had in mind Qianlong [1735–1796], who was at the time the fifth and longest-serving Qing dynasty emperor). That emperor, said Tocqueville, would not make the mistake, as the French had done in the early stages of colonization of Algeria, of destroying public records, disbanding local officials, and forcing the 'entire governing class' into exile. Parts of the French population might well obey the new emperor, he reasoned, but without the social support of a locally educated middle class skilled at governing, 'the rest of the country would soon be in a state of total anarchy'.[99]

---

97. Tocqueville, *Démocratie en Amérique*, vol. 2, chap. 21, p. 312; Tocqueville's letter to his mother (Louisville, December 6, 1831), in *Letters from America*, ed. Frederick Brown (New Haven, 2010), p. 243.
98. Alexis de Tocqueville, *Recollections*, edited J.P. Mayer and A.P. Kerr (Garden City, NY, 1971), pp. 5–6; and 'First Report on Algeria [1847]' and 'Second Report on Algeria [1847]', in Alexis de Tocqueville, *Writings on Empire and Slavery*, ed. Jennifer Pitts (Baltimore, 2001), pp. 129–198.
99. 'Second Letter on Algeria (22 August 1837)', in Alexis de Tocqueville, *Writings on Empire and Slavery*, ed. Jennifer Pitts (Baltimore, 2001), p. 14.

The rulers of the galaxy empire understand the great significance of this point. Until two decades ago, talk of the existence of a 'middle class' (*zhōng chān jiē jí*) was officially discouraged. Peasants, workers, and soldiers were deemed the only legitimate social categories. Then came the doctrine of the Three Represents (credited to General Secretary of the Chinese Communist Party Jiang Zemin, and ratified at the Sixteenth Party Congress in 2002) and the announcement that 'the great door to Chinese Communist Party membership should be opened to all advanced elements of the Chinese people'. Things quickly changed. Talk of 'modernization' and the growth of a 'moderately prosperous' (*xiǎo kāng*) society flourished. *Embourgeoisement* became publicly accepted and politically correct. The rulers nowadays publicly acknowledge the growing visibility of the middle class and its vital role in bolstering consumption and promoting 'social harmony' and 'common prosperity'.[100] Little wonder that there are moments when Party officials speak the language of the middle class. They are aware of its rising political importance and the pivotal role it is playing in driving and shaping the global fortunes of China.

The official recognition of a group once dubbed the bourgeoisie in an avowedly 'socialist' (classless) regime governed by a Communist Party may come as a surprise, but seasoned observers, accustomed to the many twists and turns of daily life in China, point out that in fact the country's middle class now includes four to five hundred million people, somewhere between 30 per cent and 40 per cent of the Chinese population. It's true that statisticians and scholars produce conflicting definitions of what it means to be middle class. Fixing a firm figure on the definition (such as US$5,000 annual income) makes little sense,

---

100. The shift towards the official recognition of a middle class generated much debate and a broad-ranging literature, including Xin Ru et al., eds., 'Middle Class: A New Group to Be Recognized', in *Blue Book of China's Society: Analysis and Forecast of China's Social Development* [*shè huì lánpìshù: Zhōngguó shèhuì fēnxī yǔ yùcè*] (Beijing, 2004), p. 58; 'Blueprint for an Overall Xiaokang Society in China', *China Daily,* December 3, 2002; Qinglian He, 'The Notion That Rise of the Middle Class Could Change China Is Just a Propaganda', *Epoch Times,* August 7, 2005; and He Li, 'Emergence of the Chinese Middle Class and Its Implications', *Asian Affairs: An American Review* 33.2 (Summer 2006), pp. 67–83.

if only because of great variations in the standard of middle class living throughout the galaxy empire. Shanghai's middle classes live more comfortably than (say) their counterparts in Dunhuang, Turpan, and Lanzhou; the diaspora middle classes who live, study, and work abroad, in cities such as Cairo, Vienna, and Sydney, live as comfortably as their local counterparts. These variations explain why other observers prefer to define the middle class as people who in matters of disposable income and consumption find themselves (say) between the twentieth and eightieth percentile of the population, or whose per capita income stands between 0.75 and 1.25 times that of others. This definition builds in a reminder that being middle class is a felt disposition. China's middle classes sense that they live somewhere in the middle of the power hierarchy of wealth, status, and power. They share certain attitudes and values in common, mingle and marry, and feel that ultimately their lives are distant from the privileged and wedged between the rich and the poor of their society.

The local and regional diversity and inner heterogeneity of this middle class are striking. Measured by Marxist standards, they are a motley group; they seem hardly to be a class at all. In the heartlands of the empire, being middle class comprises a wide range of occupations, including salaried managers, functionaries in state and private bureaucracies and self-employed entrepreneurs, teachers and administrators, accountants and architects, medical doctors and dentists, local and provincial Party-state officials and real estate agents, IT consultants and lawyers, students who have returned from studying overseas (*hǎi guī*), academics, journalists, and other professionals. Practically all these groups hold down jobs and live their everyday lives connected to the outside world, but since studies of the Chinese middle classes typically focus on domestic dynamics alone, researchers have not seen that beyond the borders of the country there is also a thriving middle class that owes everything to the global expansion of China's economic, cultural, and governmental power. The galaxy empire has opened up career pathways for millions of Chinese citizens in a wide range of fields, stretching from the diplomatic service and information technology industries through to jobs in tourism, overseas policing, military operations, and administrative positions in international organizations such as the Shanghai Cooperation Forum, the Asian Infrastructure Investment Bank, and the United Nations. Chinese people are also engaged in management roles in such corporate giants as CRRC, a state-owned enterprise that employs over 170,000 workers and is the world's largest manufacturer of railway trains and rolling stock equipment.

Despite their wide variety of callings and vocations and potentially conflicting interests, these particular occupational groups living inside and outside China enjoy a common public visibility and readily describe themselves as 'middle class', or as members of a 'middle strata' (*zhōng céng*). Wherever they live, middle-class citizens are usually educated to at least secondary level, own or rent a house or comfortable apartment, and have access to spare cash to spend on themselves and their family. These middle classes also share certain tastes and aspirations: the desire to live safely in gated communities, to send their children to the best schools and to attend university, to dress stylishly, eat well, enjoy good holidays at home and abroad, play sport, and ride motorcycles and drive fancy automobiles. At first glance, these 'bourgeois virtues' look rather similar to middle-class dispositions in Europe and North America. But there is an important difference: a striking feature of the galaxy empire's middle class is its close dependence upon the Party-organized system of state capitalism. It owes almost everything to the patronage and protection provided by this system. More than a few business entrepreneurs have directly gained from their membership of the Party and the restructuring and flourishing of former state-owned enterprises. Middle- and lower-level cadres who think of themselves as middle class are on the payroll of the Party-state. And some members of the middle class are immediate stakeholders in the political system. They serve as a nomenklatura in official posts, ranging from grassroots-level Party branch secretaries and representatives in provincial people's congresses to higher-level bodies such as the People's Political Consultative Conferences.

Unlike the English, Dutch, French, or American bourgeoisie, which historically speaking developed a taste for private property and self-government, China's middle class, despite periodic complaints and moments of misgiving about the political system—as happened in late 2022, when some middle-class citizens joined anti-lockdown protests—seems firmly committed to its preservation. They make jokes about the rulers—'Follow the Party line', runs one of them, 'but listen to your wife'—but mostly they are dead against flipping and turning things upside down (*bó luàn făn zhèng*).

Classic European accounts of the middle class help to explain the difference. Aristotle thought those who owned 'a moderate and adequate property' would be committed to balance and moderation and 'most ready to listen to reason'. The middling class would be the 'steadiest element' and 'least eager for change' within any given city-based polity. Self-government 'is attainable in those states where there is a large middle class', he added.[101] Later observers of the middle classes similarly supposed its taste for popular self-government. 'No bourgeoisie, no democracy' runs a famous formulation. Much the same idea runs through historians' descriptions of the lifestyles of the European middle class. Wedged between the old entrenched aristocratic classes and an underclass of peasants and workers, the middle class had a strong sense of the importance of bourgeois virtues, which were supposed to include such norms as hard work, private property, thrift, religious commitment, individual achievement, patriarchal family life, public respectability, and disciplined order. These historians tell us that bourgeois culture also stressed the importance of education, music and literature, table manners, titles and dress, and representative government.[102]

Current-day observers repeat the point. The Atlantic-region middle classes remain bulwarks of electoral democracy, they say. While the middle classes are sometimes tempted to 'align themselves with

---

101. Aristotle, *The Politics of Aristotle*, ed. Ernest Barker (London, 1968), IV, xi, 1295b–1296b.
102. Jürgen Kocka, 'The Middle Classes in Europe', *Journal of Modern History* 67.4 (December 1995), pp. 783–806.

authoritarian rulers who promise stability and property rights protection', more common is their support for legal rules and institutions that guard their property, civil rights, and daily lives from predatory government. Finding themselves in the social middle inclines them to moderation and balance. That is why they like the rotation of representatives and governments through the pendulum swings offered by free and fair elections. Especially when their numbers are large and they command substantial public influence and respect, 'a broad middle-class' is 'extremely helpful' in sustaining 'liberal democracy'. The conclusion: 'Middle-class societies, as opposed to societies with a middle class, are the bedrock of democracy'.[103] Or so runs the argument.

It turns out that the middle classes of the galaxy empire defy these modern social science precepts. Their background education, occupations, and assets incline them to be loyal to the system; they show few signs of wanting to walk in the footsteps of the independently minded, property-owning citizens of early modern Europe. So how do these middle classes see the world? What is their philosophy of life?

Generalizations are hazardous, but minimally one thing is clear: the middling classes of the galaxy empire don't share a common life philosophy. There is no middle-class ideology. For a start, they are pragmatists, skilled navigators through mazed connections. The middle classes are practised at the arts of figuring out how and why things happen—*tiān wēi bù kě cè*, they like to say. They are competent when handling the unexpected. They're good at practical writhing and wriggling. They scale walls, unlock doors, and open windows of opportunity. They know how and when to keep their heads down

---

103. Francis Fukuyama, *Political Order and Political Decay: From the Industrial Revolution to the Globalisation of Democracy* (London, 2014), pp. 403–408, 440–445; see John Keane's debate with Fukuyama in 'Can Democracy Survive a Shrinking Middle Class?', in *Democracy Field Notes* in *The Conversation*, September 4, 2013, https://theconversation.com/can-democracy-survive-a-shrinking-middle-class-17813. Compare the counterevidence from countries such as Thailand and the Philippines in Adele Webb, *Chasing Freedom: Philippines' Long Journey to Democratic Ambivalence* (Eastbourne, 2021) and Joshua Kurlantzick, *Democracy in Retreat: The Revolt of the Middle Class and the Worldwide Decline of Representative Government* (New Haven, 2014).

and to tailor their lives to Party-state standards. The middle classes can be hard-headed; prone to feel their reality is the only reality that counts, they scoff at the undeserved privileges of the unsophisticated, newly cashed-up rich (*tǔháo*) and ignore the poor. They call the rich and powerful 'big shots' (*dà rén wù*). They carry on as if the poor don't exist. When they live abroad, they regard the poor underclasses around them as people mostly to be avoided, if only because they're not Chinese. The middle classes can be self-righteous do-gooders, as when they donated money and material support to health care workers and citizens locked down in Wuhan during the first weeks of the 2020 Covid-19 pestilence. The middle classes can also be tough-minded opportunists. When they speak about being middle class, they say it's both a matter of wealth and income plus a mindset that believes in getting on through education, hard work, personal resolve, and who-you-know connections (*guānxi*).

Busy at being self-employed, running small businesses, and holding down professional jobs, they dream of a lifestyle where they are financially well-off and can sit pretty for the rest of their lives. They already earn enough to live comfortably, not extravagantly. They own a car or two, or a scooter. Enjoying a common commitment to house, car, and money—the three *zi*s (*fángzi*, *chēzi*, and *piǎozi*)—they like to think of themselves as consumers with buying power. In striking contrast to the 'uniformly gray and uniformly indigent' Soviet-type regimes of the twentieth century, plagued as they were by the 'chronic lack of consumer goods' and cursed by products of 'a single second-rate quality',[104] the galaxy empire middle classes know they dwell in a consumers' paradise. Shopping is a source of personal comfort. China's e-commerce market is three times larger than the entire European e-commerce market.[105] Chinese consumers use Taobao, WeChat, Alibaba's fresh-food chain Freshippo, and other portals to shop online. They unleash their spending power in super-large retail complexes

---

104. Czeslaw Milosz, *The Captive Mind* (New York, 1990 [1951]), p. 66.
105. See 'How Well-Off Is China's Middle Class?', *CSIS China Power Project* (2020), https://chinapower.csis.org/china-middle-class/.

like Guangzhou's Grandview Mall, where each year more than fifty-five million shoppers mingle and make use of hundreds of shops, rest areas, restaurants, games arcades, karaoke stations, a huge kids' park, a rainforest exhibit and natural history museum, an ice-skating rink, a fitness centre, and a live theatre complex. The middle classes have access to reasonable medical care, and they take holidays. Birth rates are declining. In households with children, middle-class couples expect them to go to university, and to do well in life. Both parents usually work long hours, which means they must rely on relatives or hire domestic help, such as cleaners and cooks. These middle classes shoulder family worries—about risings costs of housing, household debts, and care for elderly parents in a society whose dependency ratio (the number of people below age fifteen and above age sixty-five divided by the total working population) is rising fast—but family life is important to them. Getting married and not being a 'leftover woman' is especially important to young middle-class women.[106] The middle class are passionate 'foodies' (*chī huò*) who enjoy good dinners with friends and family. They have a measure of 'green' awareness; they are concerned about rotten air, polluted water, and extreme weather events. They join professional groups, hobby clubs, and other associations. They are not especially religious, though they often find themselves attracted to Buddhism, Christianity, and other forms of spirituality. It would be unfair to dub them 'philistines' (as Hannah Arendt said of the broken-down bourgeoisie of totalitarian regimes) marked by nothing more than 'single-minded devotion to matters of family and career'.[107] The galaxy empire middle classes yearn for better and more fulfilling lives. Some are Party members, but none wants a return to the days of the Cultural Revolution, a decade-long reign of Maoist terror, 'cowsheds', big-character posters, and Red Guard struggle sessions that in the name of eliminating 'capitalist roaders'

---

106. Weiyi Hu, *Being Chinese: Contested Experiences of Sexuality in Contemporary China* (PhD dissertation, University of Sydney, 2022), https://ses.library.usyd.edu.au/handle/2123/29367.
107. Hannah Arendt, *The Origins of Totalitarianism* (New York, 1973 [1951]), p. 338.

and 'counter revolutionaries' resulted in untold numbers of deaths and upended and ruined the lives of millions of people.[108]

When it comes to democracy, the disposition of the empire's middle classes is intriguing. In defiance of outdated predictions that China is on the road to 'democracy',[109] a large majority of the middle classes say they already live in a democracy, by which they mean that those who govern China are normally responsive to the needs and wishes of 'the people'. But few think of themselves as 'liberals' or as supporters of periodic elections and competitive party politics, which they are sure would bring ruinous 'disorder' to the country. Indulging private life, skilled at creating inner sanctuaries for themselves and their families and loved ones, happy in the hives of their homes, they watch what they say, and to whom. They know by heart the Chinese saying that life's troubles are caused by loose tongues (*huó cóng kǒu chū*). Keeping silent about personal convictions is part of the chess game of life. There are moments when they applaud their leaders and praise life's improvements, as if they really believe in the whole system. But they are equally capable of denouncing 'corruption' and bellyaching about excessive state meddling, even though they accept that their everyday lives have improved because of state policies, regulations, and edicts. The middle classes know how things work. They understand the flaws and benefits of the system. They have a measured sense of their own powerlessness to change things. Hence their

---

108. Ji Xianlin, *The Cowshed: Memories of the Chinese Cultural Revolution* (New York, 2016).
109. For example, see Bruce Gilley, *China's Democratic Future: How It Will Happen and Where It Will Lead* (New York, 2004), p. 31: 'The growth of a broad and stable middle class and an autonomous civil society armed with more information than ever, coupled with emergent legal, electoral, and parliamentary ideals of constrained state power, are nudging China in the desired direction. The emergence of a strong reform faction inside the CCP is doing the same'; and Li, 'Emergence', p. 82: 'At present, the Chinese middle class as a whole does not seek any radical change of the current one-party rule. It quietly endorses the leadership in Beijing. Nevertheless, if the past is the key to the future, as economic growth continues, the middle class will not only grow in size but also may change its orientation. Following the examples of its counterparts in the West and other Asian countries, the Chinese middle class may develop not only post-material lifestyle and values, but also play an important role in the struggle for democracy'.

inclination to make 'That's the way it goes' and 'That's how things are' remarks. They mostly support state-enforced law and order, which is why they can say they like democracy and in the next breath curse the disorder born of American-style 'politics'. The middle classes have an unspoken 'We're on the same page' (xīn zhào bú xuán) arrangement with the Party: in return for state support and protection of their lives, they guarantee they won't meddle in politics. They are proud of the People's Republic of China, but seldom do they or their children act as nationalist little pinks (xiǎo fěn hóng) who heap unrestricted praise on China or its government. Their refusal of electoral democracy and their taste for strong leadership and top-down rule is palpable. Guided by a mixture of motives, including occupational pride, selfish greed, family honour, and respectability, mixed with concerns about the future, the middle classes seem happy to be governed—to be left alone to enjoy the benefits of empire and to get on with private lives rotating around family, work, and consumption.

Building across Borders

Just as the galaxy empire is energized and pushed and pulled by the dynamics of state capitalism at home, so the impulses of state capitalism, backed by middle-class support, shape and drive its expansionism abroad. It's been noted already that declining empires talk big but look inwards, retreating to strongholds and building walls. Rising empires look towards horizons and fling themselves into—and onto—the world. The galaxy empire evidently fits the pattern. But there's something less obvious to note, to do with the relationship between the economic and political dimensions of empires. Some modern European empires, most notably the Dutch, British and French, expanded through two steps. Put simply, first came the founding of swashbuckling trading companies (the Royal African Company, VSO, the British East India Company, the Compagnie française pour le commerce des Indes orientales), often accompanied by missionaries.

When local and regional pressures endangered their operations, the governing bodies of the imperial heartlands stepped in to protect what de facto had already been taken. The brutal late nineteenth-century military campaigns of the British in the northern and coastal regions of Nigeria, for instance the use of Maxim guns and explosives to burn, loot, and destroy the Kingdom of Benin and massacre many of its inhabitants, were not exceptional.[110] Often using force, these European armies moved to shape, regulate, and control the empire whose foundations had already been built through investment, production, trade, and consumption. Battles were fought, cruelties dispensed, local rebellions crushed underfoot, new administrative structures erected, taxes levied, laws imposed on the 'lower races'. In Namibia, in what was then known as German Southwest Africa, German soldiers and officials waged the twentieth century's first campaign of genocidal extermination against the Herero and Nama peoples.[111] The galaxy empire operates differently. Grasping its unusual dynamics requires setting aside mainstream 'free market', neoliberal economics and neo-Marxist approaches, both of which, in their own ways, indulge what the Vienna-born anthropologist Karl Polanyi once called the 'economistic fallacy': the reductionist prejudice that all empires are at base founded on an 'economy' whose money-driven dynamics are independent and determinant of language, family life, social institutions, and governing arrangements.[112] These reductionist approaches blur

---

110. See Max Siollun, *What Britain Did to Nigeria: A Short History of Conquest and Rule* (London, 2021); Ronald Hyam, *Understanding the British Empire* (Cambridge, 2010), pp. 576; compare Eyck Freymann, *One Belt One Road: Chinese Power Meets the World* (Cambridge, MA, 2020), pp. 330 ff.
111. Jürgen Zimmerer, *Deutsche Herrschaft über Afrikaner: Staatlicher Machanspruch und Wirklichkeit im kolonialen Namibia* (Münster, 2001) and *Von Windhuk nach Auschwitz? Beiträge zum Verhältnis von Kolonialismus und Holocaust* (Münster, 2011).
112. See Karl Polanyi, 'The Economy as Instituted Process', in Karl Polanyi et al., eds., *Trade and Market in the Early Empires: Economies in History and Theory* (Glencoe, IL, 1957), pp. 243–270. Ho-fung Hung's *Clash of Empires: From 'Chimerica' to the 'New Cold War'* (Cambridge, 2022) is a commendably brave attempt to use the category of empire to make sense of China's imperial tensions with the United States. But it suffers from 'economism'. Setting aside disagreements about mentalities, communication infrastructures, and conflicting governing arrangements, among other factors analysed in this book, it explains the growing tensions between the rising

the key point: as a new type of imperial state capitalism in digital form, the galaxy empire builds and strengthens its innumerable nodes and worldwide and extra-planetary networks through the simultaneous deployment of 'economic' and 'political' instruments. For this empire, the global accumulation of capital depends upon the global accumulation of political power.

Consider China's formidable commitment to building and operating cross-border governing institutions. Through the already-mentioned Chiang Mai Initiative multi-currency-swap arrangement, for instance, China actively partners with the finance ministries and central banks of ASEAN + 3 countries: Brunei Darussalam, Cambodia, Indonesia, Japan, Korea, Lao PDR, Malaysia, Myanmar, Philippines, Singapore, Thailand, Vietnam, and the Hong Kong Monetary Authority. Founded in 2010, it's a regulatory body designed to deal with balance-of-payment and/or short-term liquidity difficulties in the region. The galaxy empire contributes actively to regional bodies such as the 1990 Protocol on Environmental Protection to the Antarctic Treaty (commonly known as the Madrid Protocol, which China helped to negotiate) and the Asia-Pacific Economic Cooperation. Guided by geopolitical calculations, financial gains, and pragmatic consent, not formal treaty alliances, the Chinese government and state-owned banks and companies are also sponsoring and leading new institutions

---

and declining empires as a simple expression of the underlying forces of 'intensifying inter-capitalist competition' driven by a 'crisis of overaccumulation'. Liberal commentators sometimes make the same 'economistic' mistake, as in Charles Clover and Lucy Hornby, 'China's Great Game: Road to a New Empire', *Financial Times*, October 15, 2015: 'Lenin's theory that imperialism is driven by capitalist surpluses seems to hold true, oddly, in one of the last (ostensibly) Leninist countries in the world'. A crude neo-Marxist 'economism' pervades Michael Hardt and Antonio Negri's *Empire* (Cambridge, MA, 2000), which argues, unconvincingly, that our planet is everywhere overrun by the 'single logic of rule' of capitalist commodity production, exchange, and consumption. 'No territorial boundaries limit its reign' (xiv). A neo-Leninist species of economism weighs down heavily on John Smith, 'Response to David Harvey on Imperialism', *URPE: Union for Radical Political Economics*, March 20 2018, https://urpe.org/2018/03/20/john-smiths-response-to-david-harvey-on-imperialism/: 'Imperialism is inscribed in the DNA of capitalism, and if China has embarked on the capitalist road, then it has also embarked on the imperialist road . . . , *a road that leads to war*'.

such as the China-Portuguese Speaking Countries Cooperation and Development Fund and the China-Africa Development Fund headquartered in Beijing, with representative offices in Ethiopia, Ghana, Kenya, South Africa, and Zambia.

To make better sense of these multifarious dynamics, let's probe these governmental dynamics in more detail. They are of three basic types: inclusion and active participation within pre-existing cross-border bodies, the construction of new cross-border governing institutions, and the establishment and promotion of international non-governmental organizations. Most obviously, some political moves involve *strengthening China's influence within existing cross-border institutions*. Its embrace of existing global institutions can be read as the empire's refusal of nationalist protectionism. The United Nations has been a special target of the galaxy empire's diplomatic moves to add Chinese characteristics to existing cross-border institutions. Setbacks happen, as when Chinese efforts to win the leadership of the World Intellectual Property Organization were blocked by a fierce opposition campaign waged by Washington. But bounce backs are common: despite American resistance, China successfully nominated the director-general (Qu Dongyu) of the Rome-based Food and Agriculture Organization in 2020, winning an outright majority of member state votes, with strong support from developing countries. Various initiatives followed: a new management model known as the Hand-in-Hand Initiative; an 'umbrella program' combining China's agricultural development priorities, Belt and Road projects, and support for African and Asian low-income countries; and a Covid-19 Response and Recovery Programme. Within the Industrial Development Organization, China has meanwhile coordinated over thirty UN agencies to sign Belt and Road memorandums and, since 2016, annually co-hosted an event called 'Bridge for Cities' designed to promote the 2030 Agenda for Sustainable Development. Within the International Civil Aviation Organization, Chinese officials have promoted a global 'sky silk road' in support of the Chicago Convention's civil aviation standards. Through the International Telecommunication

Union, China has championed the Belt and Road Initiative in areas such as 'agricultural research and development programs in the Asia-Pacific region, ICT (information and communications technology) research and training centres in Afghanistan, the Trans-Eurasian Information Superhighway, as well as research and construction projects in Africa'.[113] It has agreed deals with China's Export-Import Bank in support of African-focused projects for 'bridging the digital divide', pushed for a new internet protocol, and provided support for telecommunications and consumer electronics giant Huawei.

China's expanding role in UN conflict prevention and peace-building missions in Africa is especially noteworthy.[114] Setting aside its attachment to 'state sovereignty' in favour of intervention in zones of violent conflict, China is now (after the United States) the second largest financial contributor to United Nations operations. It deploys more peacekeeping troops than the other four permanent members of the UN Security Council combined. In 2017, China joined the UN Peacekeeping Capability Readiness System, with contributions of an eight-thousand-strong standby military force and a permanent police squad. Within UN peacekeeping operations, Chinese forces serve as engineers, medical staff, transport drivers and helicopter pilots, infantry unit troops, and as staff officers, instructors, and military observers. Eighty per cent of these blue helmet-wearing peacekeeping troops are deployed in Africa, where in 2020 alone China was involved in seven UN peacekeeping missions. China also provides military assistance to the African Union in support of its the African Standby Force. And it has funded a US$4.5 billion rail link between Ethiopia and Djibouti, its first overseas military base.

---

113. From an interview with Zhao Houlin, secretary-general of the UN's International Telecommunication Union, April 24, 2019, http://www.chinadaily.com.cn/a/201904/24/WS5cbfbb1aa3104842260b7f2f.html.
114. The State Council Information Office of the People's Republic of China, *China's Armed Forces: 30 Years of UN Peacekeeping Operations* (White Paper, Beijing, September 2020), http://english.www.gov.cn/archive/whitepaper/202009/18/content_WS5f6449a8c6d0f7257693c323.html.

Chinese officials are equally active within the United Nations Human Rights Council (UNHRC)—the body from which the United States withdrew in 2018 (it re-joined in 2022). Some analysts interpret China's participation in the UNHCR as diversionary, a tactic designed to minimize scrutiny of its own human rights record, even an effort to undermine UN human rights standards.[115] In reality, the dynamics are far more complicated. Within its various platforms, China has consistently emphasized the *economic and social dimension of human rights*. It finds justification of the 'right to development' as the precondition of 'the enjoyment of all human rights' in the wording of the original declaration, which envisaged a world wherein human beings enjoy 'freedom from fear and want'. It's why vaccines, healthcare, education, transport, and anti-poverty programmes are among the policy priorities of the Chinese government at home and abroad. Human rights in this selective sense are its priority—and a key reason why the PRC regime generates loyalty at home and respect abroad, in such regions as central Asia and sub-Saharan Africa, where the UNHRC, through China-backed bodies such as the Global Development Initiative (launched in 2021) and the Like-Minded Group of more than fifty developing countries, offers member states the opportunity to voice their opinions and interests and devise their own human rights agenda.[116] There are even moments when China takes the lead on gross human rights abuses in the widest sense, as happened when China, president of the Security Council for the month of May 2021, was joined by Norway and Tunisia in issuing a public statement and

---

115. Ted Piccone, 'China's Long Game on Human Rights', Washington, DC: Brookings, September 24, 2018, https://www.brookings.edu/blog/order-from-chaos/2018/09/24/chinas-long-game-on-human-rights/; Lindsay Maizland, 'Is China Undermining Human Rights at the United Nations?', Washington, DC: Council on Foreign Relations, July 9, 2019, https://www.cfr.org/in-brief/china-undermining-human-rights-united-nations; compare Chen Xu, 'Opening Remarks by Ambassador Chen Xu at the Intersessional Seminar on the Contribution of Development to the Enjoyment of All Human Rights', May 28, 2021, http://www.china-un.ch/eng/dbtxwx/t1879641.html.
116. Rana Siu Inboden, 'China and Authoritarian Collaboration', *Journal of Contemporary China* 31.136 (2021), pp. 505–517.

call for action to remedy the injustices produced by Israel's continuing colonization of territory and cruel military attacks against Palestinians.

In the field of cross-border governing institutions, the galaxy empire is pursuing a second type of strategy: *actively building new regional and global multilateral institutions* designed to strengthen its hand in global affairs, along the way side-stepping and outflanking the IMF, NATO, and other governing arrangements established a generation ago by the United States and today in some circles euphemistically called 'the rules-based order'.

Examples of how the galaxy empire is building its own rules-based order are plentiful. Born of a formal summit during the global financial crisis, BRICS is a multilateral grouping of the governments of Brazil, Russia, India, China, and South Africa; in August 2023, at the 15th BRICS Summit, invitations to join the bloc were formally extended to Argentina, Egypt, Ethiopia, Iran, Saudi Arabia, and the United Arab Emirates. Headquartered in Shanghai, its members are committed to closer cooperation in such fields as science/technology innovation, telecommunications and the prevention of drug trafficking and organized crime; reforming global financial institutions; promoting the case for a new 'diverse, stable and predictable' global reserve currency (to supplement or replace the US dollar); and generally strengthening what Chinese diplomats call 'true multilateralism' and the participation and visibility of poorer countries in global affairs.[117] China led the formation of the already-mentioned consortium of central and eastern European countries, originally known as Cooperation between China and Central and Eastern European Countries (China-CEE), or 16 + 1. Founded in Budapest in 2012, with its secretariat in Beijing and 'national coordinators' in each partner country, the regional arrangement aims to promote Belt and Road projects—a high-speed Budapest-Belgrade railway link, the Pelješac bridge in Croatia, and the takeover of the civil engineering division of Huta Stalowa

---

117. Kwang Chun, *The BRICs Superpower Challenge: Foreign and Security Policy Analysis* (London, 2016).

Wola, a large artillery and military equipment manufacturer in Poland. In addition to tightening cooperation with China in matters of transportation, logistics, investment, and trade, the China-CEE has other purposes, such as promoting cultural exchanges, student scholarship schemes, and tourism. Remarkably, some CEE states are members of US-led NATO; a majority are European Union member states, which suggests that the wider ambition of the regional platform is to create cross-membership and overlapping mechanisms designed to weaken US influence in the region and to loosen or 'bi-lateralize' alliances within the EU and not (as some outside observers imagine) to establish a socialist commonwealth of former communist countries.[118]

The cross-border institution building strategy is well illustrated by the Shanghai Cooperation Organisation (SCO). Also known as the Shanghai Pact, it is exemplary of China's burgeoning global power and influence—more exactly, an illustration of its refusal of Brexit-style fantasies of go-it-alone 'sovereignty' and its commitment to building cross-border arrangements that complement its expanding economic empire, along the way addressing its age-old concern with satisfying and protecting good relations with neighbouring peoples.[119] Clothed in affirmations of the triple principles of 'No Alliances, No Confrontations, and No Targeting of Third Parties', the SCO is seen by Chinese officials as a new type of cooperative multi-state partnership, not a military alliance or security community.[120] Founded in 1996 as the Shanghai Five, a pact

---

118. The member states include Albania, Bosnia Herzegovina, Bulgaria, Croatia, Czech Republic, Greece, Hungary, Latvia, Montenegro, North Macedonia, Poland, Romania, Serbia, Slovakia, and Slovenia. At the Dubrovnik Summit in 2019 Greece joined the partnership; Estonia and Latvia have since withdrawn from the consortium. Background developments are analysed in Weiqing Song, ed., *China's Relations with Central and Eastern Europe: From 'Old Comrades' to New Partners* (London, 2017).
119. See, for example, Daniel McMahon, *Rethinking the Decline of China's Qing Dynasty: Imperial Activism and Borderland Management at the Turn of the Nineteenth Century* (London, 2014); and Martin Saxer and Juan Zhang, *The Art of Neighbouring: Making Relations across China's Borders* (Amsterdam, 2017).
120. Thomas Wilkins, 'Building Regional Security Architecture: The Shanghai Cooperation Organisation. From an Organisational Theories Perspective', in Mehdi Parvizi Aminah, ed., *State, Society and International Relations in Asia* (Amsterdam, 2010), p. 165.

agreed by China, Kazakhstan, Kyrgyzstan, Russia, and Tajikistan, the SCO was initially committed to bringing greater security and political stability to the Central Asian region, strengthening economic ties between China and the natural gas- and oil-rich former Soviet republics, and rolling back the regional influence of outside powers, especially the United States. Following the SCO Charter signed in early July 2002, it expanded, to include eight member states (Uzbekistan joined in 2001; India and Pakistan joined in 2017), together with a sizeable group of 'observer states' (Mongolia, Afghanistan, Belarus, and Iran) and 'dialogue partner' states (including Armenia, Azerbaijan, Cambodia, Nepal, Sri Lanka, and Turkey). The SCO is governed by decisions taken at annual meetings of its members within a body called the Heads of State Council. Its deliberations are in two official languages: Chinese and Russian. Covering an enormous landmass, the arrangement has become a networked organization committed to dampening rival geostrategic agendas of the states within its ranks plus strengthened cooperation with the UN (wherein it's an observer in the General Assembly and a member of the Office on Drugs and Crime) and other multilateral groupings such as BRICS, the G20, NATO, ASEAN, and the African Union. The SCO conducts regular military exercises among members—four of whom are nuclear-tipped—in support of cooperation and protection against terrorism and other external threats, and to promote what its officials call regional peace and stability. It has economic aims, too. Promotion of the Belt and Road Initiative is among its key aims. Measured in terms of GDP (20 per cent of the world's total), population (40 percent of the world), and footprint size (nearly two-thirds of the Eurasian continent), the SCO is now the world's largest regional organization backed by states who feel aggrieved by their under-representation in global affairs.

In addition to its active participation within established cross-border bodies and the founding of new regional and global governing institutions, galaxy empire initiatives are making their mark in the field of international non-governmental organizations (INGOs). These cross-border organizations are without exception government initiatives;

strictly speaking they are not civil society organizations. They are better described as GONGOs: governmental non-governmental organizations. The Chinese government currently supports more than 130 of these GONGOs spread across at least one hundred countries. Confucius Institutes—their stated brief is the promotion of Chinese language and cultural exchanges—are perhaps the best known and most controversial examples. Other initiatives command little media attention outside the heartlands of the galaxy empire. One of them is a foundation called Amity. More than an acronym (accountability; motivation; integrity; teamwork; youthfulness), it is the world's largest printer and exporter of Bibles whose stated mission is ambitious: 'Printing Bibles for Chinese Christians and churches and for overseas churches and many Bible societies worldwide, serving the Chinese society and Chinese people'. Among the oldest GONGO is the China Foundation for Rural Development (formerly it was known as the China Foundation for Poverty Alleviation). Founded in 1989 and supervised by the Ministry of Agriculture and Rural Affairs, it is a registered charitable organization that carries out humanitarian relief and long-term poverty reduction programmes work in twenty-five countries, with registered offices in Cambodia, Ethiopia, Laos, Myanmar, and Nepal. Other GONGO bodies include the China Association for NGO Co-operation, a global (164-member state) network of global finance and development organizations guided by a 'Code of Conduct of Chinese Social Organizations in International Project Cooperation'. The pace of growth of GONGOs appears to be accelerating. Just before and during the Covid-19 outbreak, there was a flurry of new initiatives, including the Second Silk Road NGO Cooperation Network Forum convened in Beijing; the establishment of the China-Italy Charity Forum; the launch of the Silk Road One Family Initiative; and the setting up of government-funded overseas support bodies for Chinese students studying abroad.[121]

121. Ying Wang, 'Going Global: The International Endeavours of Chinese NGOs', *People's Map of Global China*, June 1, 2021, https://thepeoplesmap.net/2021/06/01/going-global-the-international-endeavours-of-chinese-ngo/.

Finance Matters

This book of essays has so far pictured the galaxy empire as a new kind of state-organized capitalism whose global and extra-terrestrial reach is powered by systems of digital communications harnessed by a vast constellation of government-protected businesses and cross-border governing institutions. The picture wouldn't be complete without saying a few words about the galaxy empire's government-backed banking and currency arrangements.

All previous empires invested much time and technical energy in developing their own credit and banking systems and currency arrangements. The *akçe* silver coin was the chief monetary unit of the Ottoman Empire. The Dutch guilder was the bedrock of the chartered, limited liability joint stock companies (such as the United East India Company and the West India Company that enabled the early Dutch empire, centred on Amsterdam, the financial capital of Europe, to dominate world trade until the early decades of the eighteenth century, when it was overtaken by London and its pound sterling). From the end of the fifteenth century, under the reign of King Manuel I (1495–1521), the Portuguese empire relied upon the medium of coins minted from copper known as *real* (meaning 'royal'). The currency facilitated the seizure of lands and trade and commerce in spices, textiles, porcelain, tobacco, sugar, and slaves in a vast geographic zone that extended from African enclaves and south Asian ports to islands in the Atlantic, all the way to the hinterlands of Brazil. The galaxy empire is no exception to this old rule that empires functionally require robust and durable monetary arrangements; although the fundamentals of its currency and credit model remain work in progress, several striking trends are already observable.

Most obvious and of long-term significance for the whole world is the drive to globalize the renminbi ('the people's money', or RMB) and to downgrade or even overtake the US dollar as the world's leading currency. The de-dollarization efforts date from 2009, when

Chinese bankers and government leaders and officials gave priority to protecting their banking and credit system from global market failures and possible Washington-led sanctions of the kind targeted at Iran and Russia.[122] That was the moment that featured a step jump in awareness that a new global financial system was a requirement of China's global expansion. The reasoning was fuelled by long-held Chinese concerns over the dominance of the US dollar, which left the Chinese economy, particularly its large foreign exchange reserves, vulnerable to the vagaries of domestic US policy decisions and the fallout effects of punctured speculative bubbles. The empire's officials and diplomats began lobbying hard to join the Special Drawing Right, a reserve asset facility created by the IMF to supplement its members' global reserves, a basket currency comprising the US dollar, Japanese yen, euro, and the pound sterling. It succeeded; on October 1, 2016, the RMB was finally included in the Special Drawing Rights basket.

The RMB or Chinese yuan has since come to rival the pound sterling and the Japanese yen for third place in the table of the world's most widely used currencies (after the US dollar and euro).[123] US sanctions against Chinese companies (in 2020) only served to accelerate this trend, encouraging Chinese officials and companies to see themselves, as Japan and the EU did during earlier periods of discomfort with the dollar system, to join Russia and other countries in a global rebellion against a world financial system defined by currency unipolarity in

---

122. Days before a 2009 G20 summit in London, Zhou Xiaochuan, governor of the People's Bank of China, suggested the creation of a new international currency reserve to replace the US dollar. See David Barboza, 'China Urges New Money Reserve to Replace Dollar', *New York Times*, March 23, 2009, https://www.nytimes.com/2009/03/24/world/asia/24china.html.

123. Haihong Gao and Yongding Yu, 'Internationalisation of the Renminbi', in A. Filardo and J. Yetman, eds., *Currency Internationalisation: Lessons from the Global Financial Crisis and Prospects for the Future in Asia and the Pacific* (Bank for International Settlements Paper No. 61, 2011), pp. 105–124, at https://www.bis.org/repofficepubl/arpresearch200903.05.pdf; and Hyo-Sung Park, 'China's RMB Internationalization Strategy: Its Rationales, State of Play, Prospects and Implications' (*Mossavar-Rahmani Center for Business & Government of Harvard University Associate Working Paper Series* No. 63, August 2016), https://www.hks.harvard.edu/sites/default/files/centers/mrcbg/files/park_final.pdf.

the form of US dollar hegemony. The rebellion initially targeted the East Asian and South-East Asian region, which is a 'natural habitat' for the RMB to develop into a widely used international currency.[124] But the rebellion is widening. In mid-2023, for the first time, the RMB topped the US dollar in China's cross-border transactions. In Hong Kong, RMB-denominated stocks and bonds now openly trade on a global basis. There is a surge of RMB-denominated financial assets held by overseas institutions and individuals and large increases in the quantity of RMB held by countries in foreign currency reserves, while over half the world's central banks now hold the RMB in their reserve assets. Bilateral trade agreements with countries such as Brazil and Argentina accelerate the switch from dollars to RMB. Chinese government efforts to buy oil and gas from Saudi Arabia in yuan—in effect, to weaken the US-Saudi petrodollar agreement that has fortified the US dollar since the 1970s, and that has allowed the American government to run massive budget deficits and to spend hundreds of billions annually on its military—are also intensifying.

Chinese government efforts to back the RMB with holdings of gold are also well underway. Not enough is known about the steady acquisition of a metal designed to back the imperial currency and to protect its corporations possessive and citizens' private wealth. There are estimates that whereas over 65 per cent of the foreign exchange reserves of the United States are backed by gold, barely 3 per cent of China's foreign exchange holdings are supported by gold, but that figure is probably understated. China imports more gold—by way of Switzerland, Dubai, and Hong Kong, through the Shanghai Gold Exchange—than any other polity. Since the year 2000, more than seven thousand tonnes of gold have also been mined in China. In 2007, China overtook South Africa as the world's leading gold producer and has remained so until this day. During the past decade, some 15 per cent of the world's gold has been mined in China, over

---

124. Callan Windsor and David Halperin, 'RMB Internationalisation: Where to Next?', *Reserve Bank of Australia Bulletin*, September 2018, https://www.rba.gov.au/publicati ons/bulletin/2018/sep/pdf/rmb-internationalisation-where-to-next.pdf.

half of it by state-owned enterprises such as the China National Gold Group Corporation. The export of domestic mine production is not permitted. Chinese mining companies have meanwhile been buying gold mine assets abroad, throughout Africa, Asia, and South America. The broad trends suggest that the empire's actual gold reserves are probably much higher than those reported by official bodies such as the World Gold Council. The discrepancy between official and unofficial figures is politically understandable, since the Party-state clearly has no interest in openly declaring its actual holdings, public knowledge of which would probably cause an unwanted surge in both the RMB and the price of gold and lead to a devaluation of the Chinese government's massive holdings of an estimated US$3.2 trillion foreign exchange reserves—US dollar holdings that are larger than Britain's annual GDP and greater than any other government on the planet. As in other areas, the minimum aim of the gold strategy is to achieve financial parity with the United States. Later, if circumstances and luck permit, the galaxy empire might aim for global supremacy. Whether that development would be to its advantage or serve as its curse is for the future to decide.

Those who hold the gold make the rules, it's said, which is why China is meanwhile moving to build and strengthen its currency swap arrangements. As the largest trader in the world, and a huge exporter—China is the biggest steel exporter, the leading merchandise exporter, and exporter of more than a third of global household goods—the galaxy empire naturally wants to eliminate the transaction costs associated with using the US dollar by developing bilateral trade settlement agreements in RMB and, more importantly, avoiding the 0.01 per cent fee for using the Belgium-based, US-backed Worldwide Interbank Financial Telecommunications (SWIFT) when making cross-border payments. Given the huge sums of money involved in its cross-border transactions, China has every incentive to cut costs and retain profits from cross-border payments. That is why in 2015, backed by the People's Bank of China, China launched its own Cross-Border Interbank Payment System (CIPS). Several large foreign banks are among its shareholders, including Standard Chartered, HSBC, the ANZ Banking Group, and BNP Paribas. Some 1,280 financial institutions located in 103 countries are already connected to CIPS, which processed (in 2021) a not insignificant 80 trillion yuan ($12.68 trillion). More than thirty African banks currently receive yuan funds in connection with the Belt and Road Initiative. For the moment, CIPS users still operate through the messaging systems of dollar-based SWIFT, but the new RMB-based system is a potential rival. As a clearing and settlement services system that already enables global banks to clear cross-border RMB transactions directly onshore, instead of using clearing banks in offshore RMB hubs, CIPS could in future operate more independently by strengthening its existing lines of communication with an expanded portfolio of financial organizations.

The historic significance of the galaxy empire's efforts to secure its currency foundations is confirmed by its quickening role as the globe's leading creditor. Just as the United States overtook the United Kingdom (in 1929) as the world's largest creditor, so in creditor terms China has now overtaken the United States. In the fiscal year 2019–20, the World Bank's commitments, disbursements, and gross issuances totaled just over US$77 billion.[125] Over a slightly longer period of seventeen months, between May 2019 and September 2020, the IMF approved US$165 billion in loans. By comparison, Chinese outward foreign direct investment for 2020 amounted to almost US$133 billion.[126] With a reputation as a 'muscular and commercially savvy lender',[127] Chinese banks and their subsidiaries have so far lent about $1.5 trillion in direct loans and trade credits to more

---

125. World Bank, *Annual Report 2020* (Washington, DC, 2020), p. 13; International Monetary Fund, *Annual Report 2020* (Washington, DC, 2020), p. 9.
126. C. Textor, 'Annual Outflow of Foreign Direct Investment (FDI) from China between 2010 and 2020', *Statista*, April 12, 2021, https://www.statista.com/statistics/858019/china-outward-foreign-direct-investment-flows/.
127. Anna Gelpern, Sebastian Horn, Scott Morris, Brad Parks, and Christoph Trebesch, *How China Lends: A Rare Look into 100 Debt Contracts with Foreign Governments* (London, 2021), https://docs.aiddata.org/ad4/pdfs/How_China_Lends__A_Rare_Look_into_100_Debt_Contracts_with_Foreign_Governments.pdf.

than 150 countries around the globe. This has turned China into the world's largest official creditor—surpassing traditional lenders such as the World Bank, IMF, and OECD creditor governments combined.[128] The financial capital of the galaxy empire, Shanghai, now outranks Singapore, Tokyo, and Hong Kong in global league tables; according to the Global Financial Centres Index, New York remains the world's highest-ranked financial centre, but Shanghai has been closing the gap (from nearly 200 points in 2007 to 22 in 2021) and now ranks just one point shy of second-placed London.[129]

These comparisons and considerations—China's transformation into the world's largest trading and creditor power backed by its own currency swap measures, gold holdings, and a cross-border payments system (CIPS)—must be handled with care, especially because China is not on the road to becoming yet another case of unbridled 'finance capitalism' whose economy is substantially dominated or (when things go wrong) threatened by non-state banking and credit institutions. In the OECD, for instance, Luxembourg's financial service sector is the largest, contributing around 25 per cent of the country's economic output; in the United Kingdom the equivalent figure is 8.5 per cent, while in the United States the financial services sector is the principal economic sector, contributing 22.3 per cent (in 2020) of output. At first glance, it may seem that China is trending in the same direction. In 1978, at the beginning of the country's opening to the global economy, the financial sector contributed around 2.1 per cent to China's GDP; by 2020, it had grown four times, comprising around 8.3 per cent of GDP. By global standards, household savings held by Chinese banks and credit institutions are predicted to rise to an impressive $46 trillion by 2025, while foreign capital has poured

---

128. Sebastian Horn, Carmen M. Reinhart, and Christoph Trebesch, 'How Much Money Does the World Owe China?', *Harvard Business Review*, February 26, 2020, https://hbr.org/2020/02/how-much-money-does-the-world-owe-china.
129. See the home page of Z/Yen, London's leading commercial think-tank, available at https://www.longfinance.net/programmes/financial-centre-futures/global-financial-centres-index/gfci-29-explore-data/gfci-over-time/.

into the purchase of Chinese government bonds, with foreign investors currently holding around 11 per cent of Chinese sovereign debt.[130] But, as we have already seen, in contrast to finance capitalist economies, the galaxy empire is a species of heavily government-regulated capitalism, in which financial services and equities markets, with their massive market capitalizations, are not only considerably smaller than in the United States, but much more tightly regulated, and therefore enjoy considerably less independence in the empire's overall economy.[131] The galaxy empire is not a replica of the early twentieth-century European empires described by J. A. Hobson and Vladimir Lenin as the 'highest stage of capitalism' run by 'great financial houses' and money-lending classes that drive 'the business of Imperialism'.[132]

The Party-state's efforts to control the banking and credit sectors may be seen as the manifestation of an old Confucian tradition in which the government controls key economic activities like the production of metal, salt, and tea. But when it comes to financial matters, the galaxy empire uses thoroughly twenty-first-century methods.

CEOs in the banking and credit sector are mandated by the state to guarantee financial stability and success, restrain financial speculators, and eliminate corruption. There are extensive controls on capital flows and tightly regulated financial markets. The RMB is prevented from freely floating on the world's currency markets through a so-called 'managed floating exchange rate system', whereby the People's Bank of China sets a daily central parity rate against the US dollar and limits changes to the RMB's value to within 2 per cent either side of that mark. The process of transforming the RMB into a global currency

---

130. Rupa Subramanya, 'China's Domination of Global Finance about to Take a Quantum Leap', *Nikkei Asia*, July 20, 2021.
131. Matthew Johnston, 'China's Stock Markets vs. U.S. Stock Markets', *Investopedia*, May 1, 2020), https://www.investopedia.com/articles/investing/092415/chinas-stock-markets-vs-us-stock-markets.asp.
132. John A. Hobson, *Imperialism: A Study* (London, 1905 [1902]), pp. 56–59; Vladimir Lenin, *Imperialism, the Highest Stage of Capitalism* (London, 1948 [1917]).

is slow, and (so far) deliberately restrained.[133] Government controls of money are indeed strict.

And yet: impressive are the many ways in which the galaxy empire is reshaping the worlds of currency, banking, and credit. The realignment dynamics, as in other policy fields such as cross-border governing arrangements, are evident in efforts, such as negotiated access to special drawing rights, to align and to integrate on a 'win-win' basis financial services with the economies of the United States and Europe. Probably of greater long-term importance is the building of independent financial services institutions, most important of which is the new Asian Infrastructure Investment Bank (AIIB). Established in 2016 in the face of Washington's call to boycott the initiative and Japan's refusal to join, the first Asia-based international bank separated from the US-dominated Bretton Woods institutions, the IMF and the World Bank, the AIIB attracted fifty-seven founding members, among them Indonesia, Britain, Saudi Arabia, Australia, Brazil, France, and Germany. The AIIB now has 106 members. Some observers say that the bank is a rogue competitor of the Asian Development Bank and the World Bank, a body designed to undermine Washington-led global financial institutions. In reality, the AIIB is an example of how a hybrid system led by an emerging empire might work in practice—resulting for the time being in the reshaping of a Washington-led financial order by new China-led financial institutions.

There's one other important dynamic helping to reshape the galaxy empire's financial power: the state's commitment to a digital currency. Elsewhere in the world, champions of Bitcoin, Ethereum, and other new currencies often say that these alternatives pose a positive 'paradigm' challenge to the dogma that states enjoy a 'natural' monopoly on the issue of currency and the regulation of the money supply. More outspoken cryptocurrency fans go further. They predict that cryptocurrencies are a force for 'peaceful coexistence' of citizens

---

133. See the People's Bank of China 'Report on the Internationalization of the RMB in 2020', August 14, 2020.

blessed in their private ownership of a currency that guarantees 'stability of possession' and 'transference by consent'.[134] The Chinese government stands squarely against this way of thinking. It moved quickly to introduce the digital renminbi as an official currency (also known as the e-CNY) issued by China's central bank, the People's Bank of China. The currency was formally launched in Singapore (in early 2021), well ahead of Federal Reserve plans to create a digital currency in support of the competitiveness and attractiveness of the US dollar. The galaxy empire thus became the first recorded empire to issue a digital currency as legal tender. The digital RMB is equal in value to other forms of RMB, such as bills and coins, and among its functional purposes is to facilitate both domestic and international financial transactions by lowering transaction costs and speeding up transfers. In contrast to Bitcoin and Ethereum, the e-currency is not a cryptocurrency, if by that word is meant a digital currency in which transactions are verified and records maintained by a decentralized system using cryptography, rather than by a central authority. The digital RMB is a government-controlled form of legal tender that is not only exchangeable with physical RMB; it is also distinct from digital payment systems such as WeChat Pay and Alipay, which use existing forms of money rather than their own legal tender.[135]

While still in its early stages and subject to further testing, experimentation, and revision, the digital RMB has long-term strategic advantages. The e-RMB is designed to ward off threats from Bitcoin and other cryptocurrencies. Crackdowns on unregulated cryptocurrencies are motivated less by environmental concerns—Bitcoin's annual carbon footprint is equivalent to that of the Czech Republic; a single Bitcoin transaction generates the same carbon emissions as 2.8 million credit or debit card transactions—but rather by understandable

---

134. Álvaro D. Maria, *The Philosophy of Bitcoin* (Madrid, 2022), pp. 35ff., 65ff, 101–102; see also F.A. Hayek, *The Denationalisation of Money* (London, 1976).
135. Heng Wang, 'China Meets Digital Currency: E-CNY and Its Implications for Businesses', *Law Gazette*, November 2021, https://lawgazette.com.sg/feature/china-meets-digital-currency-e-cny-and-its-implications-for-businesses/.

concerns about their vulnerability to profit-seeking pyramids and bubbles whose bursting, judging by the history of modern capitalist booms and busts, would inflict serious damage on the whole empire and the global institutions which nurture its power. Unsurprisingly, the banning of cryptocurrencies and the promotion of the e-RMB is consistent with a basic rule of the galaxy empire's state capitalism: market innovations are welcomed as triggers of dynamic change, but the euphoria unleashed must be dampened by government intervention geared to fostering political stability.

But there's something else, something more visionary about the new digital currency. Its ultimate purpose is to rival the US dollar and prevent its weaponization. The e-RMB deployment, runs the calculation, has the advantage of reducing Chinese susceptibility to future US sanctions (just as the tiny Marshall Islands and the Bahamas have done by developing a new blockchain-based currency)[136] and strengthen Chinese 'monetary sovereignty by circumventing the SWIFT network'.[137] The imperial quest to spread usage of its own currency functionally requires efforts to make new digital financial rules and set up standards on cross-border digital transactions, risk supervision, and data management, as Chinese officials first proposed when tabling proposals for new 'global sovereign digital currency governance' arrangements at the Bank for International Settlements Innovation Summit in March 2021.[138]

---

136. Thaddeus Jahn and Peter Müller, 'Central Bank Digital Currencies: The State of Play in China and Asia-Pacific', *Polis Blog*, December 10, 2020, https://polis180.org/polisblog/2020/12/10/central-bank-digital-currencies-the-state-of-play-in-china-and-asia-pacific/.
137. Robert Greene, 'What Will Be the Impact of China's State-Sponsored Digital Currency?', *Carnegie Endowment for International Peace*, July 1, 2021, https://carnegieendowment.org/2021/07/01/what-will-be-impact-of-china-s-state-sponsored-digital-currency-pub-84868. See also Daniel Broby, 'China's Digital Currency Could Be the Future of Money—but Does It Threaten Global Stability?', *The Conversation*, May 11, 2021, https://theconversation.com/chinas-digital-currency-could-be-the-future-of-money-but-does-it-threaten-global-stability-160560.
138. Rebecca M. Nelson and Karen M. Sutter, 'De-dollarisation Efforts in China and Russia', *Congressional Research Service, In Focus*, 1885 (July 23, 2021).

Resilience, Resistance

These pages have so far described and probed the most obvious contours of an empire whose remarkable rise historians half a century from now will surely record as a transformation of planetary significance. The long-term viability of the new galaxy empire and whether or to what extent it can irreversibly change the world are still to be examined, but one point should already be clear: if by the word 'empire' we mean a polity whose transformative power stretches well beyond its borders in such matters as banking and credit systems, capital investment, cultural symbols, governing arrangements, and military strength, then China, whatever its diplomats, scholars, and officials say, is fast becoming an empire with a planetary reach. Breaking news and headline statistics tell something of the trend, but truer measures of the global transformation now taking place are urgently required. That is the overall point of this book: written as a chapterless, long essay using a multiplex style that aims to mimic and draw attention to the multifaceted, multiplex qualities of the galaxy empire it is investigating, it probes developments whose historic significance can be grasped only by moving beyond the superficial thinking and slapdash reports of breaking news to delve more deeply into large trends that confirm that China, a young, emergent empire of a kind never witnessed before in world history, is much more than a 'sovereign state' or a 'big power' or monolithic 'autocracy'.

The achievements of the galaxy empire during the past half century are impressive by any standards. China is now the world's largest trading and creditor power backed by its drive to globalize the RMB through its own state-owned banks, currency swap measures, gold holdings, a new cross-border payments system (CIPS), and an e-currency. The empire's mantra of sovereignty and territorial integrity is belied by active participation in regional and global governing bodies and the building of new cross-border institutions. Neither an old-fashioned land empire nor a maritime empire, China is a leading air power dedicated to reaching into and permanently occupying the heavens. Backed by corporate telecommunications giants such as Tencent and Huawei, the new empire with post-territorial qualities is the first global empire to be born of the age of digital networked communications. It is the world's largest trading country, owner of half the world's patents, the EU's main trading partner, the principal investor and trader in Africa—three times larger than the United States—and a serious economic competitor of the United States in Latin America. And, as we are going to see, the People's Liberation Army is now the world's largest standing army, with two million troops backed by more submarines than any other power, sophisticated military hardware, nuclear weapons, and strategies of hybrid warfare bent on outfoxing enemies without firing a single shot.

A Ruling Ideology?

This much is so far clear, but now come hard questions about the resilience and durability of the galaxy empire. In European studies of the rise and decline of empires truisms abound. It is commonly noted by writers that empires flourish and survive longest when they throw off timidity (Tacitus) and act boldly, as if they are monopolists of their own destiny and history is on their side. It is said that successful empires strive to create and consolidate their own sense of time. Their rulers and their subjects are gripped by dreams of a life of endless summers. Autumnal decline and wintery death are far from their minds. But history always has other plans for them. While many empires postpone for a time the seasons of fortune, they are doomed to live within history. In recorded human history, European and other observers point out, no empire has ever lasted forever. All empires are subject to internal strains and external threats that sooner or later get the upper hand and drag them down into the dungeons of defeat. This should come as no surprise, if only because the preconditions of empire are so stringent. The famous English analyst of the Roman Empire, Edward Gibbon, emphasized how 'an extensive empire must be supported by a refined system of policy and oppression; in the centre, an absolute power, prompt in action and rich in resources; a swift and easy communication with the extreme parts; fortifications to check the first effort of rebellion; a regular administration to protect and punish; and a well-disciplined army to inspire fear, without provoking discontent and despair.'[1] These are demanding conditions, to say the least. They minimally require a strong dose of self-belief and a robust sense of what Gibbon called 'immoderate greatness'. Here the irony is that the requisite sense of superiority turns out to be a terrible toxin. Empires are typically felled by their own arrogance, which is why their defiance of time by biding their time ultimately depends on their ability to learn from their mistakes, to change course when circumstances grow threatening, to know when to back down, and, not to be underestimated, to hide their arrogance by staying close to the ground when strong winds of doubt and criticism blow their way.

It follows from these considerations that the key question that must be asked is not why some empires rise and fall quickly, or why all empires eventually come crashing to the ground, but how it is that some of them last so long. It turns out that high on the agenda of durable and successful empires are efforts to camouflage their own immodesty and to convince themselves and their clients and subjects that they are a force for good. Among the most frequently recorded ways in which empires ensure their stability and durability is to get under the skin of the people whose lives they shape at a distance. The aim must be to transform the empire into a whole way of life so that its power

---

1. Edward Gibbon, *The History of the Decline and Fall of the Roman Empire* (New York, 1841 [1776]), vol. 3, chap. 49, p. 35.

to shape the world at large—to tell stories that persuade others of its superiority and to nurture 'inferiority' and 'masochistic wallowing' among the empire's subjects[2]—comes to be seen and accepted as 'natural', and as the way things must remain.

The galaxy empire is similarly burdened by the functional requirements of public legitimacy. This is to say that at home and abroad its rulers are confronted by the fact that since power and authority are not the same thing, getting their way in the world—securing business contracts, winning support of member states within cross-border organisations, participating in joint military exercises, dealing with the United States—involves persuading others that 'the rise of China' and Chinese ways of wielding power are on balance a 'win-win' gift to the world. The point is that in order to survive and powerfully thrive in the world the galaxy empire has to win authority. It must be seen as legitimate in the eyes of others.

Here we encounter a surprise novelty: this galaxy empire isn't framed by a single dominant ideology, a comprehensive story about its past, present, and future, a persuasive summary of its global achievements and worldly benefits. By contrast, empires of old typically ruled through a set of legitimating symbols portrayed as intrinsically consistent and globally universal. Portuguese and Spanish emperors were proselytes for monarchy and the church. 'I believe in the British Empire', boasted Joseph Chamberlain, secretary of state for the colonies, 'and I believe in the British race. I believe that the British race is the greatest of governing races that the world has ever seen.'[3] The Ottoman Empire that confronted and outflanked Christian Europe in the Mediterranean, the Indian Ocean, and the lands bordering the Volga River for over five centuries (between 1400 and 1922 CE) wielded power in the form of a *gaza*, a holy war conducted in the name of Islam against its non-Muslim doubters and enemies. In palace

---

2. Frantz Fanon, *The Wretched of the Earth*, trans. Constance Farrington (London, 1967), p. 74; Tsitsi Dangarembga, *Black and Female: Essays* (Minneapolis, 2023).
3. Joseph Chamberlain, 'Speech at the Imperial Institute', November 11, 1895, in *Foreign and Colonial Speeches* (London, 1897), pp. 88–89.

training schools, the sultan's servants received instruction in the codes of conduct of Islamic government. The rulers regularly met with religious scholars (*ulema*) and the imperial faith was taught in theological seminaries (*madrasas*) and propagated through charities (*waqf*) and mosques, where sermons usually offered short prayers for the sultan. Public rituals and celebrations helped transform the faith into everyday customs. Wandering dervishes preached in the bazaars and open-air squares. Festivals celebrated the birthday of the Prophet, the night of his passage to heaven, the month of fasting known as Ramadan, and the spring equinox rite of *Nowrūz*. At the annual *Qurban* festival, as guests of the sultan and wealthy citizens, sheep were slaughtered in the thousands and distributed to the poor. Guild pageants, storytelling (*meddāh*), peasant dances, puppet shows, halvah parties, fireworks displays, and popular theatre consecrated the faith.[4]

Policy analysts and critics of the galaxy empire say that its rulers are similarly motivated by efforts to spread grand narratives infused with 'socialism' or Marxist-Leninist 'totalitarian' ideology; and there are scholars convinced that the Party leadership is now busily mobilizing television shows, movies, social media, and popular writing to retell the past to suit its mounting 'nationalism' at home and newfound confidence abroad, at a moment in history when the country's destiny of shaping the whole world comes under increasing threats from the United States.[5] Quite aside from the category mistake of supposing that China is a territorial state backed by a single ruling ideology of nationalism, these orthodox interpretations of how the galaxy empire seeks to legitimate its burgeoning global power miss the point that the ruling rhetoric comprises a hotchpotch of different symbols and styles, both at home and abroad. No doubt, these

---

4. Halîl Ỉnalcik, 'Communication in Ottoman Society', in *The Ottoman Empire and Europe* (Istanbul, 2019), pp. 23–32; Metin And, *A History of Theatre and Popular Entertainment in Turkey* (Ankara, 1963); and Eyal Ari, 'The People's Houses and the Theatre in Turkey', *Middle Eastern Studies* 40.4 (July 2004), pp. 32–58.
5. Rana Mitter, *China's Good War: How World War II Is Shaping a New Nationalism* (Cambridge, MA, 2020).

interpretations correctly note how those who run empires know that they must never be seen without clothes. 'Reputation of power, is Power', said Hobbes.[6] Power naked is power resistible; it breeds fears of corruption, manipulation, loss. Durable empires nurture feelings among their clients and subjects that the empire's power arrangements are authoritative: legitimate, right and proper, honoured and respected, or at least tolerated.

The galaxy empire rulers undoubtedly crave authority in this way, but they do so with a difference that is missed especially by those observers who report that China is driven by a single ruling ideology variously described as 'nationalism', 'Marxism-Leninism', 'socialism', or 'Xi Jinping Thought'. The empire certainly throws its cultural weight around on the global stage. Its leaders are gripped by a powerful sense that in a world crowded with public stories jostling for attention, whoever tells better stories, aggressively, unscrupulously, whatever their degree of veracity, has a good chance of coming out on top. In recent years, for example, the Chinese government humbled Mercedes Benz into making an apology for Instagramming an inspirational quote from the Dalai Lama; foreign airlines and other companies were pressured into deleting online references to Taiwan if they wanted not to lose access to the Chinese market; and the Houston Rockets basketball team paid dearly for its general manager's tweet in support of Hong Kong protesters. Media publicity, beating the gong in support of the empire, is also high on the government's agenda. While there are draconian controls over its domestic media environment, Beijing spends heavily on its state-run media presence in foreign markets as part of a global campaign to 'tell China stories well' (Xi Jinping).[7] Telling stories well means harnessing China-based media platforms to deliver breaking news to audiences around the world, praising China's economic achievements in global forums, celebrating

---

6. Thomas Hobbes, *Leviathan* (Harmondsworth, 1972 [1651]), part 1, chap. 10, p. 150
7. 'Xi Urges New Media Outlet to "Tell China Stories Well"', *Xinhua / China Daily*, January 2, 2017, http://www.chinadaily.com.cn/cndy/2017-01/02/content_27837476.htm.

its fauna and flora and landscape beauty in television documentaries. Chinese-owned news aggregator apps (such as Opera News) and government media outlets like China Radio International (CRI) and Xinhua weigh in with feel-good stories circulated through joint ventures and content-sharing deals with local-language platforms—as in Nigeria, where CRI broadcasts in Hausa, a language spoken by 30 per cent of Nigerians; its Facebook page has over one million followers. Local journalists are offered exclusive access to inside stories and invited to apply for Chinese government-funded fellowships and short courses. When the going gets rough, opinions hostile to the Chinese government and business ventures are dealt with by targeted disinformation campaigns, trolls, intimidation of local journalists, and the energetic promotion of counter-narratives on platforms such as Twitter, where editors of the hawkish *Global Times* (@globaltimesnews) wage abrasive pro-government campaigns, even though Twitter is blocked in China.

These randomly chosen examples illustrate the general rule that power always craves authority, but when examined carefully they also reveal something paradoxical and peculiar about the empire: its *mixing and stirring of different and sometimes incompatible sets of political symbols*. Gone are the days of a Glorious Myth propagated through endless repetitions of organized drumbeat euphemisms, neologisms, and prefixes. The empire is certainly not describable as a tyranny 'dressed up in fascist or communist clothing and acting out haphazardly some aspects of fascist or communist ideology'.[8] It doesn't make the mistake of the rulers of the Soviet Union, who tried and manifestly failed to impose on its empire's subjects a Communist ideology that promised that comprehensive Party-state control of government, education, media, and the means of production would bring the peace and plenty of 'international socialism' to the entire world. Unlike twentieth-century totalitarian regimes that ruled through a combination of

---

8. Victor Klemperer, *Language of the Third Reich: LTI—Lingua Tertii Imperii* (London, 2013); Michael Walzer, 'Totalitarian Tyranny', in Yehoshua Arieli and Nathan Rotenstreich, eds., *Totalitarian Democracy and After* (London, 2002), p. 191.

all-purpose terror and a dominant grand ideology that purported 'to know the mysteries of the whole historical process' and its supposed 'natural' laws, such as the coming triumph of the classless society and the inevitability of a war between 'chosen' and 'degenerate' races,[9] the galaxy empire ditches inflexible, fanatical ideologies. Its poetics of power are different, more creatively adaptable, more sophisticated, and thus much more difficult to pin down politically.

The symbols deployed by party officials, diplomats, journalists, and others to justify the worldly spread of Chinese power have a kaleidoscopic '*yīn-yáng* structure'.[10] Functionally speaking, their multiplex and shapeshifting qualities are well suited to the multiplex and shapeshifting forms of the galaxy empire. We could say that in their efforts to win support and blinker the eyes of public doubt, the empire's rulers take their cue from older Chinese empires whose rulers performed rituals perfumed with a potpourri of Daoism, Confucianism, Buddhism, and (if their dynasty had roots beyond the Great Wall) shamanism;[11] or perhaps that the rulers take a leaf from the book of Charles V, the legendary sixteenth-century Holy Roman emperor who learned so many languages to help him rule over his vast empire that he was said to speak Spanish to God, Italian to friends, German to enemies, and French to lovers. The promoters of China's galaxy empire—government, business, and cultural leaders operating at home and abroad—similarly present themselves in many guises. They come draped in multi-coloured coats woven from different languages and styles, which gives them important tactical advantages that are not describable in terms of the old Machiavellian 'art of contrivance',[12] in which a government scripts and stages pseudo-stories and

---

9. Hannah Arendt, 'Ideology and Terror: A Novel Form of Government', in *The Origins of Totalitarianism* (New York, 1973 [1951]), p. 469. Compare the account of 'vaudeville government' in Keane, *The New Despotism*.
10. The phrase was coined by the renowned Chinese scholar Liu Zehua (1935–2018); see his introductory remarks to Ge Quan, *Quánlì zǎizhì lǐxíng: shìrén, chuántǒng zhèngzhì wénhuà yǔ zhōngguó shèhuì* (Tianjin, 2003), pp. 1–3.
11. Dominic Lieven, *In the Shadow of the Gods: The Emperor in World History* (London, 2022), p. 26.
12. Daniel Boorstin, *The Image: A Guide to Pseudo-events in America* (New York, 1964).

pseudo-events that function as counterfeit versions of things as they really are. The galaxy empire's rhetoric is forged in more complex ways, for multiple purposes and with different effects.

Operating within the bounds of an empire comprising constellations of many different institutions and multiple modes of activity, leaders who play language games speaking in tongues and dressed in iridescent coats have the tactical advantage of appearing to be different things to different people at different times and places. Their conflicting images, euphemisms, intentional ambiguity, and cloudy vagueness are difficult to summarize. Their rhetoric isn't easily falsified. Double standards are difficult to criticize when the standards are double. Leaders are much harder to pin down. They can bamboozle (*hū you*) their foes. Bamboozling, as Chinese writer Yu Hua points out, throws a cloak of respectability over deception and manufactured rumour. Official 'boasting and exaggerating, puffery and bluster, mendacity and casuistry, flippancy and mischief' is a tricky form of political trickery, hype purged of its negative connotations, an ostentatious new type of advertising that makes the big-character posters of the Cultural Revolution seem comparatively tame.[13] Bamboozling enables leaders—as the Chinese expression has it—to shift a thousand pounds with four ounces. Semantic ambiguity is their great strength. They can sail with the political winds and outflank opponents by mentioning them, acknowledging them, even praising them, for a time. The rhetoric has a more journalist-friendly quality, and surprise moves can more easily be sprung, as when (in April 2022) Xi Jinping, following the signing of a security pact between China and the Solomon Islands, announced at an annual Boao Forum for Asia that China would put its energies into a new global security initiative that rejects a 'Cold War mentality' and instead defend 'common, comprehensive, cooperative and sustainable' security arrangements.

There is admittedly plenty of pragmatic, businesslike patter about 'stability' and 'development'. GDP, making money, growing rich, and

13. Yu Hua, *China in Ten Words* (New York, 2011), pp. 203–225.

prosperity are general articles of faith. Loyal subjects are encouraged to say: 'Our lives have improved. Millions have been lifted out of poverty. Even if hard times come, we'll support the government. It's brought stability. It's done a lot for our country.' But CCP leaders also spout mantras such as 'harmonious society', 'Confucian principles', 'rule of law', 'the democratization of international relations', 'ecological civilization', and 'ancient Chinese civilization'. Other precious phrases include 'territorial sovereignty', 'national pride', and 'national dignity'. As we have seen, 'sovereignty' is a favourite word in their arsenal. So are weaponized phrases such as 'rule of law' and 'law and order', 'peace', anti-imperialism, and protection from 'foreign enemies'. There is abundant talk of 'socialism' mixed with dollops of 'Marxism'. That leftist rhetoric is strained by the fact that North Korea and Vietnam promote their own versions of socialism, sometimes in opposition to China's role in global institutions, yet at home 'socialism' and 'Marxism' with Chinese characteristics are taught widely in universities, which receive special government funding for class materials and for the promotion of international workshops and public forums on the subject. Although there are signs that the rhetoric is reckoned by students, scholars, and state officials alike to be dubiously relevant and in policy terms impracticable, talk of 'socialism' and 'Marxism' helps remind audiences at home that the CCP is in charge and on a historic mission to make China great again, to ensure that it becomes a powerful world leader. The boasting has a corollary: government-enforced silences and denials of past failures, along the lines sketched in Chinese author Ma Jian's fantastical story of the forgetfulness that sets in after drinking 'China Dream Soup'.[14] In opposition to hostile images of China as an 'autocracy', there's additionally much mellifluous talk of the creation and development of a 'whole-process people's democracy' adjusted to China's 'national conditions', a form of self-government in which the 'people are truly masters of the country', a democracy 'with distinctive

---

14. Ma Jian, *China Dream* (London, 2018).

Chinese features which at the same time reflects humanity's universal desire for democracy.'[15]

How these official narratives are received and interpreted by audiences at home and abroad remains subject to the uncertainty principle. Whatever is thought of their veracity, or efficacy, the fact is that these rainbow performances underscore the way China's leaders and their media publicists are aware of the reputational dangers of ideological rigidity. Knowing that those who grow thorns reap wounds, they want to be seen as strong but flexible, benevolently tough servants of 'the people', strong-willed champions of planetary peace, wealth creation, good governance, and environmental resilience. Especially in recent years, as tensions with the United States have mounted, official calls for 'in-depth and candidly open dialogue' to blow away 'dark clouds of misunderstanding and misjudgment' have become common. Within bodies such as the United Nations and the World Trade Organization, Chinese diplomats and negotiators display strong commitment to rule-of-law precepts and often impress outsiders with their practical knowledge of procedural rules and technical details and their tough negotiating skills. But there are also moments of informality, as when the leaders are spotted and filmed pressing flesh with street crowds and participating in cultural performances of the territories they happen to be visiting. And in matters of public image there's no shortage of paradoxical and perplexing moments, as when the leaders indulge the language of 'socialism' in an empire more accurately described as a form of state capitalism; or when the Chinese government—the enemy of country-wide multi-party elections—supports voting elsewhere, as it did by outflanking the EU and the United States by providing Cambodia with computers, printers, voting booths, ballot boxes, and election monitors for its sham mid-2018 general election; and when, shortly after the outbreak of the 2020 pestilence, it donated large quantities of personal protective equipment to Myanmar for its 2020 general election.

15. See the State Council Information Office of the People's Republic of China's report, *China: Democracy That Works* (Beijing, December 4, 2021), pp. 2, 45.

Chairman of Everything?

The public performances of the supreme leader Xi Jinping display a similar iridescent style. Descriptions of him as a stern-talking 'autocrat' who enjoys unlimited power, the tough-minded 'Chairman of Everything' (Geremie Barmé)[16] who stands for no nonsense, are commonplace, but overdone. It is more accurate to say that his style is not comparable to the unchecked megalomania of past dictators such as Napoleon, Stalin, and Hitler. Xi is indeed a leader driven by ambition and the quest for glory, but in matters of public performance he is much more like Shakespeare's Duke of Gloucester, confident in his ability to frame his face for all occasions and to wet his cheeks with artificial tears, a leader who likes to 'add colours to the chameleon, change shapes with Proteus for advantages'. Xi's performances give a whole new meaning to dialectics: at home, he's a tough-minded, iron-fisted champion of 'socialism' and 'common prosperity', head of the armed forces and benevolent man of 'the people'. He is one of history's strong-man leaders, as Chinese people put things, whose one hand covers the heavenly sky (*zhē shǒu zhē tiān*). Much is made officially of his father's purging from the CCP and imprisonment during the Cultural Revolution, and Xi's triumphant 're-education' in the countryside, where (the story runs) the iron-disciplined son of the revolution learned from poor peasants in a barren mountain village in Shaanxi Province that ordinary people wanted material improvements in their day-to-day lives, not Western-style democracy or human rights. Xi proudly parades his credentials as a highly respected political thinker whose Marxist meditations on local and global challenges have been published in such newspapers as the *Zhejiang Daily* (more than two hundred pieces appeared there under the pen name of Zhijiang, including one piece entitled 'To Be a Good Official Is to

---

16. Geremie R. Barmé, 'Under One Heaven', in G. R. Barmé, L. Jaivin, and J. Goldkorn, eds., *Shared Destiny: China Story Yearbook 2014* (Canberra, 2014), p. xxi.

Be a Good Man [or Gentleman]' [February 7, 2007]). His wisdoms are now enshrined in the constitution of China and widely available in affordably priced, multiple volumes of *Xi Jinping Thought*.

Abroad, Xi dons the mantle of moral redeemer, champion of ancient Chinese civilization, and stout and stolid defender of peace through multilateral institutions. At Davos-style international gatherings, Xi speaks fulsomely about the need to use the torch of 'win-win' multilateralism to light humanity's forward path. Vladimir Putin-style macho politics is not his thing. He urges the abandonment of 'ideological prejudice' and champions 'macroeconomic policy coordination', 'sustainable, balanced, and inclusive growth' and 'peaceful coexistence'.[17] There are moments of vigorous diplomacy when affirming the need for China to 'guide the international community to jointly shape a more just and reasonable new international order' and even occasions when Xi mounts the global stage to play the part of the first Chinese leader since Mao to tackle the West, for instance (in a March 2022 video meeting) by telling the US president in tough-guy terms that China was refusing to impose sanctions on Russia because the United States was co-culpable for the Ukraine war and therefore should recognize not only that it takes 'two hands to clap' but that those who 'tied the bell to the tiger must take it off'.[18]

Xi's local and global performances are impressive in their iridescence, robustness, and range, and they naturally raise a core question: Is Xi Jinping to be considered an autocratic mystagogue, an instructor in a mix of mystical and arcane lore, perhaps even the foolhardy emperor of the emergent galaxy empire?

17. Xi Jinping, 'Let the Torch of Multilateralism Light up Humanity's Way Forward' [full text of speech delivered at the virtual Davos Agenda event held by the World Economic Forum, January 25, 2021], *CGTN*, January 26. 2021,, https://news.cgtn.com/news/2021-01-25/Full-text-Xi-Jinping-s-speech-at-the-virtual-Davos-Agenda-event-Xln4hwjO2Q/index.html.
18. Xi Jinping, 'Xi Calls for Overall National Security Outlook'," February 17, 2017, https://www.xinhuanet.com/english/2017-02/17/c_136065190.htm; 'President Xi Jinping Has a Video Call with US President Joe Biden', Ministry of Foreign Affairs of the People's Republic of China, March 19, 2022) https://www.fmprc.gov.cn/mfa_eng/zxxx_662805/202203/t20220319_10653207.html.

Emperor: the term comes loaded and laden with controversial past connotations, notably in Europe, where prior to 1200 CE the word (originally from old French *empereor* and the Latin *imperātōrem*, commander, from the stem of *imperāre*, to command, from *parāre*, to prepare or order) meant an omnipotent ruler who commanded an empire, that is, a collection of peoples living in lands stretched across vast distances. Not without bitter controversy, old European thinking supposed that empires functionally required an emperor, a ruler who was described as a *dominus mundi*, a figure who exercised supreme power over a vast geographic area often described as 'the world', or treated as 'worldwide rule'. It was even said by Frederick I, his son and successor Henry VI and their admirers, that the emperor enjoyed universal dominion (*dominium mundi*) blessed by divine power. The sacred emperor sat atop a vast temporal empire that doubled as a spiritual empire (*sacrum imperium*) that was entitled to rule over all local kings and their subjects until the forthcoming end of the world, the Day of Judgment.

It is tempting to describe Xi Jinping as a strong-willed ruler of this kind, an emperor on a mission, a sovereign leader who fancies himself as enjoying a heaven-mandated duty (*tiān jiàng dà rèn*) to rule his country and the world beyond its borders. Xi is said to act the part of an 'autocrat', a potentate 'who thinks that autocracy is the wave of the future'.[19] He indeed heads up all the key groups within the upper echelons of the CCP power structure; he has ditched the two-term president limit rule, and strictly forbids criticism and casual talk against him. Rumoured to be the world leader who has survived the highest number of attempts on his life, Xi moves around flanked by a large posse of hand-picked men dressed in black suits, elite bodyguards employed by the several-thousand-strong, shadowy force known as the Central Security Bureau.[20] He has led 'rectification' campaigns to

19. Nicole Gaouette, 'Biden Says US Faces Battle to "Prove Democracy Works"', *CNN*, March 26 2021, https://edition.cnn.com/2021/03/25/politics/biden-autocracies-versus-democracies/index.html.
20. Keane, *The New Despotism*, p. 77.

'scrape poison off the bone' and 'drive the blade' into abuses of power, graft, and disloyalty within the Communist Party. He reportedly exercises a tight grip on the armed forces and what he calls the Party's 'knife handle' law-and-order agencies, the hydra-headed spy and security agencies, police forces, courts, prosecutors, and prisons grouped under the Ministry of State Security, the Central Political and Legal Affairs Commission, a stronghold of Party power, and the newly founded policing body called the Secure China Development group chartered to strengthen efforts to quell unrest and eradicate crime. Some observers see him as a 'new Mao',[21] while others regard him as a contemporary throwback, a figure to be compared with past Chinese emperors who sought subordination and respect for defending and reclaiming China's rightful territory, as the long-serving Emperor Wu (156–87 BCE) did during the Han dynasty period by militarily seizing from the nomadic Xiongnu the strategically significant Hexi Corridor (*héxī zǒuláng*), a prized stretch of arable land wedged between the Tibetan and Mongolian plateaus and a trade route linking mainland China to the western regions of central Asia.[22]

The common comparison of Xi Jinping's rule and the reign of Emperor Wu is overdrawn. Xi will indeed be remembered for completing the forcible integration of Hong Kong into the People's Republic of China and for his efforts to erase all talk of the sovereign independence of Taiwan. He is the head architect of the Belt and Road Initiative and China's strategy of 'reclaiming'—more accurately, building artificial maritime islands—in the strategically significant trade chokepoint of the South China Sea. He makes much of working hard to bolster China's global influence and improving the lives of Chinese people by eradicating poverty and fostering a 'moderately prosperous society'. All these features of Xi's leadership are well documented, and they seem to confirm the portrayal of him as

21. Bruce Gilley, 'Meet the New Mao', *National Interest*, September 28, 2011, https://nationalinterest.org/commentary/meet-the-new-mao-5953.
22. Xinjiang Rong, *Eighteen Lectures on Dunhuang*, trans. Imre Galambos (Leiden 2013), vol. 5, pp. 19–20.

an autocratic new emperor. But the picture is one-sidedly misleading. For several reasons both formal and informal, the supreme ruler is not a solo performer on the stage of power. Xi Jinping may harbour inner masculinist fantasies about himself as an invincible lord of the whole earth. In reality, he does not enjoy absolute power; he neither has a free hand to decide everything, nor does he always get his way.

Xi is an exceptionally stubborn, ambitious, and power-hungry leader, but not to be underestimated is his entanglement and entrapment within complex thickets of institutional power. Within the heartlands of the galaxy empire, the polity over which Xi Jinping presides is neither unified nor monolithic nor guided from the top by a coherent grand strategy and undifferentiated chain of command. The country called 'China' is more complicated and fractured than the name suggests. China is not simply China. In the heartlands of the galaxy empire, government policies are typically the outcome of competition and hard bargaining among multiple Party-state apparatuses and state-owned and private businesses.[23] Some observers note that Xi's actions are further constrained and circumscribed by upper-level structures of Party-state 'socialist constitutionalism', and that these formal arrangements—complex relationships among the Party, the National People's Congress, and the State Council—are marked by older Chinese characteristics. The Tang dynasty emperors, for example, governed for nearly three centuries (from 618 CE) through an imperial bureaucracy divided into three departments. The central secretariat, under orders of the emperor, drafted policy proposals, which were then passed down to the chancellery for scrutiny. The chancellery was empowered to reject proposals approved by the emperors, or to demand revisions be done by the central secretariat. After final approval by the central secretariat and the chancellery, policies were implemented by the special ministries of the department of state affairs.[24]

---

23. Jones and Hameiri, *Fractured China*.
24. H. J. Wechsler, 'T'ai-tsung (Reign 626–49) the Consolidator', in D. C. E. Twitchett, ed., *The Cambridge History of China* (Cambridge, 1979), vol. 3, pp. 188–241; see also Gan Huaizhen, 'Huángdì zhìdù shìfǒu wèi zhuānzhì [Is emperorship despotic? in Chinese]', *History of Political Philosophy and Thought* 5 (2019), pp. 42–44; Yuri Pines,

Although times and circumstances are obviously different, Chinese government policymaking nowadays functions in a similarly multi-level, multi-jurisdictional way. Put simply, China's political system combines the rule of one (the general Party secretary), the rule of a few (twenty-five members of the Politburo, including seven Politburo members who also hold a seat on the all-powerful Politburo Standing Committee), and the rule of the many in the shape of the National People's Congress, an elected body charged with scrutinizing, revising, and approving national policy initiatives, which are then passed to the State Council, an executive body responsible for implementing policies.

Within this agglomeration of multi-tiered structures, Xi's personal leverage is further curbed and cramped by less formal pressures, especially the shadowy push-pull dynamics and intrigues within the Party ruling group which he leads, but does not fully command and control. He suffers setbacks, as when (in 2022) senior and retired Party leaders successfully defended Article 6 of the Party Constitution that banned 'any form of personality cult'. (Xi failed to insert the words *rén mín lǐng xiù* [the people's leader]; his attempt to shorten 'Xi Jinping Thought on Socialism with Chinese Characteristics for a New Era' into 'Xi Jinping Thought' was also blocked).[25] Rulers of past empires often feared power rivalries of this sort. That is why they yearned for untouchability, sometimes using extreme methods. When the Ottoman Empire's Bayezid I (1389–1403) became sultan, he ordered the execution of his brother Yakub. Sultan Mehmed III (in 1595 CE) executed each one of his nineteen brothers. The Ottoman emperors' favourite method of fratricide was strangulation by a thin silk rope. Past Chinese emperors thought they could handle things differently. Imagining themselves to be Sons of Heaven whose faces were never to be seen except by high-ranking palace officials, and never by

---

The Everlasting Empire: The Political Culture of Ancient China and Its Imperial Legacy (Princeton, NJ, 2012).

25. Katsuji Nakazawa, 'China's Elders Defend Party Charter from Xi Onslaught', *Nikkei Asia*, November 3, 2022.

commoners, they affirmed their own deathless, timeless eternality. Qin Shihuang (221–210 BCE), the founding ruler of the first imperial dynasty, laid down the ground rules: emperors are much more than monarchs (*wáng*). They are 'splendid' and 'shining', proto-divine *huángdì* blessed by the firmaments and the four points of the earthly compass. As the human embodiment of the heavens, rulers are celestial sages, which is why Qin Shihuang built a grand palace patterned on the Big Dipper and the North Star, the centre points of the nightly skies, and why he pioneered the *fēng shān* (to seal, to clear away) sacrifices by scaling Mount Tai to pay homage to both earth and the highest deity.[26] Subsequent emperors similarly believed they were mandated and duty-bound to strike a balance between Earth and Heaven. Their claimed divine authority was used to shield and protect themselves against rivals. When challenged, wrote Lu Xun, arrogant Chinese emperors usually replied: 'Did not Heaven destine me to rule?'[27]

Xi Jinping enjoys no such mandate of heaven. His brief is this-worldly, and as president and general secretary he's required to pay close attention to potential rivals, scheming factions, and what the Party calls 'political consultation work'. No doubt, those who criticize or challenge his rule quickly find themselves in trouble, on the wrong side of the political fence, politically doomed. And for sure Xi's deposition, or his death, will rock the political system to its foundations. Perhaps the time is coming when the leader decides to act as an autocrat without the means or ability to do so. Whether his future departure triggers a major succession crisis and unleashes life-and-death power struggles that threaten to bring down the whole empire, we cannot yet know. But, as things currently stand, the Communist Party of China is not simply his instrument; if anything, Chinese scholars suggest, Xi is beholden to 'the organizational emperor' of the Party, which is not a political party in the Western sense but a ruling group embedded within a multiform system of 'governance' officially committed to the 'all-round development' and 'common prosperity' of

26. Mark Edward Lewis, *The Construction of Space in Early China* (Albany, NY, 2006).
27. Lu Xun, 'On Emperors', in *Selected Works* (Beijing, 1985), vol. 2, p. 258.

'the people'.[28] The huge gaps between rich and poor, environmental despoliation, and the felt powerlessness of many millions of ordinary Chinese people go unexplained in these scholars' interpretations, but their claims do reveal how the sacred principle of the 'Two Upholds' (firmly upholding General Secretary Xi Jinping's leadership position in both the Central Committee and the Party as a whole, and respect for the Central Committee's centralized, unified leadership) operates within a labyrinth of interconnected institutions, including the influential advisory body known as the Chinese People's Political Consultative Conference, whose members include representatives of the eight officially recognized minor political parties linked to the CCP, retired CP cadres, and business and media elites. In the name of 'socialist consultative democracy', Xi and the rest of the Party leadership aim politically to integrate and co-opt these and other groups, in exchange for which the insiders are granted political recognition, eased access to Party backrooms, and material rewards such as government contracts and new business deals.

Political exchanges of this kind have a wider significance. The Party emperor in fact stands at the apex of a tall pyramid of patronage. As patron in chief, Xi Jinping is a dedicated practitioner of favours: big favours, small favours, deals, and contracts disbursed downwards through the political order with the help of friends and fixers. Throughout the political system, in the heartlands of the empire, *connections are the common currency of power*. They bind together the whole political order, *Guanxi* matters. It really matters. Getting things done involves cultivating links and rewarding others. Backscratching, bargaining, deals, kickbacks, tie-ins, favours, and gifts shape what happens above and below the pinnacles of state power. Not even Xi and other top Party leaders can escape their influence; they, too, are entangled in

---

28. Yongnian Zheng, *The Chinese Communist Party as Organizational Emperor: Culture, Reproduction and Transformation* (London, 2009), p. 34; Pan Wei, 'Why Is the Chinese Communist Party Not a "Party" in the Western Sense?', *China News Service* (August 30 2021, https://www.tellerreport.com/news/2021-08-30-exclusive-%7C-pan-wei—why-is-the-chinese-communist-party-not-a-%22party%22-in-the-western-sense-.S1xZEGg9WK.html.

webs of patronage. In a strange way, the omnipresence of *guanxi* lends connections a measure of legitimacy. They feel egalitarian, or at least universal. When it comes to getting things done, everybody knows that there are hierarchies of opportunity, that the cards are stacked in favour of the powerful. Everybody knows that connections naturally breed corruption, if by that is meant illegal or extra-legal transfers of money and other resources in exchange for favours. But everybody also knows that connections matter to everybody, that everybody is in a boat, and that when at any point in the system their boat hits a bridge, there's still (Chinese people say) a river on which to navigate forward (*chuán dào qiáo tóu zì rán zhí*). If things go wrong, or don't work out as expected, there is always backscratching: someone asks, someone offers, deals are struck, something is given, things get done. Patron-client relations of this kind are not premodern throwbacks, bonds and ties that belong to the past, symptoms of economic and political backwardness to be swept away by the forces of modernization. Patronage is a core feature of life in the heartlands of the galaxy empire, and it is an added reason why it is mistaken to interpret the Chairman of Everything as a latter-day tyrant caught in a tyrant trap of blindly self-interested hunger for absolute power. This head of the empire is different. Caught within thickets of interconnected institutions and thick webs of patronage that radiate down and out from the top of the political system, all the way to the bottom, this imperial leader does not rule alone, untouched by clients and patrons, friends and foes, or concerns about 'the people' over whom he rules. There are even times, as during the late-2022 China-wide public demonstrations against lockdown and economic stagnation, when the emperor once half-affectionately called Xi Dada ('Uncle Xi') is suddenly confronted with street-level outbursts of anger, frustration with his ruthless obstinacy and policy mistakes, and even daring satirical chants using such phrases as 'banana peels' (*xiāng jiāo pí*—the same initials as Xi Jinping) and 'shrimp moss' (*xia tai*—sounds like 'step down') designed to show that in the eyes of 'the people' the emperor is wearing no clothes.

Abusive Power

How 'the people' fit into the one-party governing arrangements of the galaxy empire is a topic of fundamental importance when considering its capacity for survival and future flourishing. Like all previous empires, the galaxy empire cannot escape a question that has been central in all previous accounts of why empires endure, and why they decline, or suddenly collapse: to what extent are its wealthy leaders and big bosses (*dà lǎobǎn*) prone to abuses of power that serve to breed disaffection and resistance among their subjects, either at home or abroad?

Historians and political thinkers teach us that when power is exercised arbitrarily—arrogantly, brutally, without self-restraint—over subjects it rapidly loses its seductive charm. There are always collaborators, cowards, and waverers, to be sure. But brutal power normally loses its capacity to cast spells on its subjects. They lose trust in its practices and its promises. They may feel disesteemed; and they may resist its abuses. Seen in this way, *high-handed and self-aggrandizing arbitrary power is the great curse of empires*, as the ancient Greek historian Polybius (c. 200–118 BCE) warned the Roman aristocracy.[29] An early work by the influential eighteenth-century French thinker Montesquieu (1689–1755) repeated the point with great eloquence. He was sure that empires ancient and modern, like all other forms of government, 'necessarily become corrupt'. The experience of Asia, where 'large empires have always been characteristic', shows that every empire necessarily requires that its 'ruler should have despotic authority; that decisions be made promptly to compensate for the distances over which they must be conveyed; that fear must be used to prevent a distant governor or magistrate from becoming negligent; that law must originate from one person, that is to say it must be constantly changing, since the larger a state is, the more unexpected events occur'. He

---

29. *Polybius: The Histories* (Cambridge, MA, 1922), vol. 6, sections 7.6–7, 6.8.5–9, and 6.9.5–7.

added: 'A large empire where the ruler did not have absolute power would necessarily become divided, either because the provincial governors did not obey, or because, in order to make them obey, it was necessary to divide the empire up into several kingdoms'.[30]

We are about to see that when it comes to China things are much less straightforward than Montesquieu supposed. An important reason is that *the galaxy empire has emerged during the era of monitory democracy*— a period in which the contagious spirit and practical substance of free elections and the public monitoring and restraint of arbitrary power by independent courts, anti-corruption commissions, and other watchdog institutions have spread to every continent of our planet.[31] Montesquieu was right to observe that imperial hubris—the failure of imperial rulers, despite their best efforts, to secure support at home and abroad for power exercised arbitrarily over great distances—was an enormous challenge confronting every known empire. What he could not have anticipated is that public refusals of 'despotic authority' and 'absolute power' accused of arrogance, incompetence, and corruption haunt every form of rule in these years of the twenty-first century. The party apparatchiks of the Soviet empire were taught this lesson during the 'velvet revolutions' of last century; citizen revolts on its western fringes spelled the end of empire. The United States is no exception to this rule. Especially because its elected governments are nominally committed to the ideals of 'democracy', their imperial adventures whip up storms of controversy, at home and abroad. Their economic grip in foreign lands is denounced as corporate exploitation. Their spreading cultural influence arouses local symbolic resistance to 'neo-colonialism' and 'imperialism'. Military adventures

---

30. From sections 8, 10, and 15 of the essay *Réflexions sur la monarchie universelle en Europe* [Reflections on universal monarchy in Europe], in *Ouevres complètes de Montesquieu* (Paris, 1955), vol. 3, pp. 361–382. Printed in 1734, the essay was immediately withdrawn by Montesquieu; fearing censorship and arrest, he destroyed every copy of the work, save for a single printed copy which remained inaccessible to readers until its republication in 1891.
31. John Keane, *The Life and Death of Democracy* (London, 2009), part 3, and *The Shortest History of Democracy* (London, 2022), part 3.

conducted in the name of democracy are variously denounced as abuses of power poisoned by fiscal wastefulness, corporate profiteering, the destruction of ecosystems, war booty grabs, and bogus stage-managed secrecy and deception (the alleged existence of Iraqi weapons of mass destruction, claims about murdered Kuwaiti babies in incubators, and North Vietnamese attacks on US naval ships in the Gulf of Tonkin). And fears are expressed that imperial hubris is gradually destroying democracy itself.[32] The galaxy empire, we are going to see, does not escape charges of hubris. Hence the pressing questions: When judged in terms of the foundational problem of arbitrary power and imperial arrogance, how does the galaxy empire measure up? As its rulers improvise their way into the future, are they aware of the paradox that the survival and flourishing of China depends on restraining the power they want to extend? That becoming an empire means being drawn inescapably into tricky situations in which the control of others and their ecosystems is as necessary as it is risky? That hubris at home and abroad may well prove to be the greatest weakness—and the great underminer—of this young galaxy empire? Do they realize that while every rising empire aims to shift the balance of power in its favour, no empire lasts forever, and that some are stillborn, because they indulge illusions of greatness and reckless power adventures?

In reply to this question, foreign journalists and politicians often jump to conclusions. Differences between the inside and the outside, dynamics at home and dynamics abroad, are usually of little interest to them. China is China. Simple-minded reductionism is their specialty. They like to say that the People's Republic of China (PRC) is

---

32. A sample of these criticisms of the incompatibility of empire and democracy include Andrew J. Bacevich, *American Empire: The Realities and Consequences of U.S. Diplomacy* (Cambridge, MA, 2003); Chalmers Johnson, *Blowback: The Costs and Consequences of the American Empire* (New York, 2000) and *The Sorrows of Empire* (New York, 2004); Tony Smith, *America's Mission: The United States and the Worldwide Struggle for Democracy in the Twentieth Century* (Princeton, NJ, 1994); and Michael Mann, *Incoherent Empire* (London, 2005), p. 13: 'The American empire will turn out to be a military giant, a back seat economic driver, a political schizophrenic and an ideological phantom'.

a worrying instance of what Montesquieu called 'absolute power'. Sometimes they speak of 'totalitarianism'. Mostly, they describe China as an 'authoritarian regime'. Their general view is that within the Chinese political system the hungry tigers and wolves of power and their corrupting effects are uncontrolled. The whole polity is in the grip of the *arbitrium*, the arbitrary power of party rulers who suppose that they can always decide and get away with things unopposed; or suppose, without losing a wink of sleep, that their own power is self-justifying, as if they have the heavens, or history, or human luck on their side. That is why, so the reasoning runs, cunning and camouflage aside, the rulers of China treat their subjects at home and abroad badly, with disrespect. Putting themselves on a pedestal, they ditch the dignity principle. They have no regard for the precept that people should be treated as beings worthy of respect because all people are capable of publicly explaining themselves and their actions to others. The rulers do not believe that those who exercise power should be required openly to give account of their actions, and to be held publicly responsible for their slipups, fraud, and mendacity, their capricious lawlessness and violence. China is thus a political system whose merchants of arbitrary power typically rig things to their advantage. Its rulers restrict or ban outright opportunities for questioning or actively refusing their own power. They boss and bully their subjects, and even resort to eliminating their opponents, through torture, imprisonment, disappearance, or death. The weak have few or no means of speaking against the strong by pressing home their concerns freely in public. Their dignity is dispensable. The regime deems people as fit only for bowing and scraping in the presence of masters. There is no room for genuinely democratic politics. The whole system (the terms are often used interchangeably) is 'autocratic', 'authoritarian', or 'totalitarian'.

These assessments by observers of China's rise rightly take aim at the issue of arbitrary power, but they are careless of language. Strictly speaking, as we have already pointed out, totalitarianism refers to a one-party political order ruled by violence, a single 'glorious myth' ideology, all-purpose terror, and compulsory mass rallies. Within the heartlands of the galaxy empire, most Chinese people would say that daily life in their country just isn't like that. The Mao days are over. There's a larger point here, for the realities of life inside China and in its outlands contradict the key terms found in mainstream political science textbooks. When seen as an emergent whole, the inner and outer parts of the empire are neither 'autocratic' nor 'totalitarian' nor describable as a Mugabe-style corrupt military-bureaucratic dictatorship nor a 'tyranny', if by that term is meant a state ruled by a strong man consumed by lawless desires. China watchers who use these terms to describe Beijing's government as a form of iron-fisted 'authoritarian' rule sustained by the material benefits it delivers to its toad-eating subjects seriously misperceive things. Not only do they marshal Orientalist prejudices (kowtowing Chinese who haven't yet realized the beauty and benefits of Western liberal democracy), but they ignore basic facts. Those who describe the Chinese political system as heavy-handed 'authoritarianism' or 'totalitarianism' get at least two things wrong.[33] They fail to see that while within the heartlands of the PRC there is certainly plenty of public and private bellyaching about how the party periodically makes mistakes and is prone to corruption, citizens who stay inside the government's electric fences enjoy a wide range of daily freedoms without fear.[34] China watchers convinced that the PRC is ruled ultimately by iron fists wrapped in lies and censorship also underestimate the preoccupation of the CCP leadership with the use of and techniques of 'adaptive governance' and other sophisticated methods of clever rule.[35] The leadership strives hard to foster the sense that government is for the

---

33. The serious flaws in the fashionable concept of 'authoritarianism' are analysed in more detail in Keane, *The New Despotism*, pp. 212–215.
34. Xuanzi Xu, *Online News-Prompted Public Spheres in China* (London, 2023); and John Keane, *When Trees Fall, Monkeys Scatter* (London, 2018).
35. See Sebastian Heilmann and Elizabeth J. Perry, eds., *Mao's Invisible Hand: The Political Foundations of Adaptive Governance in China* (Cambridge, MA, 2011), pp. 8–10 and 62–103; and Sebastian Heilmann, 'From Local Experiments to National Policy: The Origins of China's Distinctive Policy Process', *China Journal* 59 (2008), pp. 1–30.

benefit of 'the people'. It's a key reason why state violence and legal coercion are carefully calibrated, cleverly targeted at troublemakers—during street protests, and in places such as Tibet, Hong Kong, and Xinjiang. It's also why the party state uses opinion polling, elections, public forums, anti-corruption agencies, and other tools of government that lend it a people-sensitive, 'democratic' feel.

Why do the CCP leaders strive hard to be seen as accountable to the people whose loyalty at home they seek to win? The shortest answer: because they know from their history books and their immediate experience the political dangers of self-aggrandizement. *The rulers' skittishness is palpable.* While they live the illusion of their own indispensability, they constantly worry about losing power over people. They recall from their history books details of large-scale rebellions like the Yellow Scarves peasant revolt (184–205 CE) and the 1850–64 Taiping uprising, which claimed the lives of at least twenty million souls during perhaps the bloodiest uncivil war ever recorded in human history. They learned from events such as the 1989 Tiananmen uprising that the political system is vulnerable to disorder and implosion, popular resistance, and breakdown, and they well understand the general rule that political orders appear stable and legitimate until the moment they crumble and collapse. They understand that governing is less like hammering nails into wood and more like balancing on slippery eggs, as the Chinese saying goes.

The rulers also know the old dictum that power is the ability to succeed in the world, to outflank opponents, to set aside the need to learn from previous mistakes, and to ignore their costs, or to heap them onto others, or postpone remedying their consequences until a later date.[36] From the Politburo Standing Committee all the way to the bottom, state officials nevertheless know the teachings of ancient Chinese political thinkers: power (*quán lì*) backed by rough hands does not in itself breed the authority (*quán wēi*) required for enduring rule. Power can become too big for its boots. Violence is the clenched

---

36. Karl Deutsch, *The Nerves of Government: Models of Political Communication and Control* (New York, 1965), p. 21.

fist in their pockets, but they understand that its overuse can be counterproductive, and that what is gained by persuasion is always preferable to what is achieved by force. During the Yuan dynasty period, a leading Confucian intellectual Liu Ji (1311–1375) explained the dangers of ruling by force. 'Reliance on force can lead to short-lived wins,' he wrote. 'Only great virtue can command the force of the many. Virtue is inexhaustible, whereas force can be frustrated'. He told the story of the monkeys employed by a greedy master to collect berries and fruits from a nearby forest. Cruel beatings of uncooperative monkey workers by the boss were common, until one day a young monkey asked his fellow monkey workers why, aside from habit, they were willingly cooperating with a cruel master when after all the fruits they collected grew naturally in the forest and were not the property of the master. A monkeys' revolt followed. They fled, carrying with them baskets of forest fruits and berries, leaving the master in the lurch, eventually to starve to death.[37]

The CCP leadership instinctively understands this parable of power and virtue. It grasps that jobs, full rice bowls, skyscrapers, shopping malls, and talk of socialism, family life, improved healthcare, and holidays at home and abroad aren't enough to ensure their legitimacy. The rulers are aware that getting things wrong—mishandling a pestilence, inadvertently fuelling a property prices boom, failing to deal with a looming aging and demographic crisis—can easily breed public discontent. The point is to get people willingly to comply—to win their voluntary servitude—without grinding their noses into the ground. Perhaps the party rulers were taught the Confucian wisdom that virtuous rule of the people resembles a breeze that strokes and bends the grasses of the field. More likely is that the leaders know by heart a more sobering proverb: when trees fall, monkeys scatter (*shù dǎo húsūn sàn*). Mistakes can be costly. When power becomes unpopular, anything can happen. Everything can be lost. That's of course why the active public scrutiny and restraint of their arbitrary powers is both

---

37. John D. Langlois Jr., 'Song Lian and Liu Ji in 1358 on the Eve of Joining Zhu Yuanzhang', *Asia Major*, 3rd series, 22.1 (2009), pp. 131–162.

unwelcome and impermissible. In the heartlands of the galaxy empire, the CCP rulers have no taste for monitory democracy—a robust style of politics and way of life committed not only to free elections but also to active citizen and media support for the public monitoring of power, wherever power is exercised. That is certainly why they spend vast sums of money on policing and surveillance, and why they surround themselves day and night by secret agents, and by secret agents watching the secret agents, plus highly trained, well-armed guards. Xi Jinping and other CCP leaders don't like open talk of China as a system of state capitalism that in the name of socialism hatches super-rich tycoons faster than any other country (257 billionaires in 2020 alone). The slightest whiff of a challenge to the CCP's power can bring down the hammer, as evidenced by mass detention camps in Xinjiang and crushed dissent in Hong Kong.

Phantom Democracy

But here's the thing: the poligarch rulers also know that rich and powerful people must fear too much power, just as pigs fear growing fat. In the heartlands of the galaxy empire, they reject power-sharing, power-monitoring democracy, yet they fret about reckless abuses of power. Not without a dose of anxiety and self-contradiction, the rulers thus acknowledge, when all is said and done, that very little durably props up the political order except people's belief in it. *Potestas in populo* is the classic Roman formulation to summarize this rule. The Chinese version is worded differently: the water that floats the boat can overturn it as well (*shuǐ kě zài zhōu, yì kě fù zhōu*). If the power of a regime is its ability to get its subjects to act as the rulers choose, then persuasion of people rather than violence against them is ultimately the most valuable governing resource. Command and obedience turn out to be tricky elements in any political equation, for power over others functionally requires that they feel comfortable with the instructions, directives, and commands issued by those who rule. Despite their native suspicions of power, the ruled have to be persuaded that they will not be devoured by its jaws. Otherwise, they may be tempted to stir up trouble. That's why the CCP leadership treads carefully, eyes wide open, nervously looking around, and looking ahead. It is also why the leadership trumpets the heartlands of China as a 'people's democracy' and embraces a 'phantom democracy' governing style (*shènjǐngshì mín zhǔ*) that mocks but mirrors and mimics monitory democracies, where fears of election defeat and public exposure of incompetence and corruption put leaders on constant alert.

What does it mean to call domestic China a phantom democracy?[38] It's a corrupted local form of democracy that is simultaneously real and not real, believed and disbelieved, an underdeveloped and self-contradictory form of democracy that is both with substance and without substance. It is more than a sham and less than the real

---

38. The words 'phantom' and 'phantasms', with their connotations of true and false, real and unreal, fact and fantasy, aren't easy to translate into Mandarin. Family terms such as 'illusory', 'ghostlike', and 'mirage', each with different Chinese meanings, compound the translation difficulty. Chinese equivalents for phantom are *huànyǐng* (幻影) and *guǐhún* (鬼魂). According to ancient usage, *huàn* refers to 'fraud' and things that are 'misleading' (相欺诈迷惑). In modern Chinese, the phrase *huànyǐng* (幻影) refers to an imaginary image in one's mind, hence as something that is non-existent 'in reality'. An alternative common translation of 'phantom', *guǐ* (鬼), or *guǐhún* (鬼魂), is the word for 'ghost', or the superstitious (officially frowned upon) belief in what happens to humans after their death. The superstitious belief in *guǐ* is understood as the opposite of being sensible, reasonable, and even educated and civilized. Along with *huànyǐng*, *guǐ* in modern Chinese conveys the meaning of 'false', 'unreal', and 'non-existent', which is not what is meant here by 'phantom', which rather refers to something that is both real and unreal, true and false, factual and fantastic. To avoid these unhelpful connotations, this book therefore draws throughout upon the Chinese expression *hǎi shì shèn lóu* (海市蜃楼) (known as *shèn jǐng* [蜃景] for short), which is an ancient Chinese word for 'mirage'. The word *shèn* (蜃) refers to a dragon-like creature that was once a pheasant bird and now lives in the ocean in altered form. It was believed in ancient times that a *shèn* could blow off steam that produces a mirage. In modern Chinese, *shèn jǐng* is still used by artists as the name for the fantastic vision of a mirage; while in the contemporary physical sciences, it is used to refer to the phenomenon of light that bends to create a mirage. *Shèn jǐng* therefore has an agreeable double connotation. It refers to something that is factual, 'true', and perceptible, and to a fantasy that is intangible and elusive. Hence the decision of this book to use *shèn jǐng* to represent 'phantom', and the phrase *shènjǐngshì mín zhǔ* (蜃景式民主) to represent the phenomenon of 'phantom democracy'.

thing. Phantom democracy has polychromatic, *yīn-yáng* characteristics which, as noted by Liu Zehua and other scholars, have long marked Chinese rulers' ways of handling power.³⁹ Current-day examples are plentiful. Most obvious is the proto-democratic style of the present leaders—their constant affirmation that they believe in the people, and that their sole purpose as rulers is to serve the people, whose support they claim to enjoy.

The strange thing is that inside the People's Republic of China, as Yu Hua has noted, the phrase 'the people' (*rén mín*) has a phantasmagorical quality. They are 'ubiquitous yet somehow invisible', present but absent, the supreme source of authority and of limited or no significance at all.⁴⁰ 'The people' and 'democracy' (*mín zhǔ*) are at the heart of the prevailing language of the Party-state, which is said to be the living manifestation of 'the people'. In briefings, seminars, and workshops, officials wield such formulations as 'serving the people wholeheartedly . . . is the leading purpose of the Party', and the Party represents the interests of the people 'rather than special interests of certain vested groups'. During the Xi Jinping period, which has witnessed a personality cult rejuvenation, life tenure for the supreme leader, and tightening state controls of the economy, the Party leadership has repeatedly said that its struggle against corrupt 'tigers and flies' is 'what the people demand and what they support'. When Xi Jinping (in February 2016) made a studio appearance at China Central Television (CCTV), he emphasized that state media is 'a reflection of the voice of the people' and therefore (note the logic of substitution) the function of media is to 'protect Party power and protect

---

39. See Liu Zehua's introduction to Ge Quan, pp. 1–3; and Pines, *The Everlasting Empire*, who notes (p. 5) how the *yīn-yáng* qualities of traditional Chinese thinking and institutional practices—for instance, the way reverence for monarchy came mixed with periodic rebellions against bad emperors, and respect for commoners was combined with their forcible exclusion from government—were among the important sources of resilience of the imperial polities that ruled various parts of China for more than two millennia, until the end of the Qing dynasty (1912 CE), when three major Western empires—ruled by the Ottomans, Habsburgs, and Romanovs—also collapsed.
40. Hua Yu, *China in Ten Words* (London, 2013), p. 3.

Party unity'. Shortly after the eighteenth National Congress of the Chinese Communist Party, Xi announced the China Dream project. 'I believe that realizing the rejuvenation of the Chinese nation has been the greatest dream of the Chinese people since the beginning of the modern era', he reportedly said. 'This dream concentrates a long-cherished expectation of many generations of the Chinese people, and encapsulates the overall interests of the Chinese nation and its people'.[41] There are odd but understandable moments when Chinese journalists are ordered by the censors to alter the phrase 'Chinese people' to 'some people' (so as to preserve the unsullied purity of the key phrase), and to scrub references such as 'Xinjiang people' or 'Gansu people', phrases that are seen to encourage regional differences and to violate the sacred abstract universal principle of 'the people'.[42] There are also occasions when the rhetoric of 'the people' is mobilized by the Party leadership to counter its sworn enemies, as when Chinese officials called the harsh military crackdowns in Xinjiang a 'people's war', or when Xi Jinping described the aim of the Party's 'zero Covid' strategy as putting 'the people and their lives above all else', as an 'all out people's war to stop the spread of the virus'.[43] The implication is clear: the ode to 'the people' harbours a deep ambivalence, even perhaps a secret contempt, for flesh-and-blood people, whose opinions can be mistaken and produce disharmony, and who therefore need guidance by the leaders of the true people, preferably by winning their hearts but, if necessary, by tugging at their ears.

In the heartlands of the galaxy empire, public opinion guidance (*yú lùn yǐn dǎo*) is a prime preoccupation of Party officials and state media outlets. 'The correct guidance of public opinion benefits the

---

41. These sentences and phrases reappear in 'Xi Jinping's Speech on the CCP's 100th Anniversary', *NikkeiAsia*, July 21, 2021, https://asia.nikkei.com/Politics/Full-text-of-Xi-Jinping-s-speech-on-the-CCP-s-100th-anniversary; see also Huaguang Huang and Jianzhang Luan, *The Roadmap of the 18th CPC National Congress and the Chinese Dream* (Beijing, 2013), p. 2.
42. John Keane, *Democracy and Media Decadence* (Cambridge, 2013), p. 207.
43. Alexandra Stevenson, 'China Is Sticking to Its "Zero Covid" Policy', *New York Times*, October 16, 2022.

Party, benefits the nation, and benefits the people', former general Party secretary Hu Jintao famously remarked. 'Incorrect guidance of public opinion wrongs the Party, wrongs the nation, and wrongs the people'.[44] The foundational principle is that government stability rests on public opinion (*mín yì*). Often ignored by those who view China as a country run by authoritarian autocrats and totalitarian bullies, this principle is of utmost importance in understanding why the Party-state comes equipped with shock absorbers that make it more politically resilient than many outside observers suppose. When Xi Jinping speaks of 'the people' and says that the resilience of China depends on 'winning public support', he gives an old Party maxim a new twist. If opinion is the foundation of stable government, then the government must create stable opinion. In the name of 'the people', the imperative is to keep an ear to the ground so that the goal of 'guiding public opinion' towards harmonious rule becomes a reality. In this way, the present-day rulers of China acknowledge that power doesn't ultimately flow from the barrels of guns, or from Xinjiang-style interrogations, arrests, and internments. They are well aware that it's not enough to have the army, secret police, journalists, and censors on their side. They admit that little sustains the political order beyond the population's loyalty—their willingness to believe that the system addresses their complaints, and that democracy with Chinese characteristics is therefore better than its ailing American-style 'liberal' alternative.

But what does 'public opinion guidance' imply in practice? In the heartlands of empire, since the early 1980s, the one-party phantom democracy has built a giant information-gathering apparatus using a variety of methods of measuring and 'guiding' public opinion. In the hallowed name of the people, for instance, the Party showboats. It practises the common touch, as when President Xi—who

---

44. David Bandurski, 'Propaganda Leaders Scurry Off to Carry Out the "Spirit" of Hu Jintao's "Important" Media Speech', *China Media Project*, June 25, 2008, https://chinamediaproject.org/2008/06/25/propaganda-leaders-scurry-off-to-carry-out-the-spirit-of-hu-jintaos-media-speech/.

has amassed more titles and formal powers than any Chinese leader since the 1940s, including Mao—springs a well-crafted 'surprise' appearance and presses the flesh in a Beijing bun shop, rides a bicycle with his daughter, tips a humble trader in the back streets of Nanjing, praises state television journalists, or is seen on national television kicking a Gaelic football during an official visit to Ireland; or when his partner, former opera star and singer Peng Liyuan, turned her first state visit (to Trinidad and Tobago in 2013) into a media sensation, bringing 'kindness and language capability', high heels, and proto-democratic style for the first time into the field of high-level Chinese diplomacy and foreign policy.[45]

But public opinion guidance extends well beyond leadership style. The Party experiments with what it calls 'consultative democracy' (*xié shāng mín zhǔ*).[46] The broadly defined methods include neighbourhood assemblies, public hearings, 'anti-corruption' mechanisms built into state bureaucracies, and experiments in participatory budgeting. Throughout China, almost a million legal mediation (*fǎ lǜ tiáo jiě*) committees assisted by 'people's mediators' now handle most conflicts (perhaps 90 per cent) inside and outside courts, at no cost [two words to the litigants, in disputes over property and labour, divorce, and minor criminal and civil matters. The methods of 'consultative democracy' are deployed more widely, both at the political top, for instance in the annual 'democracy life meetings' (*mín zhǔ shēng huó huì*) used by Politburo members to ponder and criticize their own work performances, and in the world of state-regulated business, where, for example, the telecommunications giant Huawei features a governing board, called the Representatives Commission, comprising 115 employee representatives elected through secret ballot by the company's nearly one hundred thousand shareholder employees, who are scattered across more than 170 countries. The government's vigorous

---

45. Zhao Yanrong, 'First Lady Turns on the Charm, Impresses Hosts', *China Daily*, June 4, 2013.
46. Baogang He and Mark Warren, 'Authoritarian Deliberation: The Deliberative Turn in Chinese Political Development', *Perspectives on Politics* 9.2 (2011), pp. 269–289.

promotion of a culture of top-down 'inspection' is part of the same trend. An example is the determined efforts of the Chinese government to bring greater transparency to the massive (around $2 trillion) private fund management industry by promoting 'investor education' and 'honest and safe' business practices and bringing together 'sunshine investors' and legal, taxation, and regulatory compliance experts and organizations in Beijing Fund Town, one of at least eighty purpose-built fund towns (*jījīn xiaozhèn*) dotted across the country.

In the heartlands of the galaxy empire, the spirit of phantom democracy feeds as well on the clever use of digitally networked media as sophisticated tools to shape public opinion and policymaking and to serve as early warning devices. It is an open secret that the rulers issue secret written and unwritten instructions about which information can and cannot be circulated through official media platforms. The Party censors crack down on 'inappropriate' and 'disruptive' and 'foreign' messages. Street-level surveillance is omnipresent. Dawn raids by plainclothes police, 'cups of tea', disappearances, illegal detentions, and violent beatings by unidentified thugs happen. Less well known outside China is the way its CCP rulers use digital media not just as propaganda tools but as learning mechanisms, as listening posts, as platforms through which people are urged to chat and to vent their grievances against the government, to come closer to the rulers, to 'improve their governance', even to fight against their corruption and misuse of power.[47]

Chinese government officials working in 'management teams' (*yīng jí lǐng dǎo xiǎo zǔ*) watch for signs of brewing unrest or angry public reactions. Their job is to neutralize the disruptive effects of digital activists who use sophisticated proxies to spread tales of official wrongdoing by means of videos, screen shots, jokes, songs, satires, and euphemisms. So-called rumour refutation departments pitch in, zapping 'harmful' posts and issuing knockdown rebuttals of claims made

---

47. 'Public Opinion via Internet', *China Daily*, December 16, 2010. Some examples cited here are drawn from John Keane, 'Digital Innovations', in *The New Despotism* (Cambridge, MA, 2020), pp. 150–154.

by netizens. Their aim is to take the wind out of the sails of those who accuse the rulers of hypocrisy—who insist that the Party leaders must listen to normal people and live up to their promises to provide a good life for everyone. Government officials also use microblogs to spread the opinions of influencers. *Study Times*, the newspaper of the Central Party School in China, speaks of the urgent need for officials to get involved in the business of shaping public opinion—for instance, by employing big-time bloggers to spread positive energy, paying them according to their productivity as representatives of the 'silent majority'.[48] Still other government platforms spread public information. A team of researchers at China's Center for Disease Control and Prevention played an important role in publicly confirming evidence of the prevalence of SARS-CoV-2 in the Huanan Seafood Market in Wuhan during the early stage of the outbreak of the pestilence.[49] The official microblog of the Beijing Emergency Medical Centre earned high praise for its role in quickly informing anxious citizens in the aftermath of the 2011 Fukushima nuclear catastrophe in Japan. The government body known as the Institute of Public and Environmental Affairs does something similar. Its Blue Map app, designed to inform citizens in real time about water quality, local sources of pollution, and emissions from polluting companies, has been downloaded many millions of times. The data collected through the app, which enables users to add updates via their smartphones, is then shared with hundreds of companies in the power, steel, chemical, and petrochemical fields, to encourage them to cut levels of poisonous emissions.

Hugely relevant for understanding how things work within the heartlands of the galaxy empire is the role played by government platforms designed to stimulate public involvement by luring 'the people' inside the structures of government. The tools include virtual petition

---

48. Guohong Zhao, 'Enhance the Party's Social Management Capability in the New Communication Environment', *Study Times*, March 14, 2011 (in Chinese).
49. George Gao et al., 'Surveillance of SARS-CoV-2 in the Environment and Animal Samples of the Huanan Seafood Market', February 25, 2022, https://doi.org/10.21203/rs.3.rs-1370392/v1.

sites, e-consultation platforms, online Q&A sessions, and webcasts that come packaged in official assurances about the need to encourage transparency. The billion-people audience '315 Gala' event annually hosted by state broadcaster CCTV on World Consumer Rights Day uses undercover investigations to target and shame companies peddling defective products and services. Other tools include the widespread reliance upon opinion polls comprising hundreds of registered polling firms—such as the Canton Public Opinion Research Centre, the largest such independent research agency in China, and the *People's Daily* Online Public Opinion Monitoring Centre, which uses data-harvesting algorithms to send summaries of internet chatter to officials in real time, often with advice about terms to use and avoid during public brouhahas. Clothed in official talk of 'answering people's questions', 'listening to people's voices', and remedying 'public grievances', these mechanisms show that the one-party state is capable of using digital media not just as tools of top-down decision-making and control but also as a way of involving people 'from below' in the processes of government administration.

Pioneering examples include the anti-corruption web reporting platform (www.12388.gov.cn) hosted on the official website of the CCP's Central Commission for Discipline Inspection and the Ministry of Supervision of the People's Republic of China (www.ccdi.gov.cn). These platforms encourage citizens to report wrongdoing by government officials at all levels. The range of possible matters is defined widely, to include 'political discipline', 'democratic rights', financial and tax regulations, family-planning regulations, and government procurement and bidding procedures. The sites also invite complaints about bribery, hidden property and other assets, assaults on other people's rights, pornography and prostitution, and 'abuse of power, negligence, and power-seeking'. The point is to convince citizens of the need to criticize and make suggestions about how to build 'clean and honest government'. The experiments operate at lower levels of the domestic polity. In the southern Chinese province of Guangdong, known for its innovative public involvement schemes, Party officials use public policy 'network hearings' (*wǎng luò tīng zhèng*), broadcast live, with hand-picked presenters expressing their views on proposed reforms, with the public invited to make comments and to vote online for the policies they support. Similar innovations have happened in the Yangzi Delta cities of Hangzhou and Nanjing, which use electronic 'mayor's mailboxes' to promote bottom-up feedback, make public administration more accountable (*gōng sī*), and persuade people that local government is actually efficient and effective.

Domestic Troubles

Within the heartlands of the galaxy empire, these mechanisms of phantom democracy regularly fail. Here we encounter the most serious contradiction that troubles the homelands of the empire: the deeply ironic fact that state-backed efforts to deploy digital platforms designed to encourage people to vent their grievances and to blow the whistle on corrupt and incompetent officials—to put into practice a limited and local version of the ideals of monitory democracy—regularly produces blowback, public outbursts that shame local officials and sometimes shake the whole governing system to its foundations.

Within the strongholds of the empire, nothing's ever calm for long. Small-scale public mutinies are chronic, and there are times when they morph into bigger media storms. While the reasons for these protests against arbitrary power are often circumstantial, having to do with particular grievances and the courage, technical skill, and sheer determination of digital activists, a much deeper dynamic is at work. Throughout the galaxy empire, we have already seen, all institutions, from government ministries and state-owned corporations to China Global Television Network reportage from various parts of the world, functionally depend upon information flows structured by digital communication networks whose multiple nodes enjoy a measure of mutual independence. When for any reason particular information nodes suffer technical problems, or are blocked by censors, the rest of the network continues to operate. Within these distributed networks, the ability of actors to exercise power by doing things with information is thus never fully controllable by centralized, top-down regulation. Of course, governments always have the option of shutting down the operating networks, as has happened several times in the past in China, in the regions populated by Tibetan and Uighur majorities. The trouble is that in the end shutdowns prove to be both self-paralysing and technically fraught: digital networks can't be fully controlled by any single user or organization. At any point in the galactic system of information flows, digital disruption and public mutinies are always possible.

Harnessing a wide range of available tools, including smartphones, tablets, desktop computers, VPNs, and other sophisticated software, China's web people (*wǎng mín*) regularly find ways of projecting themselves into daring campaigns that spread messages to wider publics, sometimes with dramatic effects. The growing sophistication of government censorship tactics is matched by activists' cat-and-mouse resistance, which sometimes has 'swarm' effects. Rowdy media storms the rulers call 'mass incidents' are the result. These are not 'revolutions' in the early modern sense. The mutinies are often brief, with limited aims, but they always come politically charged, first erupting online then quickly spreading through daily life, sometimes to the point where the storms grow so fierce that worried officials scurry to restore political order, or suddenly change political direction, as happened in late 2022 when protests against the government's 'zero Covid' policies in many cities forced officials to abandon strict lockdown and testing policies. The disturbances proved that 'real people' could force the self-appointed leaders of a fictive 'People' to listen, to change their minds, minimally to act more prudently.

During the past decade or so, the lesson has been repeatedly delivered to the ruling powers. Consider the arrest and trial (in early March 2012) of Chongqing Communist Party boss Bo Xilai: online media carried so many tens of thousands of anti-government comments and even rumours of a possible coup d'état in Beijing that the government scampered to enforce social media blackouts. In 2015, a huge public debate was sparked by *Under the Dome* (*qióng dǐng zhī xià*), an online documentary about pollution from coal-fired power plants watched by at least 150 million Chinese viewers; later blocked by government censors, which aroused even greater annoyance, the mutiny resulted eventually in press-conference assurances that the Chinese government was committed to reducing air pollution. There are moments when it feels as though the foundations of the People's Republic of China are being rocked by people power in digital form. An example was the mid-2018 vaccine scandal centred on the Changsheng Biotechnology Company, whose *baibaipo* children's vaccine was reported by local journalists to be defective. The company was also accused of falsifying data. The company was hit by revelations that it had already received a large sum (48.3 million yuan) of new government subsidies designed to boost the global market position of Chinese vaccine companies, and that its executives had financial interests in these competitor corporations. That was why Changsheng was initially protected by the State Drug Administration and by the local Changchun pharmaceuticals administration, which initially ordered only a small fine (3.4 million yuan). 'We are deeply ashamed', confessed the company in a stock exchange announcement, adding that the defective product had been discontinued. Social media activists quickly pointed out that there was no mention of a recall. All hell broke loose. Within hours, an online article viewed over one hundred thousand times, the limit displayed by WeChat, poured scorn on the company. The public mood was well summarized by a Weibo user: 'If the state does not protect its citizens, how can we love our country?' By the next day, Changsheng's website displayed a 404 page and the Weibo article had been scrubbed. Then Chinese state media and local authorities sprang into action. They urged Weibo users to 'not let anger and panic spread.' The *People's Daily* called on local regulators to 'rapidly take action, do a complete investigation, and announce authoritative information in a timely manner to pacify public anxiety'. Premier Li Keqiang chimed in with talk of 'illegal and criminal acts that endanger the safety of people's lives', while Xi Jinping interrupted his state visit to Rwanda to order severe punishments 'to safeguard the public interest and social security'. The upshot: the company was stripped of its assets, compulsorily delisted on the Shenzhen Stock Exchange, its chief executives were banned for life from the securities industry, and several national and provincial-level government officials were fired.

The public occupations of Hong Kong's streets and squares during the summer–autumn 2014 Umbrella Movement, and the equally dramatic protests of 2019 in support of civil society, social justice, and free and fair elections, were undoubtedly the most serious digital mutinies the imperial rulers have so far faced at home. The networked—dispersed and flexible—qualities of the mainly non-violent uprising relied heavily on the creative deployment of digital tools. Drones and the encrypted Telegram app were used for the first time in China to organize and publicize crowd actions; at one point during the protests, citizens even responded to rumours that the local Hong Kong government was about to cut the city's cellular networks by downloading the Firechat app, which uses Bluetooth and Wi-Fi technology to allow smartphone users to connect anonymously by relaying messages from one user to another without a cell signal or internet connection. The uprising was eventually crushed using a variety of strategies and tactics that millions of Hong Kong citizens felt amounted to a process of colonization of their way of life. In mid-2020, a National Security Law was imposed on the city. With the backing of special police units, hand-picked prosecutors, and judges, pro-democracy figures were arrested, convicted of 'uttering seditious words' and 'holding unauthorized assemblies'. Many were forced into exile. Freedoms of expression and peaceful assembly were gutted, and *Apple Daily* and other independent media platforms were shut down. *Ta Kung Pao* and *Wen Wei Po* and other state-owned media waged fiercely pro-Beijing campaigns. Groups such as teachers and civil servants faced pressure to pledge allegiance to the 'Hong Kong Special Administrative Region of the People's Republic of China', and 'electoral reforms' stipulated that only candidates loyal to Beijing could in future run for the local rump Legislative Council parliament.

Faraway Troubles

The future role of a tamed Hong Kong within the new galaxy empire continues to arouse disagreements among observers, some of whom point out that the forecast 'death of Hong Kong' is premature.[50] Robed like an emperor in pomp and ceremony, Xi Jinping travelled there (in late June 2022) to mark the triumph of Chinese rule, but the city remains a global financial hub with its own convertible currency, transparent regulations, and a substantial financial services sector with accounting, legal, and insurance firms not found elsewhere in China. Hong Kong has another long-term significance: fuelled by local fears of becoming just another Chinese city, its public mutinies of recent years are harbingers of a broader challenge confronting the rulers of the emerging galaxy empire, a problem faced by all hitherto existing empires, but this time on a global scale: how to win the hearts and minds of the colonized, how to get under the skin of people and organizations in far-flung places where there is no automatic love for a rising China, spaces where Chinese business executives, government officials, journalists, and other galaxy empire figures are greeted with suspicion because their financial, political, and cultural power is deemed illegitimate.

Beyond its own state borders, much more than at home, the galaxy empire is dogged by legitimacy problems. Scholars have noted that for two millennia Chinese emperors were guided by the political principle of 'stability in unity' (Mengzi) and beliefs in the omnipotence and universality of their own rule; and some say this principle lives on in the heads and hearts of the Chinese political class until our days.[51]

---

50. Compare Ho-fung Hung, *City on the Edge: Hong Kong under Chinese Rule* (Cambridge, 2022) and Karen Cheung, *The Impossible City: A Hong Kong Memoir* (New York, 2022).
51. Pines, *The Everlasting Empire*, pp. 1–10.

Truth is that the exact meaning and practicability of the principle remain in doubt, not least because at many points on our planet, China's leaders are now regularly reminded that rejection and resistance are the price of influence and control—and that methods trialled in Tibet, Xinjiang, and Hong Kong for shaping and controlling the habits and hopes of people don't work elsewhere, in far-distant zones of the empire. Nobody knows whether Chinese government officials, diplomats, and businesspeople have read *The Vizier's Elephant* (1947) by Nobel Prize winner Ivo Andrić, a classic tale of resentment against the pinched promises and shameless hypocrisy of occupiers, to grasp how easily imperial power can be doubted, satirized, worn down, and defeated.[52] Feeling their way in the new world, encountering situations never before experienced, Chinese empire builders are slowly but surely being forced to recognize that the age of digital networks and communicative abundance makes public resistance to arbitrary power—mutinies against the maltreatment of local workers and bribery scandals, for instance—much easier. Digital tools give new life to the Chinese writer Lu Xun's principle that 'discontent is the wheel that moves people forward'. Local disenchantment with the empire can readily follow—as happened, for instance, in Kazakhstan in 2019, with large-scale protests against the construction of Chinese factories and the maltreatment of Muslim and Turkic peoples in Xinjiang; and in Zambia, where bitter clashes between local mining workers and their Chinese employers have been rife for decades.

These local legitimacy problems have everything to do with the general problem of abusive power. In the heartlands of the empire, we have seen, abuses of power by Party-state officials and poligarchs regularly breed disaffection and public resistance, often at the local level. Similar dynamics of abusive power trouble the outer zones of the empire, too. This should come as no surprise because every previous empire not only experienced conflicts generated by misuses of power by the central rulers. Power struggles at the periphery of the

---

52. Ivo Andrić, *The Vizier's Elephant* (New York, 1961 [1947]).

imperial order were also chronic. The Dutch East India Company was regularly dogged by disputes with distant ship captains, company representatives, and local governors abusing their power. During the 1770s, British mishandling of its American colonies ended badly. In southern Africa, its colonial administrators later faced constant jostling for power and wealth among land-hungry colonists, ruthless colonial employers, and Bible-banging missionaries.[53] China's difficulties in Libya in 2011 provided a similar centre-periphery lesson: when state-owned companies invested in the local petroleum industry and infrastructure projects, they never anticipated that the collapse of the Libyan regime would require a military rescue operation that inadvertently publicized suspected Chinese arms sales to the Gaddafi regime and embarrassed the Ministry of Foreign Affairs. The galaxy empire stumbled. Talk of 'non-interference' in 'sovereign' states was dropped. After declining to veto a UN Security Council resolution sanctioning NATO bombing of Gaddafi's forces, it then urged compromise with the regime and condemned the air strikes. As the regime collapsed, Chinese forces intervened to protect seventy-five Chinese companies and deliver thirty-eight thousand workers to safety.

In the coming years, legitimacy problems linked to the misuse of power and tensions between centre and periphery are bound to trouble the Chinese empire. The challenges will surely be exacerbated by local and regional concerns about such matters as how mounting debt conflicts are to be handled—by persuasion, legal proceedings, debt restructuring, or force. Cross-strait troubles over the future of Taiwan remain unresolved. Revelations about networks of shadowy policing operations inside the European Union are stirring up public troubles.[54] As we are going to see, there are serious environmental

---

53. John Comaroff, 'Images of Empire, Contests of Conscience: Models of Colonial Domination in South Africa', *American Ethnologist* 16 (1989), pp. 661–685.
54. Francesco Collini, Christoph Giesen, Tobias Großekemper, Roman Lehberger, Nadia Pantel, Maik Baumgärtner, and Ann-Katrin Müller, 'China's Secret Police Stations in Europe', *Spiegel International*, November 4, 2022, https://www.spiegel.de/international/world/beijing-s-long-arm-china-s-secret-police-stations-in-europe-a-d6732094-ca32-4c0a-8e6f-58b395b946aa.

concerns, too. China invests much more in renewable energy than the United States, yet at least a third of its groundwater is unfit for human consumption. And there are bio-challenges abroad, in places such as Antarctica, where the Chinese-owned Shanghai Chonghe Marine Industry Company, which operates the world's largest krill-fishing boat, is sure to encounter protests against its profit-driven plans to mega-harvest the small crustacean currently suffering population decline in delicately balanced biomes.

Seen in terms of the general problem of arrogant, selfish, and abusive power, these particular unresolved challenges are symptomatic of the major overall weakness of the galaxy empire: its *often lukewarm and self-contradictory embrace of public accountability mechanisms.* The problem of phantom democracy at home is mirrored in the problem of phantom democracy abroad. As a one-party regime with a penchant for secrecy, dissimulation, and unchallenged exercises of arbitrary power, the galaxy empire remains globally vulnerable to charges of corruption and power blindness. That is a key reason why China's leaders repeatedly say they want open connectivity and uncorrupted cross-border institutions based on consultation and adherence to rule-based procedures. Along the same lines, several leading Chinese international relations scholars have told the principal author privately that their country can't succeed globally unless it opens its power structures to much greater public scrutiny, both at home and abroad. Its currency must be eternal vigilance, wise deference to complexity, humble open-mindedness, they say. Echoing earlier European critics of empire—think of Jeremy Bentham's historic speech (in 1793) to the National Convention of France about the dangers of empires run by 'degraded despots'[55]—they have a point: *the fundamental weakness of every rising empire is bombast, hubris, and vulnerability to public exposure and public rejection.* This flaw is especially threatening to an empire born within the digital information age, and it helps explain why in more than a few overseas settings Chinese

---

55. Jeremy Bentham, *Emancipate Your Colonies! Addressed to the National Convention of France* (London, 1830 [1793]).

officials practise a form of phantom democracy: they do what they can to deal with threatening uncertainties, charges of corruption, and nasty surprises by mimicking the methods of accountable rule.

In places such as Sri Lanka, poster campaigns announce the coming of 'extensive consultation, joint contributions, shared benefits'. There are moments and settings in which things happen at a distance that are not permitted in the heartlands of the empire. Especially striking is China's escalating contributions to the field of cross-border governing and legal arrangements. In the heartlands of the empire, the rulers have opened the legal-services field to Baker McKenzie, to Paul, Weiss, Rifkind, Wharton & Garrison, and to other large foreign law firms, which work alongside local partners, with global effects. Although at home there are stiff penalties for such criminalized offences as 'publishing state secrets' and 'subverting state security', abroad there is abundant talk by officials of the need to 'respect the law' and to 'strengthen laws', even calls for locking power in 'a cage of regulations' (Xi Jinping)[56] within a stable global 'community of common destiny' and a 'new model of international relations' (*xīn xíng guó jì guānxi*) based on multi-polarity and careful calculations of the costs and benefits to China's 'national interest'.[57] In recent decades, the galaxy empire has agreed (in 2022) to allow US regulators to inspect the Chinese government's own audits of large publicly listed companies such as JD.com, Alibaba, and Baidu. The empire has negotiated and now operates cross-border rule-of-law deals, such as the 1998 Legal and Judicial Cooperation Program with the European Union. Officials have learned how to play the legal rules of the foreign policy game. With the notable exception of the Organisation for Economic Cooperation and Development, the galaxy empire now plays a robust role in leading Bretton Woods institutions (the World Bank, from which it

---

56. An Baijie, 'Xi Jinping Vows 'Power within Cage of Regulations', *China Daily*, January 23, 2013.
57. Xi Jinping, 'Working Together for a New Progress of Security and Development in Asia', speech in Dushanbe, June 15, 2019, https://www.fmprc.gov.cn/mfa_eng/zxxx_662805/t1673167.shtml.

is now the largest recipient of projects and loans, and the International Monetary Fund), as well as the World Trade Organisation and the Asian Development Bank. It extracts investment, loans, and aid from a wide variety of multilateral agencies—larger sums than any other state in the world—and plays a vital role in key global security and arms control treaties. It is committed to building and buttressing new cross-border institutions such as the Shanghai Cooperation Organisation, a partnership of China, Russia, India, Pakistan, and the Central Asian states, and to the twenty-seven-member Conference on Interaction and Confidence Building Measures in Asia.

How do Chinese officials behave within these organizations? Reports suggest that the empire's diplomats and other negotiators often impress outsiders with their knowledge of procedural rules and technical details, their circumspection, and their tough bargaining skills. Chinese officials are said to be 'thorough, exceedingly well-prepared and well organized'.[58] Chinese negotiators equally demonstrate their respect for rule-of-law principles and practices within such venues as the World Trade Organisation Dispute Settlement Body, in which China has become a highly active participant with a surprisingly low volume of complaints and full acceptance of legally binding decisions.[59] China even wins cases against the United States, as when (in December 2022) the adjudicating panel of the WTO, in a case pursued by China, Norway, Switzerland, and Turkey, ruled that United States' Section 232 tariffs on steel and aluminium imports were an unwarranted misuse of national security precepts for political purposes and a clear violation of international trade rules specified by the General Agreement on Tariffs and Trade 1994.[60]

58. Olson and Prestowitz, *Evolving Role of China*.
59. Xiaojun Li, 'Learning and Socialization in International Institutions: China's Experience with the WTO Dispute Settlement System', in Mingjiang Li, ed., *China Joins Global Governance* (Lanham, MD, 2012), pp. 75–94; Xiaojun Li, 'Understanding China's Behavioral Change in the WTO Dispute Settlement System', *Asian Survey* 52.6 (December 2012), pp. 1111–1137.
60. Liu Zhihua, 'WTO Ruling against US Tariffs Lauded', *China Daily*, December 12, 2022, https://www.chinadailyhk.com/article/304829#WTO-ruling-against-US-tariffs-lauded.

These trends suggest to some observers that those who govern the new Chinese empire are capable of outdoing the Ottomans and the British by cleverly paying homage to their clients and subjects everywhere, employing surprising degrees of self-scrutiny, procedural experimentation, and rule-bound action. Perhaps indeed the galaxy empire is in the throes of developing a commanding resilience many outside observers hadn't anticipated. Perhaps its rulers, tempered by skittishness and smart governing methods, will succeed not only in harnessing phantom democratic mechanisms at home to legitimate and strengthen their single-party rule, but also abroad, in the far-flung districts of their empire. If that happened, China might well perfect the art of what has been called 'administrative absorption': the ability to turn political problems into administrative matters, and to outflank and win over resistance, to convince governments and citizens everywhere that Chinese infrastructure projects, ways of life, and commitments to multilateral governance are universally good, or on balance not bad, that China is a responsive and responsible global player, an imperial alternative clearly superior to the confused and hypocritical American alternatives on offer.

It is indeed imaginable that in the coming years and decades foreign suspicion of the galaxy empire will falter, grow divided and fatigued, and that the shrinking economic might and repeated military foolishness of the United States combined with solid domestic support for dreams of restoring China to greatness will together serve to fertilize the new empire's tremendous power and help it triumphantly beat a path towards a world dominated by unequalled Chinese power. There's no certainty this is going to happen anytime soon. We earthlings are by definition forbidden to know the future, but when it comes to the galaxy empire things may not be clear-cut, promising, or straightforward. The brutal fact is that unexpected events at different points on our planet are already damaging the good reputation, public reassurances, and grand promises of its rulers. A corruption scandal here, the collapse of a corporate behemoth there, or sudden social resistance to infrastructure projects can set back the galaxy empire's reputation and offset its resilience. Small beginnings can hatch big dramas. Supported by investigative journalists, civil society organizations, professionals, and elected political leaders, the push for accountability can put the brakes on the galaxy empire. And the times are surely coming when troubles somewhere in its outlands even spread back across borders, into the heartlands of the empire.

Whether the troubles will accumulate and coalesce into serious global opposition to the galaxy empire as 'imperialist' is at this stage unknowable. What is however certain is that on every continent the levels of suspicion and open public criticism of the galaxy empire are growing. Let us take just a small handful of examples, chosen randomly to clarify the trend, beginning with the case of Africa.

Within the ranks of Africa's rising generation, the perception that China is now more influential in their countries than the United States is growing.[61] More than three-quarters of young people view Chinese influence either as positive (35 per cent) or somewhat positive (41 per cent). In countries such as Rwanda (97 per cent), Malawi (95 per cent), and Nigeria (90 per cent), a huge majority think that China's role is beneficial. With foreign direct investment from China flowing rapidly into the continent (it increased from US$75 million in 2003 to US$2.7 billion in 2019), it is unsurprising that young Africans praise the affordability of Chinese products; the positive effects of Chinese loans, investments, and assistance for infrastructure development; and (their main overall concern) the creation of skills training and employment opportunities for workers in their country. But there are grumblings about the return of what many call colonialism. More than a few African young people (around 25 per cent overall) say Chinese companies are extracting natural resources without fair compensation or benefit to local communities. They are anxious about the future inability of their countries to repay loans to China and

---

61. See the survey research findings published by the Ichikowitz Family Foundation, which sampled thousands of respondents between the ages of eighteen and twenty-four across fifteen African countries, *2022 African Youth Survey* (Johannesburg, 2022), p. 66.

they express concerns about Chinese companies and workers taking job opportunities away from locals and the lack of respect of Chinese businesses and government officials for local values and traditions.

Here's a second example of how, when it comes to doing business in foreign quarters, beyond China's borders, things don't always go the empire's way. It is well known that Chinese companies usually play tough, according to the rules of the game. They specialize in strenuous negotiation and bargain hard to secure deals in their favour. The extent to which *guanxi* laced with corruption operate is never entirely clear, but there are plenty of negotiations in which Chinese companies win contracts because they are better capitalized, better equipped and professionally prepared, and generally more experienced and highly motivated. They are equally willing to take risks. An example, by no means exceptional, is the contract won by the China Road and Bridge Corporation to build a bridge at the Adriatic city of Neum, to link together divided parts of Croatia at what was once described as the world's most ridiculous border. Construction began in July 2018 after the company won an open competitive bid to construct the 2.4 kilometre (1.5 miles) bridge. Fully functional by mid-2022, opened three months ahead of schedule in a grand midnight ceremony featuring folk songs and fireworks, the bridge now enables the free flow of people and goods up and down the Adriatic coast, from south of Dubrovnik all the way to Split, Zadar, and Rijeka, unobstructed by two border crossings staffed by Bosnia immigration and customs officials and rules and time-consuming and traffic-jammed border checks. The deal for the construction project was brokered and mainly financed by the European Commission, marking the Pelješac bridge as the first time a Chinese company had won an open-tender bid and completed a project underwritten by the European Union.[62]

62. Leonardo Dinic, 'Chinese Builders Complete the Pelješac Bridge to Fully Connect Croatia's Dalmatian Coast', *China US Focus*, August 18, 2021, https://www.chinausfocus.com/finance-economy/chinese-builders-complete-the-peljeac-bridge-to-fully-connect-croatias-dalmatian-coast.

Elsewhere in the world, Chinese contracts and deals struck are dogged by public controversies fuelled by accusations of hypocrisy, manipulation, and abuses of power. The protests come charged with feelings about Chinese double standards: it is said that promises of 'development', 'progress', and 'accountability' are mere signs taken for wonders, empty promises contradicted by the harsh reality that local peoples don't count for much when it comes to Chinese power and profiteering. There is blowback from the margins of the empire: resistance that can be likened to revolts in the plantation colonies of Guadeloupe, Martinique, and Saint Dominigue, where African slaves demanded that the rulers of metropolitan France live up to the revolutionary principles of the 'rights of man and the citizen'.[63] In today's Caribbean, there have been many reported cases of Chinese projects marred by unexplained secrecy, questionable procurement procedures, and fears of future unpayable debt. The scale of Chinese involvement in the Caribbean has been growing rapidly; bilateral trade has burgeoned; thousands of Chinese workers have been moved into the region; and during the period 2005–18 Chinese state-owned banks (China Export-Import Bank and China Development Bank) became the largest lenders, offering low interest rate loans subsidized by China's foreign aid budget. In the fifteen-member state Caribbean Community, more than half (Antigua and Barbuda, Barbados, Dominica, Grenada, Guyana, Jamaica, Suriname, and Trinidad and Tobago) have signed onto the Belt and Road Initiative. Hotels, highways, bridges, seaports, shopping malls, hospitals, tourism projects, even a prime minister's house, are among the large infrastructure projects funded by galaxy empire capital. More than a few have sparked public bellyaching about excessive secrecy, the failure of government ministers and senior state officials to read draft agreements, and the biased terms and conditions of contracts. The contract for the US$630 million North–South Highway project signed by the government of Jamaica with the China

---

63. Frederick Cooper, *Colonialism in Question: Theory, Knowledge, History* (Berkeley, 2005), especially part 3.

Harbour Engineering Corporation included a waiver of important rights of immunity, so that in the event of late delivery of debt repayments or outright defaults, it was agreed that publicly owned assets can in principle be seized by the Chinese government (as happened in Sri Lanka, where the failure of the government to repay its $1.2 billion debt enabled China to secure a ninety-nine-year lease of the strategically important Indian Ocean port of Hambantota). When delivery problems and bankruptcy hit the Bahamas project to build the US$3.5 billion Baha Mar hotel, the largest in the Caribbean, proceedings were heard in Hong Kong, where a court awarded sale of the project to Chow Tai Fook Enterprises, a Hong Kong real estate, transport, and jewellery retailing conglomerate enjoying close ties to Beijing.

Tightly guarded secrets are features of most of the deals cut between the government of Suriname and Chinese banks and corporations. When Suriname's foreign minister Yidiz Pollack-Beighle was pressed by journalists to explain these non-disclosure agreements, she emphasized (in strikingly Chinese terms) the double imperatives of sustainable economic growth and respect for territorial sovereignty. 'Since Suriname has the principle of non-interference in the internal affairs of sovereign states, no statement can be made regarding what's happening in other countries'. Loud controversies about Chinese investments have also erupted in Guyana, where the East Coast Demerara Highway Project contract expressly stated that in the event of arbitration disputes between the construction company (China Railway First Group Limited) and the government, Chinese laws would apply and hearings be held in Beijing courts. The most bitter disputes were sparked by the refurbishment of Guyana's national airport. Eyebrows first raised when the mega-deal between China Export-Import Bank and the government of Guyana to construct a runway extension and a new terminal with improved boarding bridge and security facilities was announced outside the country, in overseas Jamaica. The contract was hastily signed on the eve of a general election (in November 2011). Feasibility and environmental impact studies were only conducted later. Tight secrecy camouflaged the lopsided terms and conditions of the agreement. Investigative journalists later revealed that the contractor (China Harbour Engineering Corporation) was paid the full contract price in advance, in Chinese RMB, with exchange rate fluctuation risks borne entirely by the Guyana government. The company was freed from paying any duties, taxes, royalties, and local fees. More than half the employed workforce, and all technical staff, were imported from China. In return, the Guyana government agreed, at its own expense, to secure all necessary local permits and licences, to demolish and remove the old terminal, to provide sand and other building materials to the company, and to construct, again drawing on taxpayers' funds, access roads plus a new car park, cargo buildings, and a fuel zone area. More than a decade after the contract was agreed, with extended delays, the expiry and renegotiation of the contract with China Harbour Engineering Company, haggling over the quality of works and a belated value-for-money auditor general's report, the refurbishment project was finally completed.[64]

Here's a third example of troubles at a distance from the heartlands of the empire: throughout the region of central Asia, China is gradually nudging aside Russian military and economic power, easily outflanking India's 'Connect Central Asia' programme and pushing aside the United States, the European Union, and other Western powers.[65] Due to the region's role as a key energy and commodity node in the galaxy empire's Belt and Road programme, trade with China has risen more than twenty times during the past two decades (from US$1.7 billion in 2000 to almost US$40 billion in 2019). It is not just

64. Carla Bridglal, Ivan Cairo, Steffon Campbell, Alix Lewis, and Neil Marks, 'China's Opaque Caribbean Trail: Dreams, Deals and Debt', *Caribbean Investigative Journalism Network*, December 5, 2019, https://www.cijn.org/chinas-opaque-caribbean-trail-dreams-deals-and-debt/; and Richard Bhaini, 'We Are Not Discussing Any Extension', *Guyana Chronicle*, October 21, 2021, https://guyanachronicle.com/2021/10/21/we-are-not-discussing-any-extension/.
65. See Li-Chen Sim and Farkhod Aminjonov, 'Statecraft in the Steppes: Central Asia's Relations with China', *Journal of Contemporary China*, October 20, 2022, https://doi.org/10.1080/10670564.2022.2136937; Raffaello Pantucci and Alexandros Petersen, *Sinostan: China's Inadvertent Empire* (Oxford, 2022); and Sébastien Peyrouse, 'Discussing China: Sinophilia and Sinophobia in Central Asia', *Journal of Eurasian Studies* 7.1 (2016), pp. 14–23.

that local bazaars are stuffed full of Chinese consumer goods. Over 80 per cent of Tajikistan's gold is mined by Sino-Tajik ventures; 90 per cent of Turkmenistan's gas is exported to China; and an estimated 25 per cent of Kazakhstan's gas and oil reserves are owned by Chinese companies. China is now among the region's largest source of loans and investment. Although charging higher interest rates than most bilateral and multilateral lenders, the loans offered by Chinese banks and credit institutions are usually preferred, not only because they are tied to commodity purchases and the profits of local state-owned companies but also because lending for roads, tunnels, railways, and other infrastructure projects is not conditional on human rights or political and economic reforms. China is also a rising military power in the region: the frequency of SCO and bilateral military exercises is growing, and arms sales are booming (now 18 per cent of the region's annual purchases, up from 1.5 per cent between 2010 and 2014). The galaxy empire operates an undeclared military base in Tajikistan along with several outposts on the Afghan-Tajikistan border. Chinese private security companies protect assets in the region, and Chinese state-owned cyber security companies supply surveillance and facial recognition software used in 'smart city' programmes, public transport, schools, and policing operations.

The trends are as striking as the local resistance to their effects. Within a region that Halford John Mackinder and others long ago considered geopolitically and globally vital—'who rules the Heartland [Eurasia] commands the World-Island; who rules the World-Island commands the world', he wrote[66]—the galaxy empire is encountering a barrage of local complaints. The region's most highly educated young people express doubts about the negative environmental and social impact of Chinese mega-projects; the more Chinese investment grows, the more it breeds their dislike.[67] Many of the region's states

66. Halford John Mackinder, *Democratic Ideals and Reality* (London, 1919), p. 150; and his earlier essay 'The Geographical Pivot of History', *Geographical Journal* 23.4 (April 1904), pp. 421–437.
67. Marlene Laruelle and Dylan Royce, 'No Great Game: Central Asia's Public Opinions on Russia, China, and the U.S.', August 2020, https://www.wilsoncenter.org/sites/

do what they can to retain a measure of independence, or to 'hedge': while they are members of galaxy empire-led initiatives such as the Asian Infrastructure Investment Bank, the Shanghai Cooperation Organisation, and the Quadrilateral Cooperation and Coordination Mechanism in Counterterrorism, the region's states, sometimes to the annoyance of Beijing, contribute to multilateral forums that do not include China, such as the Cooperation Council of Turkic Speaking Countries and the European Union's Transport Corridor-Europe-Caucasus-Asia programme. There are moments when Chinese investment is snubbed: in Uzbekistan, China's state-owned company Singyes Solar was initially awarded then denied the right to build and operate a solar farm in Samarkand in 2016, preference being given to France's Total Eren. There are loud public protests against the galaxy empire, too. In Kyrgyzstan, local protesters forced the cancellation (in 2020) of a China-funded US$275 million free trade zone on the Kyrgyz-China border at Naryn, where Chinese mining operations had to shut down temporarily. In neighbouring Kazakhstan, fears of Chinese landgrabs sparked countrywide protests; and in April 2020 a formal complaint was lodged with the Chinese ambassador by the Kazakh Foreign Ministry following an article on a Chinese website that claimed Kazakhstan was a historical vassal eager to 'return' to China. And throughout the region not to be underestimated is the force of an irony: complaints about how, despite its BRI commitments, China is a curiously passive power, an 'inadvertent empire' run by confused, hesitant, and excessively cautious Chinese officials.

And now a final example, drawn from the galaxy empire's main global rival, the United States, where allegations and complaints

default/files/media/uploads/documents/KI_200805_cable%2056_final.pdf> and Julie Yu-Wen Chen and Soledad Jiménez-Tovar, 'China in Central Asia: Local Perceptions from Future Elites', *China Quarterly of International Strategic Studies* 3.3 (2017), pp. 429–445, https://www.wilsoncenter.org/sites/default/files/media/uploads/documents/KI_200805_cable%2056_final.pdf> David Trilling, 'Poll Shows Uzbeks, Like Neighbors, Growing Leery of Chinese Investments', *Eurasianet*, October 22, 2020, https://eurasianet.org/poll-shows-uzbeks-like-neighbors-growing-leery-of-chinese-investments&gt.

about China's abuses of power are the most numerous, loudest, and politically consequential. There are observers—former US secretary of state Henry Kissinger is among the most prominent—who are convinced that we have entered the Chinese Century and that the world will have to learn to live with China and its distinctive ways of handling power. There is no sensible alternative but to accept the facts of China's global rise and to recalibrate policies and strategies designed to cope with the new reality.[68] More vocal, and for the moment more influential, are China critics who are convinced that Xi Jinping's galaxy empire is bound to suffer the fate of China's past dynasties because its sources of resilience and durability are limited. Still others are convinced that despite—or because of—its contradictions, China is fast becoming an aggressive expansionist power bent on controlling large swathes of territory and greedily extracting resources on a global scale.

Their suspicion and contempt for China is often strangely underpinned by the conviction that the empire is unsustainable. Their predictions of China's coming demise come wrapped in wishful thinking. 'I'd give the regime a couple of years, no more than a decade', a prominent Chinese-American scholar said more than five years ago. The scholar has been saying that for four decades. The bravado is the flip side of the ill-fated 1990s prediction that market reforms would turn China into an American-style liberal democracy. Regime collapse is also on the political agenda of American hawks, who liken China to a house of cards, liable to be scattered by a firm flick of the wrist. They want ideological confrontation, more advanced weapons systems, and a new Cold War. The political and military perils of simple-minded, friend-versus-enemy thinking and Big China, Bad China politics aren't of interest to these hawks. Suffering a form of 'imperial trauma',[69] they're convinced of the moral superiority of

68. Henry Kissinger, *World Order: Reflections on the Character of Nations and the Course of History* (London, 2014), especially chap. 6.
69. Sanjay Subrahmanyam, 'A Tale of Three Empires: Mughals, Ottomans, and Habsburgs in a Comparative Context', *Common Knowledge* 12 (2006), pp. 66–92.

American democracy. They regard China as a dragon power responsible for the theft of American technology and jobs and for hatching and spreading a global pestilence they call 'the China virus'. When dealing with China, they are uninterested in practising what former Australian prime minister Kevin Rudd liked to call durable partnerships (*zhèng yǒu*) built on unflinching advice and frank awareness of basic interests and ambitions. They insist that breaking off and breaking up with China is necessary. Governments, businesses, non-government organizations, and citizens committed to engaging with China cooperatively in such fields as scientific research, higher education, and renewable energy are therefore accused of undermining 'patriotism' and capitulation and appeasement that feed 'treason'. Like former Trump adviser Stephen K. Bannon, they are sure that 'the lies, the infiltration and the malevolence'[70] of its rulers render China just as vulnerable to collapse as its Soviet predecessor. They don't admit of their own ignorance about the galaxy empire. Its great complexity and shape-shifting resilience, its crisis management capacities, and the empire's structural weaknesses all seem to be of little or no interest. Anathema is the thought that the galaxy empire has protean and polymorphic features—that multiformity and variegation are among its leading features and sources of strength.

The hawks ignore the possibility that the galaxy empire may be a repeat, perhaps in more sophisticated and more global ways, of the striking absence of a 'very regular pattern' within the mid-nineteenth-century British way of governing its empire, which for instance simultaneously operated penal colonies in Australia and elected legislatures in Upper and Lower Canada.[71] For these hawks, none of this complexity is interesting. The case is closed: the galaxy empire is a dangerously homogeneous, centralized, and nasty regime of power.

70. Rosalind S. Helderman, Josh Dawsey, Gerry Shih, and Matt Zapotosky, 'How Former Trump Adviser Steve Bannon Joined Forces with a Chinese Billionaire Who Has Divided the President's Allies', *Washington Post*, September 13, 2020, https://www.washingtonpost.com/politics/steve-bannon-guo-wengui/2020/09/13/8b43cd06-e964-11ea-bc79-834454439a44_story.html.
71. Herman Merivale, *Lectures on Colonisation and Colonies* (London, 1861), p. v.

That is why these critics trade in exaggerations and say things like 'the wheels are falling off the BRI' and 'China is in decline'. Their aim is to stir up public sentiment against the 'totalitarianism' and 'authoritarianism' of the CCP-led regime. They see nothing but acts of silent espionage and takeovers of businesses, governments, universities, newspapers, churches, and civil society bodies beyond China's borders. They warn of 'communist' threats to American 'sovereignty' and, if nothing is done, the coming death by Chinese strangulation of liberal democracy.

There are grains of truth in these exaggerated warnings. They rightly sense that *empires always try to shift the balance of power in their favour*. The trouble is this new Cold War politics is beset with questionable assumptions and assertions. The resilience of the phantom democracy that anchors the CCP regime at home is discounted. The warriors imagine—wrongly—that China will go the way of the Soviet Union, even though its empire was plagued, and eventually felled, by an excessively centralized Party-state economy that suffered consumer goods and services shortages, funding shortfalls for its armed forces, and organized resistance from its disaffected national minorities. More generally, the warriors' poor sense of the history of empires, masterfully probed in such works as John Darwin's *After Tamerlane* (2007) and Dominic Lieven's *In the Shadow of the Gods: The Emperor in World History* (2022), leads them mistakenly to suppose that the galaxy empire is a replay of the tragic process by which the mightiest empires of the past were undone by their excesses—by such factors as rising costs and revenue shortages, second-rate quarrelsome advisers, corruption, and cumbrous administration, by unrest and resistance on their margins. Their simple-minded talk of 'getting tough with China' is designed to discomfit and debase China. It serves as a panicky cry of insecurity from within 'the West' about the possible decline of 'the West', a rallying call for a way of life that is said to be confused and unnecessarily melancholy about its past civilizational achievements and present-day advantages. In practice, knowingly or not, the American-style attacks on China tend to attract xenophobes, racists, and old-fashioned Orientalists whose opinions, it should go without saying, contradict the image of 'the West' as the homeland and haven of 'democracy'. These bull-in-a-China-shop warriors also seem thoughtlessly blasé about the probable consequences of the desired downfall of the galaxy empire. 'The collapse of a world empire', notes a prominent German scholar, 'usually means the end of the world economy, associated with it'.[72] The warriors seem not to notice or care about that point. Whether the downfall of the galaxy empire would bring chaos to the twenty-first-century world economy is at least an open question left unaddressed by the sworn enemies of China. And whether, therefore, the sworn enemies of the galaxy empire may be picking a fight that delivers political, economic, and reputational setbacks to China's principal rival, the United States, or hastens its demise as an imperial power, or ends up engulfing our planet in nuclear catastrophes or intra-galactic Star Wars, also remains unanswered.

Borderlands

Seen in terms of the galaxy empire thesis presented in this book, the American-led concerns and complaints about China's abuses of power in and beyond its borderlands should be unsurprising. Their protests are entirely to be expected. As fledgling empires begin to stretch their wings, they typically pay attention to stabilizing and controlling their immediate environs, and well beyond. The empire of liberty (as Thomas Jefferson called the early United States) purchased Louisiana from the government of France, pushed violently westwards against the resistance of indigenous peoples, annexed Texas and invaded Mexico, militarily confiscating over half of its territory, including parts of present-day Arizona, California, New Mexico, Colorado, Nevada, and Utah. The galaxy empire is engaged in similar efforts to

---

72. Herfried Münkler, *Empires: The Logic of World Domination from Ancient Rome to the United States* (Cambridge, 2007), p. 48.

secure its borderlands through what scholars continue to call 'internal colonialism'. Think of Tibet and Xinjiang: so-called autonomous regions that together comprise nearly three million square kilometres, more than 30 per cent of the PRC's territory.

These are globally important borderland zones with disputed histories and a recent history of public resistance to Beijing controls. During the period of Xi Jinping's leadership, these borderlands have become maximum security zones. 'To govern the country well we must first govern the frontiers well', Xi told the National People's Congress in 2013.[73] Governing well has multiple meanings, but the overriding principle is the unconditional rejection of any talk of the independence of these 'autonomous' territories. There can be no 'middle way'. China must not be 'split'. Stability is in unity. Phantom democracy has its limits. Tough rule is necessary. Separatism is not up for discussion. It is treasonous. It is out of step with history (it is claimed), which shows that these domains have always been connected to China. What is now on offer to the underdeveloped peoples of the Tibet and Xinjiang regions is 'modernization', 'poverty alleviation', 'development', and 'democracy'.

The vision is backed by methods, both familiar and unfamiliar. As happens elsewhere in the empire, the Chinese government places great emphasis on the harmonizing effects of connections and flows of people, products, and services made possible by efficient and effective transportation infrastructures. As was to be expected of an empire uniquely born of the digital age, communications featured prominently in the campaign to 'modernize' Tibet and Xinjiang launched by Jiang Zemin in 1999. Now known as the 'Western Development Campaign' or 'Great Leap West', it included pledges to promote four thousand kilometres of railways, including the world's highest-altitude, two-thousand-kilometre railway line linking Qinghai and Tibet; thirty-five thousand kilometres of roads; and the upgrading and construction of airports. Enhanced connectivity has been geared

---

73. 'Timeline: Xi Jinping and Tibet's Development', *China Today*, March 29, 2019, http://www.chinatoday.com.cn/ctenglish/2018/ttxw/201903/t20190329_800163688.html.

to the exploitation of natural resources and the promotion of economic growth. Chinese officials say that Tibet, formerly a 'feudal-theocratic' territory that lacked industry to make even matchsticks, is now on the highway of development. The province is now crisscrossed by paved highways and feeder roads; its people enjoy modern houses and safe drinking water. Tibet is now a zone of economic growth centred not only on tourism, the region's traditional pillar industry, but also clean energy production and digital industries, including the world's highest big-data centre in Lhasa, the regional capital. A new rail-line connects Xinjiang and Tibet. Airports link Tibet to nearly forty Chinese cities. Model *xiǎo kāng* (moderately prosperous) villages are serviced by roads, power, and the internet, some of them constructed in disputed areas in Bhutan. Meanwhile, in Xinjiang, growth strategies designed to transform the region into a distinctly 'export-oriented economy' (*wai xiàng xing jīngji*) feature ambitious mega-projects, including the construction of new factories in industrial centres such as Karamay, Urumqi, and Bayangol; oil and gas pipelines; coal mining; solar-powered green hydrogen (in Kuqa city) and petrochemical plants; large-scale farms producing cotton, wheat, corn, and rice; and the massive expansion of the production of textiles and polysilicon used in solar panels, a commodity in which Xinjiang commands a key spot in global supply chains.[74]

Government strategies in both regions—misleadingly called 'autonomous regions', implying that they enjoy a measure of self-determination—have heavily underscored the importance of altering their demographics. Their peoples are the targets of a *settler colonialism with Chinese characteristics*. Operating under the banner of such slogans

---

74. See also Laura T. Murphy and Nyrola Elimä, 'In Broad Daylight: Uyghur Forced Labour and Global Solar Supply Chains', Sheffield Hallam University Helena Kennedy Centre for International Justice (Sheffield, May 2021), https://www.shu.ac.uk/helena-kennedy-centre-international-justice/research-and-projects/all-projects/in-broad-daylight; and Ana Swanson and Chris Buckley, 'Chinese Solar Companies Tied to Use of Forced Labor', *New York Times*, January 28, 2021, https://www.nytimes.com/2021/01/08/business/economy/china-solar-companies-forced-labor-xinjiang.html.

as 'poverty alleviation', 'cultural consolidation', and 'advancement' through 'ethnic interaction, exchanges and blending' and 'studying Chinese culture' (Xi Jinping), the multi-pronged migration programme has involved a 'zero illegal births' policy (led by a Civil Affairs Ministry programme in Xinjiang) and the transfer of considerable numbers of workers to labour in factories and farms elsewhere in the country (the details of how to 'reduce Uyghur population density in Xinjiang' are sketched in the government's Nankai Report). The programme also includes subsidized migration of large numbers of Han Chinese migrants into these regions. The effects have been dramatic. In Tibet, according to the 2020 census, massive subsidies from the central government have sharply increased the Han Chinese population share, from a small base to around 12 per cent of the population. Han Chinese farmers have been relocated into Tibet through the Western Poverty Reduction project, while in the capital of Lhasa Han Chinese now comprise at least a quarter of its nearly one million inhabitants. In Xinjiang, locally born Uyghurs now constitute roughly 45 per cent of the population of 24 million, or around 10.5 million, while the Han component went from 5 per cent in 1947 to above 40 per cent now. Immigrants are offered substantial incentives: jobs with generous monthly salaries, bonuses and supplements, coverage of relocation costs, new homes for families, free utilities and insurance payments, tax-free plots of land, plus generous guarantees of extended free education for children.

The mass migration programmes have boosted rates of urbanization. The movement of Han Chinese people into the borderland zones has involved enforced depopulation of rural areas and the rapid growth of cities. As part of a 'Xinjiang Management Plan', the Xinjiang Production and Construction Corps has built new desert cities such as Kurumkash, Bash'egim (Bayinguoleng Menggu), Tumshuk, and Aral, a city built on an existing Uyghur village that now is the home of nearly two hundred thousand people, only 5 percent of whom are Uyghurs and other ethnic groups.

Government policies have meanwhile invested heavily in so-named cultural re-education and pacification programmes founded on the building of communication grids, surveillance technologies, and strictly monitored bans on spiritual worship and everyday movements. The galaxy empire, to repeat, is the first-ever modern empire founded on a digital communications infrastructure. Trends in the borderlands reveal a dark side of the galaxy, the use of surveillance methods that aren't, however, accurately describable as 'Orwellian'. In contrast to the era of radio and television broadcasting and totalitarian control, the forms of information collection and control squarely belong to the twenty-first-century age of networked communications. In Tibet, triggered by several episodes of local resistance to Beijing's rule, there are ongoing experiments with new political 'grid' (*wǎng gé*) systems of neighbourhood information-gathering units, led by 'grid captains'. Thousands of street-side 'convenience police posts' (*biàn mínjǐng wù zhàn*) equipped with computers and video technology have been set up in towns, rural areas, and temples and mosques. Featuring millions of cameras, the grid systems operate 24/7, as they do increasingly elsewhere in the heartlands of the empire. These grid systems are linked in turn to 'voluntary civilian' networks called 'red armband patrols', whose job at the grass-roots level is to anticipate 'sudden incidents' (self-immolations or public demonstrations, for instance) and to conduct 'doorstep interviews' and searches of homes in search of politically forbidden materials, including photographs of the Dalai Lama and copies of the Qur'an. Local Party officials say that the state-of-the-art surveillance system is designed to 'improve public access to basic services'. They describe the dragnets as components of the country-wide drive towards 'social stability maintenance' (*wéiwěn*) and 'scientifically guiding public opinion'. A 2021 White Paper and other Party documents speak of the importance of 'nets in the sky and traps on the ground' to 'strengthen information and intelligence work to achieve in practical terms smart ears and clear eyes to gain the initiative'. There is much talk of building a prosperous Tibet, protecting its environment, developing 'ethnic unity' and 'enduring peace and stability', adapting 'religions in a Chinese context' to 'socialist society', and driving out villains, above all the Dalai Lama and other 'Western anti-China forces'.[75] Observers on the ground report the way the surveillance systems target 'special groups', such as ex-prisoners, 'nuns and monks on the move', and Tibetans who have returned from exile in India. Outsiders have few extra details of the new data-gathering system, but what's clear is that the grid systems aim to draw, slowly but surely, all Tibetans into *a bottom-up system of surveillance synchronized with a managed political system of top-down control.*

Similar but more extreme methods have been applied in Xinjiang. Large-scale government campaigns to erase Muslim culture and religious practices, along with the arbitrary detention of an estimated 1.5 million Uyghurs and other Turkic minorities in camps and prisons, have sparked global rows about their functions and wider ethical and political significance. The Chinese government has repeatedly denied that it has committed human rights abuses and insists that Uyghurs and other minorities have been consigned to detention facilities that function as vocational training centres for the elimination of 'troublemakers', the prevention of violent extremism, and (familiar language in the history of modern empires) the 'rescue' and moral improvement of backward peoples 'deceived by extremist ideology'. Voices in the United States and most Western countries have counter-charged that local resistance—suicide attacks by Xinjiang militants in Beijing and Kunming, unarmed protests against seizures of ancestral lands, enforced family planning, police harassment, and general discrimination in favour of Han settlers—have resulted in harsh crackdowns and a so-called People's War on Terror that amounts to crimes against humanity and genocide.

75. See also the White Paper 'Tibet since 1951: Liberation, Development and Prosperity', May 2021, State Council Information Office of the People's Republic of China, http://www.xinhuanet.com/english/2021-05/21/c_139959978.htm; White Paper, '50 Years of Democratic Reform in Tibet', Information Office, State Council of the People's Republic of China, March 2009, https://www.mfa.gov.cn/ce/ceun//eng/gyzg/xizang/t539939.htm; and Tsering Shakya, *The Dragon in the Land of Snows: A History of Modern Tibet since 1947* (New Delhi, 2000).

The clashes of interpretation are bitter, with sounds of sabres rattling, but it is accurate to say that policies of surveillance and internment, compulsory re-education, forced labour, disappearances, and compulsory sterilization have been conducted on a vast scale in Xinjiang. Local ethnic communities reportedly live under constant threats of interrogation, arrest, and confinement. Policies designed to prevent the Muslim minorities from living as Muslims have been a priority. When visiting Xinjiang on two occasions, the principal author of this book learned that since about 2017 up to sixteen thousand mosques, roughly two-thirds of the region's total, have been destroyed or damaged. Kashgar's historic Id Kah Mosque, which dates to 1442, has been permanently closed for worship. Other mosques have been shut but left standing; a few famous mosques remain open but they are under surveillance, without regular prayer services permitted. The whole region is heavily policed. In many of its towns and cities, police checkpoints operate at every street corner. Body scans and police frisking greet visitors at the entry point of every office building, hotel, and shopping area. To prevent emigration (more than ten thousand locals have reportedly fled across the border via Myanmar to Turkey), the government has confiscated the passports of the few Uyghurs and Kazakhs who once held them. Their movements within the region are restricted by digital checkpoints, surveillance camera systems, face and voice scanning, and a pass card system. It is reported that over ninety thousand assistant police have been recruited to carry out the scanning of locals' IDs and mobile phones using software designed by large, private digital forensics and cybersecurity companies such as Meiya Pico (which exports its tools globally, to countries such as Malaysia, Korea, India, Italy, Indonesia, Singapore, and France).

Many tens of thousands of Uyghurs, Kazakhs, and Hui people deemed 'unreliable elements' have either been flung into prisons or targeted by state-sponsored, forced labour schemes that are called Poverty Alleviation through Labour Transfer programmes (*tūopín zhŭanyí jiùyè*) and Vocational Skills Education and Training

Centres (*zhíyè jìnéng jiàoyù péixùn zhōngxīn*).⁷⁶ Coinciding with Chen Quanguo's appointment (in 2016) as Xinjiang Party secretary, plans were strictly applied to 'train all who should be trained' (*yīngpéi jìnpéi*) and 'transfer all who should be transferred'. Backed by big-data analysis and 'real-time monitoring',⁷⁷ Party cadres (four hundred thousand were at work in 2021) are regularly despatched to investigate and monitor the poverty and income situations of more than ten million rural households through an 'early prevention, early intervention, early assistance' campaigns. Their aim (say government documents and Party speeches) is to reward initiative and to punish 'lazy people' (*lǎn rén*) by ensuring that China does not go down the path of 'welfarism' (*fúlì zhǔyì*). China has formally ratified (in April 2022) the International Labour Organization's Forced Labor Convention and Abolition of Forced Labor Conventions, with its foreign ministry stating that in Xinjiang there is no 'forced labour', only 'voluntary employment and free choice in the labour market'. But evidence shows that workers categorized as rural surplus labourers who refuse state-mandated labour transfer placements risk internment in re-education camps. Unknown numbers of Xinjiang citizens have been disappeared. Perhaps five hundred thousand children have been placed in residential boarding schools. There have been large-scale criminal prosecutions, the house arrest of the elderly and disabled, and hundreds of thousands of locals have been required to work in factories associated with the 'Transform Through Education' camps, as Chinese officials and media call them. The networked archipelago of at least three hundred camps bears more than a passing resemblance to

---

76. Adrian Zenz, 'Unemployment Monitoring and Early Warning: New Trends in Xinjiang's Coercive Labor Placement Systems', *China Brief* 22.11 (June 5, 2022), https://jamestown.org/program/unemployment-monitoring-and-early-warning-new-trends-in-xinjiangs-coercive-labor-placement-systems/?mc_cid=ea3cf8f008&mc_eid=23d4fcca88.
77. Xue Wang, 'Xinjiang's Dynamic Monitoring of "One Household, One Policy" to Prevent the Return of Poverty', *China Youth Daily*, January 11, 2022, https://web.archive.org/web/20220112021101/https:/cn.chinadaily.com.cn/a/202201/11/WS61dcd2d4a3107be497a01931.html.

previous Guantánamo-style concentration camps (*reconcentrados* they were first called towards the end of the Spanish Empire) in which people, in large numbers, are indefinitely confined and pushed to the limits of their endurance, against their will, often in overcrowded and unsanitary settings. Available evidence suggests that these maximum security, hard strike, militarized 're-education' camps in Xinjiang have incarcerated at least as many victims as the British captured and punished in Kenya during the 1950s.[78]

Ecological Civilization

The martial feel of these strategies of pacification naturally sparks concerns about whether they presage a global future where Chinese ways of handling power bring great violence to the world, with catastrophic consequences. The matter of violently abusive power has understandably always been central in the analysis of previous empires. The most short-lived empires, ancient and modern, were usually those whose rulers tried but failed to boss and bully their subjects into submission. Their megalomania miscarried. Heavy hands bred hubris, administrative failure, economic stagnation, non-compliance, and active resistance. An example: from the 1870s, in support of business interests amidst geopolitical rivalry for 'unclaimed territories', the German empire expanded globally, especially to many points in Africa, whose peoples suffered great violence and (in German Southwest Africa, today Namibia) the first recorded case of twentieth-century

---

78. Gardner Bovingdon, *The Uyghurs: Strangers in Their Own Land* (New York, 2010); Sean Roberts, *The War on the Uyghurs: China's Internal Campaign against a Muslim Minority* (Princeton, NJ, 2020); Joanne Smith Finley, 'Securitization, Insecurity and Conflict in Contemporary Xinjiang: Has PRC Counter-terrorism Evolved into State Terror?', *Central Asian Survey* 38.2 (2019), pp. 1–26, https://doi.org/10.1080/02634937.2019.1586348; and Darren Byler, *In the Camps: China's High-Tech Penal Colony* (New York, 2021). On *reconcentrados* and other historical examples of camps, see John Keane, 'Concentration Camps and Democracy', *The Conversation* April 29, 2014, https://theconversation.com/concentration-camps-and-democracy-25576.

genocide.[79] Several decades later, feeding upon widespread popular resentment bred by the loss of empire, the Nazis attempted to build a new German empire. Between 1939 and 1945, using blitzkrieg tactics, its empire builders rampaged through annexed territories; enslaved massive numbers of foreign workers; murdered millions of victims using summary executions, gas chambers, eugenics programmes and death camps; and (as in Greece, where perhaps three hundred thousand Greeks perished through famine) starved the conquered to feed Germans. For a brief period, the Nazi empire controlled more territory than the United States. Its *Grossraum* ('great space') was richer and more densely populated than any other place on our planet. By 1941, the empire controlled the lives of half of Europe's population. But its violent continental reign was cut short by a catastrophic global war which led to serious defeats during the second half of 1942 (El Alamein, Stalingrad) and its unconditional military surrender to Allied forces in early May 1945.

Historically speaking, heavy-handed rule of peoples by declining empires desperate to prolong their wealth and power also usually failed. Violence accelerated their decline and disappearance. An example is the way the violence used to prolong the global power of the British Empire backfired badly. For over a century, it had been the largest empire in human history, straddling a quarter of the world's landmass and ruling over seven hundred million colonized subjects, often violently; during the nineteenth century alone, there were sustained efforts to exterminate indigenous peoples and more than 250 wars were waged in the name of 'civilizing' the empire's subjects. At the end of the Second World War, with the empire seriously in debt and in decline, martial law, forced deportations, torture, and other forms of violence were common techniques of rule in disobedient colonies. Fearing the end of empire, a pathway described by George Orwell as the reduction of 'England to a cold and unimportant little

---

79. Hans-Ulrich Wehler, *The German Empire, 1871–1918* (Berg, 1985); George Steinmetz, *The Devil's Handwriting: Precoloniality and the German Colonial State in Qingdao, Samoa, and Southwest Africa* (Chicago, 2007).

island' whose people would be forced to 'work very hard and live mainly on herrings and potatoes'[80], successive British governments did everything they could to preserve and strengthen their empire and its 'civilizing mission'. British officials and security forces wanted their subjects to experience the costs of their resistance, to teach them lessons in obedience. British officials had a term for this. They spoke of the 'moral effect' of violence, which was unleashed in great quantities upon subjects who rebelled, not just in the Indian sub-continent but also in such places as Aden, Northern Ireland, Cyprus, Malaya, and Kenya, where during the so-called Mau Mau Emergency of the 1950s over a million Africans were detained without trial.[81]

Is the galaxy empire destined to fall into the same fateful trap of self-indulgent bossing and violent bullying? Will dependence upon unrestrained abusive power prove to be its nemesis? Is the twenty-first-century trajectory of the galaxy empire—today Tibet and Xinjiang, tomorrow the world—a repeat of past German empires, or is perhaps the half-century-old galaxy empire so short-lived that it is already experiencing the fate of the British Empire in its self-destructive, final years? Might it resemble Betelgeuse, the petulant red supergiant star ancient Chinese astronomers called *shēnxiùsì* that nowadays, blowing its top and spitting out dust clouds, is at the beginning of the end of its evolution?

These cardinal questions require some reflection on the double meaning of violence. Strange and surprising as it may seem, they have an ecological dimension. When modern European empires spread their worldly wings, without exception they left violent marks not only on the bodies and souls of people they conquered. These empires gouged precious metals from the lands they seized, felled forests, ploughed fields, redirected waterways, transformed ancient patterns of flora and fauna. The colonizers imported harvestable grains, weeds, cattle, goats, sheep, horses, rats and pigs, together with smallpox, rabies,

---

80. George Orwell, *The Road to Wigan Pier* (Oxford, 2021 [1937]), p. 110.
81. Caroline Elkins, *Legacy of Violence: A History of the British Empire* (New York, 2022)

and other deadly pathogens unknown to the colonized. *All modern empires were in this sense not just large-scale geographical units comprising peoples and lands. They defined what counted as geography, often with brutal energy laced with boastful pride.* 'The colony of a civilized nation which takes possession either of a waste country, or of one so thinly inhabited, that the natives easily give place to the new settlers, advances more rapidly to wealth and greatness than any other human society', wrote the famous eighteenth-century political economist Adam Smith. 'The colonists carry out with them a knowledge of agriculture and of other useful arts, superior to what can grow up of its own accord in the course of many centuries among savage and barbarous nations'. The heartlands of empire also gained from the manifold exchanges with their own colonies, he added. They received 'a variety of commodities which they could not otherwise have possessed, some for conveniency and use, some for pleasure, and some for ornament, and thereby contribute to increase their enjoyments'.[82]

Only much later would critics of empire come to denounce not only the great violence waged by the colonizers against indigenous peoples but also the large-scale environmental disruption and violent despoliation inflicted upon their habitats. These critics would speak of 'ecological imperialism',[83] a new phrase that emphasized the dangerously unpredictable and perhaps irreversible local and planetary effects of the poisoning of groundwaters, the razing of ancient forests, the replacement of green pastures by deserts, the extinction of species, and the carbon-charged warming of our atmosphere originally triggered by imperial expansion.

---

82. Adam Smith, *An Inquiry into the Nature and Causes of the Wealth of Nations* (Chicago, 1976 [1776]), vol. 2, book 4, chap. 7, part 2, pp. 75–76 and part 3, p. 104.
83. The pathbreaking study is Alfred W. Crosby, *Ecological Imperialism: The Biological Expansion of Europe, 900–1900* (Cambridge, 1986). More recently, see Amitav Ghosh, *The Great Derangement: Climate Change and the Unthinkable* (Chicago, 2016) and James Beattie and Eugene Anderson, 'Environments and Empires in World History, 3000 BCE–ca. 1900 CE', in Peter Fibiger Bang, C. A. Bayly, and Walter Scheidel, eds., *The Oxford World History of Empire* (New York, 2021), vol. 1, pp. 460–493.

During recent decades, the rulers of the emergent galaxy empire have begun to acknowledge the growing dangers of environmental violence. 'Plant trees everywhere and make our country green in the interest of future generations', urged Deng Xiaoping, addressing a People's Liberation Army gathering in the early 1980s. A national forum speech by Jiang Zemin in March 1997 further underscored the need to 'reduce environmental pollution and ecological disruption'. The goals of 'short term economic development' must not 'compromise the environment', he said. 'Environmental deterioration must stop within the next 15 years'. A decade later, Hu Jintao told the United Nations General Assembly (September 2009) that 'China stands ready to work with all countries to build an even better future for the generations to come'. Guided by his country's 'sense of responsibility to its own people and people across the world', he promised the domestic implementation of a new 'climate change programme' backed by 'climate-friendly technologies', 'renewable energy and nuclear energy' schemes, reduced 'discharge of major pollutants', and 'increasing forest coverage'.[84] In a wide-ranging address to nearly three thousand delegates of the mainly rubber-stamp National People's Congress (March 2014), broadcast live on state television, Li Keqiang announced the closure of some outdated steel plants, inefficient coal-fired furnaces, and polluting cement production factories. 'We will resolutely declare war against pollution as we declared war against poverty', Li said, adding that the government was committed to the conversion of marginal farmland to forest and grassland, the recovery of wetlands, and the fight against desertification. (He did

---

84. Deng Xiaoping, 'Plant Trees Everywhere' (November–December 1982), in *Selected Works of Deng Xiaoping*, vol. 3, https://dengxiaopingworks.wordpress.com/2013/03/08/plant-trees-everywhere/; 'President Jiang Zemin on Family Planning and Environmental Protection', *China Population Today* 14.2 (April 1997), p. 2; 'Hu Jintao's Speech on Climate Change', *New York Times*, September 22, 2009), https://www.nytimes.com/2009/09/23/world/asia/23hu.text.html; 'China to "Declare War" on Pollution, Premier Says', *Reuters*, March 5, 2014, https://www.reuters.com/article/us-china-parliament-pollution-idUSBREA2405W20140305; 'Xi Focus: Xi Jinping Champions Harmony between Man and Nature', *Xinhuanet*, October 14, 2021, http://www.china.org.cn/china/Off_the_Wire/2021-10/13/content_77807402.htm.

not explain that the announced cuts to outdated steel production, although equivalent to Italy's production capacity, amounted to less than 2.5 per cent of China's total; or that cement production cuts were less than 2 per cent of the previous year's total production.)

Xi Jinping's speeches follow much the same narrative, fortified by Greenpeace-style references to a new 'ecological civilisation'. The phrase was first officially adopted in November 2012 at the eighteenth National Congress, which announced action plans such as bans on stubble burning, reafforestation programmes, and setting aside 15 per cent of China's territory as nature reserves, scenic areas, and forest parks.[85] Since that time, Xi's speeches on ecological civilisation have become customary. Their tone is unflaggingly earnest, at times melodramatic. 'Lucid waters and lush mountains are invaluable assets'. 'Ecological advantages can never be traded for gold'. 'We want green water and mountains, golden hills and silver mountains. We prefer green water and green hills to golden hills and silver mountains, and green water and green mountains are mountains of golden hills and silver mountains'. 'To move towards a new era of ecological civilization and to build a beautiful China are an important part of realizing the Chinese Dream of the great revival of the Chinese nation'. 'China's modernization has many important characteristics, and one of them is man-nature harmony'. 'If we humanity do not fail nature, nature will not fail us'. 'COVID-19 reminds us of the interdependence between man and nature. It falls to all of us to act together and urgently advance protection and development in parallel, so that we can turn Earth into a beautiful homeland for all creatures to live in harmony'. Listeners and viewers easily get the picture whose flashed images are sometimes framed in a forward-looking nostalgia. During an inspection trip (in April 2021) in south China's Guangxi Zhuang Autonomous Region, Xi recalled swimming in a local river with his teenage friends. 'The river was blue and clear, glistening in the

---

85. Natarajan Ishwaran, Tianhua Hong, and Zhijun Yi, 'Building an Ecological Civilization in China: Towards a Practice-Based Learning Approach', *Journal of Earth Sciences and Engineering* 5 (2015), pp. 349–362.

sun. Fishermen's baskets by the river were full of golden carp. It felt just like a fairy tale'. China was once beautiful, he said. It must be made beautiful again. Nothing less than an historic transition from industrial civilization to an ecological civilization was now imperative. 'When we talk about ecology', he said, 'the most fundamental thing is to pursue harmony between man and nature'. He added: 'Such a philosophy is not only in line with the current trend in the world, but also originates from the cultural tradition of the Chinese nation that has lasted for thousands of years'.

Within the homelands of the galaxy empire traces of ancient Chinese understandings of nature have indeed survived the ravages of the wars of the twentieth century, the Cultural Revolution, and fast-paced industrial transformation. While historians have shown that the history of China has been laced with environmental catastrophes— think of the early 1330s CE, when a bubonic plague (combined with a brutal civil war) that killed an estimated half of China's population spread to Europe, where cities such as Siena witnessed the death of half their residents—romantic images of rustic times past have survived until the present day.[86] Chinese people, especially from younger generations, often express admiration for old principles that nowadays have a distinctively contemporary, down-to-earth, and 'green' feel. The runaway success of *Wolf Totem*, the prize-winning novel by Jiangsu-born Lü Jiamin (better known by his pseudonym Jiang Rong), is one indicator of these lingering, newly pertinent eco-sentiments. The novel broke all previous sales records, selling many millions of copies, plus untold millions more on the pirated black market. Considered as an allegorical warning, a sad tale of how emergent empires can destroy themselves environmentally, the book depicts a double extinction: the ruination by modern Chinese farming methods of the

---

86. Drawing upon written records spanning three millennia, Mark Elvin's *The Retreat of the Elephants: An Environmental History of China* (New Haven, 2006) shows the extent to which Chinese agricultural methods, wars, and water-control systems conspired to destroy ancient forests, the habitats of elephants, and many forms of wildlife to the point where, by the eighteenth century, China was probably more environmentally damaged than north-western Europe.

lives of Mongol nomads, the last remaining progeny of the largest-ever contiguous land empire of the twelfth to thirteenth century CE, and the parallel extinction of wolves, believed by the Mongols to be magical creatures sent by the heavens to protect and nurture the vast local grasslands.

The entanglement of humans and 'nature' is a recurrent theme of ancient Chinese philosophy. There is of course the well-known Confucian saying that humans and nature are conjoined in one whole (*tiān rén hé yī*) and that rulers who fail to respect this whole will find themselves surrounded by troubles. Chinese people today know something of the ancient texts (probably) written by Daoist philosopher Zhuangzi during the late Warring States period (c. 369 BCE–286 BCE). Not only do they tell the famous story of Zhuang Zhou, a man who wore patched clothes and earned a living by making straw shoes, and who dreamed he was a butterfly, and when awakened could not be sure whether he was unmistakably human or a butterfly dreaming he was Zhang Zhou. Zhuang Zhou taught that the whole cosmos is defined by *dào*, the 'transformation of things' (*wù huà*) through unending rhythms of self-emergence and self-destruction. People cannot escape *dào*. Their positive recognition of its cosmic force offers uncluttered freedom, disengagement from the hustle and bustle of life's artificialities, the nurturing of one's 'life tendencies', the capacity to live with the sky and earth, to 'ride on clouds and fog, by sun and moon', to wander unimpeded 'across the Four Seas', 'lasting out one's natural years', untroubled by concerns about death and life.[87] And there are surviving writings by scholar officials of the calibre of Dong Zhongshu, who during the Han dynasty, serving as chief minister to Emperor Wu (c. 140–187 CE) and founder of an imperial college (*tàixué*) for training promising students, melded notions of *yīn* and *yáng* with Confucian precepts so as to underscore the interdependence of humans and their natural environments. For Dong, sky (*tiān*) and humanity on earth (*rén*) are an entangled whole dynamically

---

87. 'Discussion on Making All Things Equal' [Qíwùlùn], in *The Complete Works of Chuang Tzu* (New York, 1968), chap. 2, pp. 36–49.

divided into *yīn* (female, dark, negative) and *yáng* (male, light, positive), four seasons and five elements ('wood, fire, soil, metal and water'). On this basis, Dong counselled that emperors who respect these sky-earth arrangements and act as their ambassadors by obeying the five connected elements will find that their people are obedient and peaceful, and the weather good. When emperors refuse to follow the order of the five elements their realm will suffer troubles and their rule endangered by unusual natural disasters like droughts, volcanic eruptions, and earthquakes.[88]

The lingering magnetic effects on Chinese people of these old precepts and the spell cast by new talk of 'ecological civilization' are hard to measure. Whatever their degree of attractiveness, striking is their contrast with the more mixed and contradictory realities of life within and beyond the galaxy empire's homelands. When consideration is given to present-day government efforts to reconnect humanity with what is called nature, in support of 'ecological civilization', there are undoubtedly some positive achievements. The galaxy empire is arguably the first up-and-coming empire in modern times to pay close attention to its environmental foundations. Chinese media is awash with stories of quick-time progress in government efforts to make 'environmentally sustainable' its resource-hungry local form of state capitalism. In effect, but not in name, these reports are admissions that Mao's 'people's war' against nature—the disastrous late 1950s and early 1960s Great Leap Forward that resulted in the death by starvation of at least thirty million people[89]—is over. Headlines are given to China's reduced dependence on fossil fuels and its expanding protections of depleted biomes. China is praised as the world's largest producer and consumer of renewable energy, a serious investor in

---

88. See the chronicles dating from the period of the Zhou dynasty state of Lu (722–481 BCE), some of which are attributed to Dong Zhongshu, *Luxuriant Gems of the Spring and Autumn* [Chūnqíu fán lù] (New York, 2015)
89. Judith Shapiro, *Mao's War against Nature: Politics and the Environment in Revolutionary China* (Cambridge, 2001) and Jasper Becker, *Hungry Ghosts: Mao's Secret Famine* (New York, 2000)

green technologies, the largest employer of green jobs globally, and the leading global source of reduced-cost, high-quality solar panels. Companies like Biyadi, headquartered in Xi'an in Shaanxi Province, are headlined for surpassing Tesla to become the world's top seller of electric vehicles. The government is applauded for clearing smoggy city skies, driving down the cost of renewable energy through its tremendous manufacturing capacity, banning (in 2018) imports of plastic waste, and passing laws against single-use plastic bags, as well as clamping down on business polluters and enforcing country-wide ecological conservation 'red lines'. A quarter of China's land area is now said to be subject to environmental protections. The Great Green Wall, comprising a five-thousand-kilometre-long stretch of newly planted forests is celebrated, along with the planned 'socially harmonious, environmentally friendly and resource efficient' Tianjin Eco-city co-funded by the Singapore government. Protected waterbird sites have meanwhile tripled, and species habitat rewilding schemes are burgeoning. China, a major power in squid fishing and processing, has enforced seasonal fishing restrictions designed to protect and more sustainably use squid populations. Special tributes are extended to the past several decades' efforts to nearly double the country's iconic, much-loved giant panda population living in the wild (there are fewer than two thousand remaining). Future government plans rank as newsworthy on front pages, too. Space is given to the application for World Heritage status for migratory bird route wetlands on the Bohai Sea in north-eastern China. A revision of the country's Fisheries Law, designed to improve management of distant-water fishing and protect ocean resources, is under way.[90]

Official fanfare also greets the regional and global environmental deals negotiated by Chinese diplomats. The empire's biggest cross-border success thus far is the agreement reached (in mid-December 2022) at the fifteenth meeting in Montreal of the UN Conference

---

90. *Towards a Blue Ecological Civilisation*, China Dialogue Ocean report, September 2020, https://chinadialogueocean.net/content/uploads/2022/03/Towards-a-blue-ecological-civilisation-China-Dialuge-Ocean-Journal.pdf.

of the Parties to the Convention on Biological Diversity, or COP15. With China holding the presidency of the talks, President Xi Jinping opened proceedings with a video message to ministers from nearly two hundred countries. 'We need to push forward the global process of biodiversity protection', he said. 'All living things should flourish without harming each other'. Expectations of failed negotiations reportedly ran high. The sticking point—emphasized by a coalition of states led by Brazil, India, and Indonesia—was whether rich member states would be willing financially to support poor countries to protect their vanishing species and damaged habitats. Efforts to make the principle of biodiversity binding on corporations also proved controversial. At first, the Chinese delegation reportedly held back, to watch and wait for others to hedge bets, stall or reveal their hands, and make their final moves. Then came a flurry of late-night activity and high-drama diplomacy. Despite last-minute vocal objections from the Democratic Republic of Congo—it was curtly overruled by China's environment minister and conference chair, Huang Runqui—a revised deal drafted under Chinese supervision was tabled in the wee hours of the morning. Although it contained some watered-down commitments and targets, the first global biodiversity agreement—an 'historic' deal, said European Union officials—was quickly agreed to with loud applause.

What has come to be called the Kunming-Montréal Global Biodiversity Framework (GBF) included measurable commitments to protecting 30 per cent of our planet's land, coastal areas, and waterbodies; regenerating at least 30 per cent of degraded ecosystems; agreeing to a High Seas Treaty to establish marine protected areas covering almost two-thirds of the oceans located beyond territorial state boundaries (this happened in March 2023); and building a Global Biodiversity Fund to fund a variety of new instruments such as green bonds and biodiversity credits. Other commitments included strengthening the rights of indigenous and local communities to protect their habitats; halving food waste; halting deforestation; and reducing ecologically harmful subsidies (in the future including coal) by states and cross-border bodies such as North American Free Trade Agreement and the WTO. The GBF also agreed to curbs upon invasive alien species and trading in wild species to reduce pathogen spillovers; protecting pollinators by reducing the 'overall' use of pesticides and risky fertilizers; and the establishment of a fund to monitor what some delegates called 'genetic colonialism', the exploitation of animals and plants of lower-income countries by multinational corporations in the fields of genetics, cosmetics, and medicine.

Journalists from local and global outlets reported Canada's environment minister as saying that he had 'never seen a presidency text tabled and have so much support for it from the get-go'.[91] More downbeat reporters noted the agreement's poorly specified monitoring mechanisms and its failure to impose biodiversity obligations on corporations, banks, and financial institutions (in the end, it was agreed, according to Target 15, that states would be tasked with enforcing the newly agreed commitments). Still other journalists were struck by the strange and surprising paradoxes: breaking ranks with its main supporters, the Group of 77 poorer countries, China had closed out the deal to protect 30 per cent of land and oceans by 2030, with a $30 billion financing pledge, and it did so as a one-party 'people's socialism' political regime operating on North American soil, with the United States reduced to the role of a supportive onlooker hamstrung by its

---

91. The global coverage of the agreement included '30-by-30: Key Takeaways from the COP15 Biodiversity Summit', *Indian Express*, December 20, 2022, https://indianexpress.com/article/explained/explained-climate/30-by-30-key-takeaways-un-cop15-biodiversity-summit-8333204/; Perrine Mouterde, 'COP15: À Montréal, des engagements historiques pour la biodiversité', *Le Monde*, December 19, 2022, https://www.lemonde.fr/planete/article/2022/12/19/cop15-a-montreal-des-engagements-historiques-pour-la-biodiversite_6155018_3244.html; 'Statement by President von der Leyen on the Kunming-Montreal Biodiversity Agreement', December 19, 2022, https://ec.europa.eu/commission/presscorner/detail/en/statement_22_7827; 'How Chinese Diplomacy Helped Seal Historic Nature Deal', December 20, 2022, https://www.france24.com/en/live-news/20221219-how-chinese-diplomacy-helped-seal-historic-nature-deal; and 'President Xi Jinping Addresses Opening of High-Level Segment of Part II of COP15', Ministry of Foreign Affairs of the People's Republic of China, December 16, 2022, .https://www.fmprc.gov.cn/mfa_eng/zxxx_662805/202212/t20221216_10991195.html.

diplomats' awareness that their legislature (due to political opposition by Republicans) would be disinclined to ratify the agreement.

The future, longer-term efficacy of the Kunming-Montréal Convention on Biological Diversity agreement and the Chinese government's 'ecological civilization' initiatives can be debated, but much more controversial are the immediate bio-challenges faced by the galaxy empire. The long string of Chinese government policy failures in the hatching and handling of the Covid-19 virus breed suspicions and misgivings.[92] To what extent the ecological problems it faces can be overcome, and whether the galaxy empire becomes the first recorded empire in modern times to damage beyond repair, or destroy outright, its own bio-foundations, remain open questions. The challenges are both numerous and serious, both at home and abroad.

Within the heartlands of the empire, the unchecked extinction of species flagrantly contradicts the official commitment to a 'beautiful China'. Decimated by such factors as intensive farming and overfishing, fertilizer runoff, and the spread of invasive species, untold numbers of plants and animals have either quietly disappeared during recent decades or are now on the list of critically endangered species. In matters of environmental policy, government guidelines are often no more than comprehensively ignored blueprints. Vested Party interests in polluting industries are a fact of life, data is notoriously unreliable, and inspection systems are often corrupted. The practice of 'saving face' (*bǎo miànzi*) by local Party officials who are in charge of everything but make things much worse, initially by doing nothing, is widespread. Bamboozling (*hū you*) by officials, con tricks, hyping things up and laying them on thick, and cleverly 'using four ounces to shift a thousand pounds' to cover up the abusive power that is having ruinous effects on ecosystems are rampant. Government failures to devise and implement systems of regulation and certification that enable Chinese consumers to know the source of products, and how environmentally safe they are, are chronic. China has the world's largest

---

92. John Keane, 'Democracy and the Great Pestilence', *Eurozine*, April 17, 2020, https://www.eurozine.com/democracy-and-the-great-pestilence/

long-distance fishing fleet, for instance, yet the sources and harvesting methods of boats remain largely unregulated. China is a massive importer of such agricultural products as palm oil, soybeans, coffee, crustaceans, and fish, yet harvesting methods, the use of fertilizers and pesticides, and the resulting environmental damage are matters left undisclosed. Equally difficult to ascertain are the toxic wastes left behind by industrial production and mining ventures. Unknown is the full extent of environmental damage already done by the unregulated production of rare earth metals—in which China controls 90 per cent of world trade and around 35 per cent of reserves. Rare earths are in fact not that rare, but better described as costly and dirty to extract and to refine for use in smartphones, guided missiles, wind turbines, and other high-tech products. China's rare earth industry is dominated by six major state-owned companies whose mining of elements such as dysprosium and europium—in sites stretching from Inner Mongolia, Sichuan, and Jiangxi to Kenya, the Democratic Republic of Congo, and Greenland—has already dumped untold quantities of ammonia and nitrogen compounds into local ground and surface waters, as well as released other pollutants, such as lead and cadmium, long-term exposure to which poses health risks.

The widespread poisonings of air, soil, and water are also well documented by independent sources. Although per capita carbon emissions are only half US levels, around eight tonnes per person, China is the world's largest air polluter and emitter of greenhouse gases. Water is a powerful cultural symbol in the lives of Chinese people; it is a life-giving material substance and a spiritual force, a cleansing reminder of the contingency of life. Yet—despite abundant talk of an ecological civilisation—shortages and pollution of the country's waters remain chronic. Desertification is a curse: around a quarter of the total land area of China, nearly three million square kilometres of land, is vulnerable to loss of vegetation in a country with the least per capita forest area in the world.[93] Despite costly engineering projects

---

93. Y. Yin et al., 'Projections of Aridity and Its Regional Variability over China in the Mid-21st Century', *International Journal of Climatology* 35 (2015), pp. 4387–4398;

such as the South-North Water Project, imbalances of high-quality water supply between the water-rich south and the comparatively dry north remain problematic. The iconic Yellow River, which flows from Qinghai Province in the north-west of the country eastwards to Shandong, is the main source of water for over fifty large and medium-sized cities and around one-sixth of the country's farmland. It has already (twice during the 1990s) dried up. Plagued by the destruction of its headwaters, over-extraction of groundwaters, pollution, and poor management practices, its receding water levels continue to arouse worries. Climate change, erratic monsoons, droughts, and extreme weather events are bound to make things worse. An estimated 20 per cent of China's surface waters remain so badly contaminated that people are advised not to drink or go near them.

Soil pollution is equally worrying. Figures are sometimes treated as state secrets, but a government survey reported (in 2014) that one-fifth of arable farmland soils and one-sixth of the country's soils are heavily contaminated. It attributed the pollution to factory waste materials, excessive use of pesticides and fertilizers, the irrigation of land by contaminated water, and livestock breeding in tainted farmlands. According to the survey, over 80 per cent of the contaminated soils contained significant quantities of arsenic, nickel, and cadmium, whose levels had risen sharply in recent decades. Fears of poisoned food chains run high, traceable to areas such as Hunan Province in central China, a large rice-growing area whose farmland soils are among the most heavily polluted by local nonferrous metal production.[94]

>Alisher Mirzabaev and Jianguo Wu, 'Desertification', in *Climate Change and Land: An IPCC Special Report on Climate Change, Desertification, Land Degradation, Sustainable Land Management, Food Security, and Greenhouse Gas Fluxes in Terrestrial Ecosystems*, at https://www.ipcc.ch/site/assets/uploads/sites/4/2022/11/SRCCL_Chapter_3.pdf.

94. Among the first independent reports were by Liu Hongqiao, 'The Polluted Legacy of China's Largest Rice-Growing Province', *China Dialogue*, May 30, 2014, https://chinadialogue.net/en/pollution/7008-the-polluted-legacy-of-china-s-largest-rice-growing-province/; and He Guangwei, 'Special Report: The Victims of China's Soil Pollution Crisis', *China Dialogue*, June 30, 2014 https://chinadialogue.net/en/pollution/7073-special-report-the-victims-of-china-s-soil-pollution-crisis/.

The tasks of mapping and measuring air, water, and soil pollution within the heartlands of the empire are hampered by government secrecy and obfuscation. Independent civil society reports are normally blocked. Topics such as domestic food contamination and cancer hotspots are usually considered much too sensitive to report by mainstream journalists. Public silence and official media dissembling about environmental problems elsewhere in the empire, well beyond Chinese borders, are equally chronic. Whatever is said by diplomats about the Chinese vision of a 'beautiful earth' where nations live in harmony with their habitats, growth for growth's sake, whatever its polluting effects, remains the money-spinning orthodoxy in the Belt and Road Initiative and other projects. A commonly stated aim of these initiatives is to create 'modernized' economies in partner countries in which environmental regulations are weak, corruption is rife, and investigative journalism underdeveloped.

Coal-fired power plants financed by Chinese banks and built by Chinese companies are exemplary. Whereas at home radical cuts in carbon dioxide emissions are the reality—in the drive to transition from heavy industry manufacturing to consumer and service industries, China met its 2020 carbon intensity target three years ahead of schedule—the trends abroad run in the opposite direction. Beyond its borders, coal is big business. The dirtiest fossil fuel generates golden profits. China invests heavily in renewables such as wind and solar energy; and it is true that in 2020, following international pressure, the Asian Infrastructure Investment Bank agreed to discontinue funding for coal-fired power plants. But truth is also that China remains the world's largest investor in coal power, offloading its own coal overcapacity notably in places linked to the Belt and Road project. Its launch triggered huge investments in the financing, construction, and ownership of a sixth of the world's coal-fired power stations. By the end of 2016, Chinese banks and construction companies were involved in 240 coal-fired power plant projects in twenty-five of the BRI's sixty-five countries.[95] Ignoring the dangers of global warming and stranded assets weighed down by heavy debts, countries that agree to buy and build new Chinese coal plants function as local contract compradors. In the same way that Qing dynasty compradors profited from deals struck with the British Empire, their governments and local business classes profit from contracts with Chinese firms such as the China Development Bank and the state-owned power company China Huaneng Group.[96] Advocates of the Chinese model of state capitalist development, they ignore Chinese government guidelines about the need to promote 'green' Belt and Road projects. These compradors behave like buccaneers who are still in the grip of the outdated Kyoto Protocol, which recognized a difference between annex 1 'advanced economies' and non-annex 'developing countries' entitled to exercise their right to develop and to decide whether, or to what extent, locally appropriate mitigation measures should be adopted. For these local governments and businesses, it does not seem to matter that Chinese state-backed development banks typically operate in unaccountably opaque ways, or that in countries such as Tanzania, Serbia, and Pakistan they are willing to defy the high principles of 'ecological civilization' by financing overseas coal-fired projects with few or no environmental protection standards.

The wanton violation of these standards serves as yet another illustration of the central weakness of the galaxy empire: *its chronic reliance upon Party-sponsored and Party-controlled institutions that are prone to reckless power adventures because they are unchecked by independent monitory ('watchdog') mechanisms.* The problem of abusive power is rightly seen by scholars as the gravest danger facing every previous empire. China's new galaxy empire is no exception to this old rule. Considered as

---

95. Ren Peng, Liu Chang, and Zhang Liwen, *China's Involvement in Coal-Fired Power Projects along the Belt and Road*, Global Environment Institute (Beijing, May 2017); see also Isabel Hilton, 'How China's Big Overseas Initiative Threatens Global Climate Progress', *YaleEnvironment360*, January 3, 2019, https://e360.yale.edu/features/how-chinas-big-overseas-initiative-threatens-climate-progress.
96. Yen-p'ing Hao, *The Comprador in Nineteenth Century China: Bridge between East and West* (Cambridge, MA, 1970).

a large-scale polity that already shapes the bodily habits, ways of thinking, and habitats of many millions of its subjects, at home and abroad, China's rulers are prone to blind arrogance. They want to change the world, and to change the world in their favour. But we have already seen that these same rulers are aware that accountability matters. Living in an age of monitory democracy marked by the invention of many new forms of bio-representation,[97] they recognize that if they arrogantly abuse the habitats in which they operate, then they will destroy their own authority as well as risk unleashing organized 'green' resistance to their rule, of the kind that has already bitterly erupted in Kenya, Gambia, Zambia, Serbia, and other places.[98]

It is this recognition—however dim—of vulnerability to resistance that helps to explain why, in contrast to every previous known rising empire, *the rulers of the galaxy empire are the first to speak of the imperative of ending the human project of violently destroying our planetary ecosystems.* Bodies like the National Development and Reform Commission, a powerful macro-economic policy agency that operates under the State Council, have for some time been saying that China is setting best-practice standards, that polluters must pay, and that new mechanisms must be established to compensate victims of environmental damage and to hold local officials publicly accountable. Xi Jinping weighs in with calls for 'accountability systems' that 'hold responsible those who blindly ignore decisions in the ecological environment and cause serious consequences'.[99] Party officials, bureaucrats, diplomats, and corporate directors speak much the same language. It is as if they

---

97. John Keane, 'The Greening of Democracy', in *Power and Humility: The Future of Monitory Democracy* (Cambridge, 2018), pp. 249–269.
98. Bruno Martorano, Francesco Iacoella, Laura Metzger, and Marco Sanfilippo, 'Areas in Africa with More Chinese-Backed Projects Were More Likely to Experience Protests', *Our World: United Nations University*, August 16, 2021, https://ourworld.unu.edu/en/areas-in-africa-with-more-chinese-backed-projects-were-more-likely-to-experience-protests; and Sonja Gocanin, 'Amid Environmental Concerns, a Chinese Mining Company in Serbia Looks to Repair Its Image through Sport', *Radio Free Europe*, October 23, 2022, https://www.rferl.org/a/serbia-chinese-mining-zijin-sports-reputation/32096079.html.
99. Cao Qianfa, 'Xi Jinping's Ecological View', *Mao Zedong Thought Study* 34.6 (2017), pp. 51–59.

understand that in matters of environment China holds the key to globally negotiated improvements—that it is big enough to succeed, and much too big to fail. Realities are unfortunately more complicated, and much fickler. The contradiction between the grand vision of an 'ecological civilization' and a resource-hungry galaxy empire driven by one-party rule and state capitalist profiteering at the expense of our biosphere remains unresolved. Hence one of the most pressing and pertinent political questions of our century: whether China will carry on contributing to the cascading ruination of life on our planet, or whether instead, using the agile methods on display at the Kunming-Montréal Convention, it plays a key role in reversing environmental degradation and encouraging people everywhere, inside and outside the empire, to acknowledge the simple truth that they are living on planet Earth.

Cold Peace, Hot War

In matters of violence and abusive power, there's one remaining issue raised by this analysis of the galaxy empire: the decisive and divisive deeply political matter of whether this young empire is on balance a force for peace or, rather, an expanding power hellbent on disrupting the global order or hurling its military might at the world. In recent years, pundits, especially in the United States, have been quick to pass judgment. The dream of peaceful coexistence with China has come to an end, they say. Once upon a time, it was plausible to suppose that China's future prosperity and stability required its integration with the existing global order. China's peaceful rise seemed guaranteed. But things have since changed. Like all great powers on the rise, China is plotting takeovers and is no longer to be trusted. It is bellicose, a power-hungry, and weapons-heavy force bent on disruption, disorder, and deadly conflict. It may be the prime catalyst of the Third World War.

Among the boldest versions of this Big China, Bad China story is the claim that the young galaxy empire is caught in the 'peaking power trap'.[100] The argument hinges on the point that China's rejuvenation several decades ago rested on the lucky convergence of favourable factors. The country enjoyed cordial relations with the United States, which offered the Chinese economy entry into the WTO, vast business opportunities, and access to advanced technologies. The young empire was equally blessed by a 'demographic dividend'; for every senior citizen over the age of sixty-five, the Chinese economy employed ten working-age adults. Water, agricultural land, and other natural resources were plentiful. Environmental conditions were comparatively unspoiled. But hindsight shows that these were the halcyon days of rapid development, poverty reduction, technological innovation, and the massive growth of cities, or so runs the argument. The boom is over. China is suffering the early symptoms of economic and political decline. Its geopolitical vacation is ending; China is now hemmed in by new military alliances such as AUKUS (Australia, United Kingdom, United States) and the Quadrilateral Security Dialogue (QUAD). Its domestic economy is weighed down by a productivity crisis, GDP growth is sluggish, the workforce is shrinking, environmental degradation is worsening, and the Party-state is facing huge spending increases in support of a rapidly aging, unproductive population. Prospects of recovery and renewal are bleak—and that's why China has now entered a 'danger zone'. The so-named Thucydides trap—the claim that most rising powers ruffle the feathers of competitor powers—is wrong. The equation's the reverse. The case of China shows that rising powers are infused with self-confidence and are therefore prone to accommodation and compromise, whereas falling powers suffer bouts of rash anxiety and compensatory urges to fight back, to postpone their decline. The whole idea is that China is a 'risen power', and that's why it's dangerous, both at home and abroad. Domestic repression of citizens is backed by resource grabbing, economic sanctions, military interventions,

---

100. Hal Brands and Michael Beckley, *Danger Zone: The Coming Conflict with China* (New York, 2022).

and other acts of foreign aggression. The remedy? Outside powers led by the United States must strengthen their military capabilities, talk tough, deter menacingly, bargain hard, all the while looking their Chinese opponent in the eyes, without blinking.

The peaking power thesis is arguably a string of simplifications driven by political motives tailored to American foreign policy and military goals. This book stands at right angles to its exaggerations. It has presented a markedly different picture, backed by carefully researched evidence, of an emergent empire that is more robust and multiplex than the simplistic peaking power thesis suggests. The peaking power thesis, runs the Chinese saying, is trying to measure an ocean by using a cup. The conclusion that the young empire is on the warpath is especially problematic. There's more than a whiff of the old Orientalist prejudice that China, rulers and people alike, are by nature (as Hegel claimed) without self-consciousness, an undifferentiated and blindly underdeveloped 'substance' fit only for the 'despotism of the Sovereign'.[101] The simplified picture of a failing, falling, and bellicose China is a misdescription in another sense: it fails to understand that in military matters the new empire's rulers are practising a twenty-first-century version of ancient *yīn-yáng* principles. Their distinctive vision and strategy can be called *militarized peace*.

Making sense of this oxymoron and grasping its practical significance for understanding the galaxy empire's military preparations and peace-making efforts requires careful reflection on the *yīn-yáng* doctrine mentioned several times earlier in this book. This doctrine is not a comprehensive cosmology that teaches its believers how correctly to act in the world. Contrary to simplistic and commercialized Western usages of the phrase *'yīn-yáng'*, the doctrine is rather a modest vocabulary for clarifying the relationships among things and making good sense of the world in ways freed from black-and-white, either-or thinking. First formulated systematically by scholars

---

101. G. W. F. Hegel, *Philosophy of History*, trans. J. Sibree (New York, 1956), p. 116.

just before and during the Han dynasty (206 BCE–220 CE), this way of seeing the world highlights the entanglement and co-dependence of phenomena. Matters such as birth and death, summer and winter, the human body and the body politic, Heaven and Earth are regarded as correlative and assimilated and differentiated in chains of interdependence. The tenth-century BCE *Book of Poetry* speaks of *yīn* as rain and *yáng* as the sun that evaporates the morning dew; *yīn* and *yáng* also denote the shaded and sunlit sides of a mountain.[102] Note how the *yīn* and *yáng* are not binary opposites. Each is without a fixed form. They are defined in terms of each other. They wax and wane together, which implies not only that each has no fixed essence but also that change in one element redefines the form and substance of the other element. The *yīn-yáng* relationship is thus dynamic, charged with energy, constantly changing—exactly like the galaxy empire, whose rulers are today making peace and preparing for war.

Consider an example: the PLA-organized evacuations of citizens and officials from war-ravaged Sudan in early 2023. A Chinese helicopter peacekeeping unit rescued United Nations troops trapped near the border between South Sudan and Sudan. The PLA destroyer *Nanning*, backed by a supply ship, *Weishan Lake*, meanwhile sailed into the Red Sea from a base in Djibouti to rescue over a thousand Chinese, Pakistani, and other citizens from the nasty uncivil war. The naval destroyer displayed a big banner: 'Chairman Xi sent this naval ship to bring everyone home'. Through a loudhailer, a Chinese naval officer, playing the role of the caring 'father-mother official' (*fù mǔ guān*), told the evacuees, some of them tearful, many cheering and waving red five-star flags: 'Compatriots, no matter where you are, the great motherland will always be your strongest backup!' The Chinese Foreign Ministry's director general for European Affairs, Wang Lutong, chipped in by noting that China had come to the

---

102. *She King* (*Book of Poetry*), in *The Chinese Classics*, trans. James Legge, vol. 4, 2nd ed. (Taipei, 1935), pp. 55, 276, 488; see also Angus C. Graham, *yīn-yáng and the Nature of Correlative Thinking* (Singapore, 1986).

rescue of European citizens 'out of our vision of a global community with a shared future'.

These evacuation operations were undoubtedly driven by a mixture of peaceful motives, among them the humanitarian rescue of civilians from violence and the protection of business personnel in a country whose largest trading partner is China, with more than 130 companies investing in Sudan as of mid-2022. But these evacuations were also military operations, the third such mission in just over a decade (similar exoduses happened in Libya in 2011 and Yemen in 2015). They are a reminder that the young empire, acting under the banner of peace, is already heavily entangled in the foul business of war.

Chinese officials and military strategists are unusually forthright about these entanglements and their empire's need to protect its flanks by simultaneously developing and perfecting the arts of making peace by gearing up for war. They know the old local saying that trees prefer calm but winds blow; and they're generally familiar with the teachings of Sun Bin's *Art of Warfare*, a classic military strategy text from the Warring States period (475–221 BCE), parts of which have been newly uncovered. It features a discussion with King Wei of Qi, who is told: 'Only victory in war can bring about authority and prosperity'. But Sun warns that since 'warmongers will inevitably lose and those who expect to make a fortune out of war will also suffer defeat and disgrace', caution must be exercised. Going to war requires not only 'a storage of materials' and 'a just cause for war'. Imperative is the need to be 'well prepared in all affairs before launching an attack'.[103] Official documents similarly make clear that the preparation for war during peacetime is a vital component of fighting wars. *Yīn-yáng* ways of thinking are consistently on full display. They complement the vast web of entangled institutions and activities—the distinctively galactic qualities—of the young empire. A government White Paper (2019) reports that in a dangerously uncertain world China is striding 'forward

---

103. Sun Bin, *The Art of Warfare* (Albany, 2003), chap. 2.

along its own path to build a stronger military' and 'world-class forces' in support of 'world peace' and 'common development'.[104]

Such reports typically leave unnamed the prime source of military danger, but undoubtedly lurking between the lines is the United States, the other empire that from its eighteenth-century beginnings has fought hundreds of wars and today spends more on its military apparatus annually than the next ten countries combined, with around eight hundred military bases located in more than seventy-five countries and territories abroad.[105] Against this geopolitical backdrop, in which the United States is now pushing for the globalization of NATO to encircle China, leading Beijing institutions such as the PLA's National Defence University and the Academy of Military Sciences conduct military teaching and research and proactively publish reports trawling through matters such as the weaponization of social media, cyberattacks, slow-motion strategies and tactics, artificial intelligence warfare, and the need for tighter integration and harmonization among the various branches of the armed forces, with the Party at the helm. High-ranking PLA officers weigh in with calls to 'achieve victory without fighting' (much-used words from Sun Tzu's *Art of War*)[106] and reminders of the importance of conducting a people's war: fighting wars in the name of the people, for the people, and by the people, so making war the political art of peacefully binding together government and citizens and combining the people into an indestructible force.[107] In the field of law, there's stress on the need to prepare for war by harnessing the

---

104. State Council Information Office of the People's Republic of China, *China's National Defense in the New Era* (Beijing, 2019), p. 37, https://english.www.gov.cn/archive/whitepaper/201907/24/content_WS5d3941ddc6d08408f502283d.html.
105. David Vine, *The United States of War: A Global History of America's Endless Conflicts, from Columbus to the Islamic State* (Berkeley, 2020); Rollo, *Terminus*.
106. Sun Tzu, *The Art of War* (London, 2000 [1910]), p. 8: 'Supreme excellence consists in breaking the enemy's resistance without fighting'. The importance of Sun Tzu for PLA thinking about war is documented by Baogang Shi and Xiaoyan Zhang, *Art of War and Modern Military Education Thinking* (Shanghai, 2011; in Chinese).
107. Yongsheng Hu, 'Reflections on Unleashing the Power of People's War under Conditions of Information Technology', *National Defence* 5 (2019), pp. 11–14 (in Chinese).

methods of 'legal warfare' (*fǎ lù zhàn*). Warfighting requires clever uses of legal instruments to outflank and crush the enemy, it's said. The militarized peace arsenal comprises various weapons: waging and winning cases against opponents, peddling legal threats and legal confusion, tying them up in court, wasting their time, distracting their attention, and damaging their public reputation. Other tactics include claims to 'historic title' and 'historic rights' of control over island and maritime zones, as in the South China Sea, the use of *notes verbales* and other official state declarations of sovereign control.[108] Legal warfare is also said to include rigorous tertiary-level training of lawyers specializing in the field of lawfare, the synchronization of China's domestic laws with its strategic goals abroad, boycotting and non-compliance with selected foreign court decisions, and contributing, in the name of global peace, to the building and preservation of rule-bound cross-border institutions protective of China's military security.

Scholar officials and military academy teachers meanwhile counsel military commanders and Party leaders to think long term and to pay particular attention to the fluctuating rhythms of war and peace. They are attached to a Chinese version of a well-known maxim found in Leo Tolstoy's *War and Peace* (1869), which speaks of time and patience as the strongest of warriors. Time is an invaluable resource. Timing counts for a great deal, they say. Melons forced from the vine won't taste sweet, runs the Chinese saying. Armies have a taste for quick victory, and there are indeed moments when in the digital age speed is of the essence in warfighting. But success in war demands *self-control, forbearance, and the ability and willingness to wait during periods of peace*. Only fools rush into war. Planning and pre-emption are of prime importance; when the world is at peace, a sword needs to be within reach. In war, as in life more generally,

---

108. Florian Dupuy and Pierre-Marie Dupuy, 'A Legal Analysis of China's Historic Rights Claim in the South China Sea', *American Journal of International Law* 107.1 (2013), pp. 124–141.

proper preparation prevents poor performance. Patience is an indispensable virtue, say these scholars and teachers. They use words from Sun Tzu to remind military officers and troops alike that recklessness and a hasty temper are among the principal 'sins ruinous to the conduct of war'.[109]

There's one other feature of these high-level, high-energy discussions of peace and war. Especially striking is the omnipresent talk within high military and Party circles of the strategic importance of *public opinion warfare* (*yù lùn zhàn*). Under the rubric of what Chinese military analysts call 'network consensus warfare', there are constant reminders of the peacetime imperative of binding together military and civilian institutions and following the lead of the Central Military Commission commanded by the Party's leader, Xi Jinping. Military-civil fusion is defined broadly, to extend from state-owned enterprises and scientific-technological innovation to the mobilization of television, radio, news platforms, and Weibo, WeChat, Bilibili, Twitter, and Facebook.[110] Sun Tzu's advice that warfare necessitates deception has a new pertinence, it's said. Now that we are living in the age of *metaverse wars*, peacemaking and warfighting are digitized, gamified, and propagandized.[111] Police and military operations are even morphed into entertainment—turned into big-screen movies like Ao Shen's thriller *No More Bets* (2023) and Wu Jing's *Wolf Warrior 2* (2017), a blockbuster account of a Chinese soldier of fortune who finds himself in an unnamed African country fighting to protect medical aid workers and civilians against local gangs and arms dealers. There are warnings that China remains vulnerable in the Western-dominated global news and commentary media, which (military strategists add) produce a

---

109. Sun Tzu, *The Art of War*, pp. 31–32.
110. Bicheng Li, 'Brief Introduction to Integrated Joint Operation of Comprehensive Network Consensus', *National Defence Technology* 38.2 (2017), pp. 85–88 (in Chinese).
111. Shi Zhan, 'Appearance Is Essence, Performance Is War', *The Paper* (Shanghai), February 27, 2022, https://m.thepaper.cn/newsDetail_forward_16877837 (in Chinese); and John Keane, 'We Live in the Age of Nasty Metaverse Wars', *South China Morning Post*, June 11, 2022, https://www.scmp.com/week-asia/opinion/article/3181225/we-live-age-nasty-metaverse-wars-there-no-escape-hell.

huge percentage of the world's daily output, with more than half the information circulated via the internet in the English language compared to less than 4 per cent in Chinese.[112] The implication is clear: wars are conducted and victory won not just on battlefields but through public opinion management. Hence the calls for ramping up the use of digital platforms as mediums through which civilians can express their opinions and Chinese military strategists can make announcements, explain their concerns, issue warnings about enemies, and generally persuade 'the people' of the need to think peace while preparing for war.[113]

It may be thought that all these orange-alert reports and commentaries on militarized peace are mere talk and that, as always, deeds speak louder than words. But within the young empire, words count. They have strategic potency. Designed to win hearts and minds at home and beyond, for instance on the African continent, in central Asia, and in the Arab world, words are a pragmatically useful form of symbolic power complemented by other forms of action on the ground, at sea, in the air, and beyond, into the outer heavens. The orange alerts are a constitutive component of the fact that the galaxy empire is today actively engaged in building up its military forces and fine-tuning its military strategies in order to protect its own flanks, all in the name of peace. Party leaders, government officials, and scholars are adamant about the empire's irenic qualities. 'Over the past 70-plus years,' notes a prominent official, 'China has never initiated a war or occupied an inch of a foreign land. It is the only country that has incorporated peaceful development in its Constitution, and the only country among the five nuclear-weapon states to pledge no first use of nuclear weapons. China's track record on peace can stand the

---

112. See the essays by Xunlong Xiao and Shouqi Li, 'Brief Introduction to Cyber Public Opinion Warfare', *National Defence Technology* 35.2 (2014), pp. 5–8, and 'Thinking on Strategies of Media War in Safeguarding Maritime Zones', *National Defence Technology* 34.5 (2013), pp. 99–102 (both in Chinese).
113. Yingxue Xu and Fen Lan, 'WeChat: A New Weapon of Network Consensus War', *National Defence Technology* 35 (2014), pp. 17–20 (in Chinese).

scrutiny of history, and its peaceful rise is an unprecedented miracle in human history'.[114]

The claim that China has never waged war on its opponents requires qualification. During the decades after the 1949 revolution, the People's Republic of China was in fact no stranger to war. The PLA struck out several times: in a direct confrontation with the United States in Korea (1950–53) and in still-unresolved, high-altitude border conflicts with India (1962, 2020). There were bloody military confrontations with the Soviet Union in the late 1960s on the Xinjiang border; and several maritime conflicts and a month-long ground war with the Socialist Republic of Vietnam in 1979, dubbed by Chinese officials as a punitive 'self-defensive counterstrike' in response to Vietnam's toppling of Beijing's Khmer Rouge client state in Cambodia.

China's heavy casualties (an estimated thirty thousand deaths and thirty-five thousand wounded soldiers) and failure to oust Vietnam from Cambodia during that war triggered a reorganization and retooling of the PLA. Subsequently, it hasn't gone openly to war in defence of the galaxy empire's homelands or its outer reaches. But like all previous empires, the young empire has become ensnared in the business of war and the pity of war. Precautionary moves are in hand, among them, in preparation for a possible future war with the United States, Beijing's pursuit of its own version of 'decoupling' and 'de-risking' in a wide range of policy areas. The replacement of GPS by the Beidou satellite communications system, the de-dollarization of investment and trade deals, and the mining and independent processing of rare earths are examples already discussed in this book. This 'everything-but-America strategy' (Hank Paulson) also includes the redesign of domestic and global supply chains to guarantee food and energy security in the event of war and the building of 'parallel' cross-border governing institutions such as the Asian Infrastructure Investment Bank and

---

114. Wang Yi, 'The Path of Peaceful Development Has Worked and Worked Well', *Ministry of Foreign Affairs of the People's Republic of China*, February 18, 2023, https://www.fmprc.gov.cn/mfa_eng/wjdt_665385/wshd_665389/202302/t20230221_1 1028273.html.

Shanghai Cooperation Organisation. Of rising importance is the formidable role played by China's 'civilian army' in crafting strategies of *military diplomacy*: snubbing the United States in favour of high-level meetings with military officials and diplomats from France, Japan, the European Union, and other US allies for the purposes of winning new friends and spreading divisions within the West, gathering military intelligence by stealth, and enhancing global negotiation and cooperation in such matters as the reform of the UN Security Council and the prevention of nuclear war and weapons proliferation.[115]

That's not all. In the name of peace, the young galaxy empire is building a formidable war machine backed by a *military-industrial-aerospace complex*. Aggregate military spending reached an estimated $252 billion in 2020, around 1.3 per cent of Chinese GDP, but the details are more significant. We've seen already that China's navy is the world's largest, that it holds an estimated 350 nuclear warheads, and that it has more cruise missiles and middle-range ballistic rockets than the United States. Along the high-altitude border with India, Chinese troops are being replaced by drones and robots armed with machine guns.[116] The galaxy empire is also rapidly building a state-of-the-art aerospace industry. Symptomatic is the rise of an 'aerospace faction' within high-level Party and state positions.[117] The promotion of former state-owned enterprise officials with engineering and science-technology backgrounds and close ties to the military sector—figures such as Jin Zhuanglong (minister of industry and information technology) and Huai Jinpeng (minister of education)—are symbols of the current efforts to boost military-civilian integration, overtake the United States in the aerospace domain, and prepare for a possible future digital war in outer space. Measured in terms of output

---

115. Peter Martin, *China's Civilian Army: The Making of Wolf Warrior Diplomacy* (Oxford, 2023).
116. Stockholm International Peace Research Institute, *SIPRI Yearbook 2021: Armaments, Disarmament and International Security* (Oxford, 2021); Pravin Sawhney, *The Last War: How AI Will Shape India's Final Showdown with China* (New Delhi, 2022).
117. Shunsuke Tabeta, 'Xi Promotes "Aerospace Clique" to Counter the U.S. as a Defence Power,' *Nikkei Asia*, October 22, 2022.

volume, officials boast, China is already the world's premier high-tech manufacturer. They applaud the launch of China's first domestically built passenger jet—the Comac C919—and predict that China will soon overtake the United States in strategically important areas such as semiconductors, quantum computing, and aerospace engineering. It is most definitely a 'full-spectrum peer competitor' (Eric Schmidt) in the fields of 5G, robotics, and artificial intelligence. Sophisticated cyber weapons designed to counter, control, or hijack enemy satellites are also within reach.[118] The military's high command is acutely aware that metaverse wars livestreamed by digital information flows (as in Syria and Ukraine) are the new normal. Unsurprisingly, China's space force—the Space Systems Division of the People's Liberation Army's Strategic Support Force—was established in early 2016, some four years before the creation of the US Space Force equivalent.

Back on planet Earth, China now boasts one of the largest and most diverse *military-linked production* sectors: approximately one thousand companies currently employ about three million people, including over thirty thousand engineers and technicians.[119] These companies—sporting trade names and acronyms such as China North Industries

118. Graham Allison, Kevin Klyman, Karina Barbesino, and Hugo Yen, *The Great Tech Rivalry: China vs the U.S.*, Belfer Center, Harvard Kennedy School report (Cambridge, MA, December 2021), https://www.belfercenter.org/sites/default/files/GreatTechRivalry_ChinavsUS_211207.pdf; Mehul Srivastava, Felicia Schwartz, and Demetri Sevastopulo, 'China Building Cyber Weapons to Hijack Enemy Satellites', *Financial Times*, April 21, 2023, https://www.ft.com/content/881c941a-c46f-4a40-b8d8-9e5c8a6775ba; Henry A. Kissinger, Eric Schmidt, and Daniel Huttenlocher, *The Age of AI: And Our Human Future* (Boston, 2021); and Zhixin Li, 'Key Aspects of Building the System of Military-Civil Integrated Deep Development of Science and Technology Mobilization', *National Defence Technology* 37.6 (2016), pp. 91–95 (in Chinese).
119. The following paragraph draws upon David Welker, 'The Chinese Military-Industrial Complex Goes Global', *Multinational Monitor* 18.6 (1997), pp. 9–14; Emily Weinstein, 'Testimony before the US-China Economic and Security Review Commission on "US Investment in China's Capital Markets and Military-Industrial Complex"' (Washington, DC, 2021), *SIPRI Yearbook 2021*, p. 15; Covell Meyskens, 'Experiencing the Cold War at Shanghai's Secret Military Industrial Complex', *Cold War History* 21.4 (2021), pp. 429–447; and Maryanne Xue, 'China's Arms Trade: Which Countries Does It Buy From and sell To?', *South China Morning Post*, July 4, 2021, https://www.scmp.com/news/china/military/article/3139603/how-china-grew-buyer-major-arms-trade-player.

Group Corporation (NORINCO), Aviation Industry Corporation of China (AVIC), China South Industries Group Corporation (CSGC), and China Electronics Technology Group Corporation (CETC)—perform well on the local stock exchanges. AVIC, for example, is a state-owned enterprise that manufactures drones, helicopters, jet fighters, and bomber aircraft. Employing a five-hundred-thousand-strong workforce worldwide and comprising some two hundred subsidiaries, its Shenzhen Stock Exchange share value reportedly increased tenfold between 1997 and 2022, which raises tricky questions about the vested interests of the empire's military sector, and whether its profit-seeking, shareholding domestic and overseas business strategies are at odds with the Party-state's foreign policies and declarations of peaceful intent.[120] For the moment, what's certain is that companies such as AVIC and NORINCO are major players in the *global arms trade*. China accounted for 5.2 per cent of all international arms exports between 2016 and 2020, compared with the United States at 37 per cent. Its 'customer base' is diverse. In recent years (2016 to 2020), arms exports from the empire's heartlands have predominantly gone to Pakistan (38 per cent), Bangladesh (17 per cent), and Algeria (8.2 per cent). But the number of countries to which China exports arms is expanding, from forty between 2010 and 2014 to fifty-three between 2015 and 2019. During the past decade, China supplied eleven countries with weaponized drones, including Egypt, Saudi Arabia, and Uzbekistan. Some of these arms deals are strangely puzzling. In Myanmar, Chinese state-owned enterprises such as the China Aerospace Science and Technology Corporation and NORINCO, the owner of two copper mines in the country, are among the largest suppliers of arms and military equipment to the armed forces (Tatmadaw). But China also supplies surface-to-air missiles, heavy artillery, and armoured vehicles to the thirty-thousand-strong United Wa State Army, which from its base in the north-east region of the country, on China's southern border, is militarily

---

120. Colin Hawes, *The Chinese Corporate Ecosystem* (Cambridge, 2022)

supporting a coalition of ethnic rebel armies fighting against the Myanmar government, with Chinese peace negotiators caught in the middle of two allies in a country where the galaxy empire has significant investment and trade interests bound up with access to the Indian Ocean.

The challenges confronting peace negotiations in potential and actual war zones extend well beyond Myanmar. The empire's overall commitment to militarized peace—simultaneously advocating peace while building a war machine, all the while knowing that although peace in the age of nuclear weapons is mandatory, war may be just around the corner—is coming under intense pressure at various points on our planet and beyond, into outer space.

The galaxy empire's growing encounters with the *push-pull of peace and war, war and peace* have an extraterrestrial dimension. We've seen already that China's rulers have their sights on the high ground of outer space. Since China's first solo astronaut flight in 2003, the number of space missions has grown exponentially; China's taikonauts have perfected the arts of orbital docking and spacewalking; radio-satellite communications and other technologies have steadily become more sophisticated; a galaxy empire robot now roams the surface of Mars. But following a US Congress decision in 2011, the International Space Station, a platform principally built and operated by the United States, is now a no-go zone for the Chinese space programme. The NATO encirclement of China is extending into the heavens. The official reasons given by lawmakers for the boycott of China centred on 'national security' concerns. The justifications came wrapped in tough military talk and US government war drum warnings about how the rulers of China view space power as a means of 'bolstering the political prestige of the CCP' and enabling 'more effective military operations at increasingly greater distances from Chinese shores'. Equipped with advanced 'precision strike assets', 'space-based surveillance', a 'survivable communications architecture', 'electronic warfare capabilities', and an 'ambitious counterspace program, including a ground- and space-based space surveillance systems', it was said,

China is rapidly developing the 'ability to project firepower at greater distances and with growing lethality and speed'. Since space capability is a significant metric of the power to shape the future of our planet, noted the government report, the United States must now be on high military alert. 'Beijing's lack of transparency over military budgets, and potential risks associated with the military applications of space technology, remain major causes for concern'.[121]

Earthly tensions triggered by the empire's militarized peace strategies are also rising. Troubles within the China-Pakistan Economic Corridor (CPEC) are an example. An assortment of infrastructure projects connecting south-west China to the Arabian Sea, CPEC had the unintended effect of fostering frictions among the country's provincial governments because of concerns that some provinces, Punjab for instance, were unfairly benefitting from Chinese investment. Chinese diplomats responded by abandoning their stated policy of peaceful non-interference in Pakistan and launching ground-level negotiations between its central government and the provinces and territories.[122] The policy shift reportedly resulted in a more agreeably equitable allocation of CPEC funding and projects, but new troubles erupted. CPEC projects have been vandalized. Chinese nationals working in Pakistan are targets of harassment and violence. Local media platforms publish reports about the low levels of understanding of the 'religious sensitivities of Pakistanis' among Chinese nationals and embassy staff. Local journalists also table complaints about the way private security firms deputed to protect Chinese projects are often either untrained or insufficiently equipped with weapons and ammunition.[123] China's

---

121. Mark A. Stokes with Dean Cheng, *China's Evolving Space Capabilities: Implications for U.S. Interests*, a report for the U.S.-China Economic and Security Review Commission (Washington, DC, April 2012), pp. 50–51.
122. Zahid Shahab Ahmed, 'Impact of the China-Pakistan Economic Corridor on Nation-Building in Pakistan', *Journal of Contemporary China* 28.117 (2019), pp. 400–414; Babar Khan Bozdar and Sadia Kazmi, *China-Pakistan Economic Corridor: Potentials and Prospects* (Islamabad, 2016), p. 8.
123. See, for example, Munawer Azeem and Mohammad Asghar, 'Security of CPEC Projects on High Alert', *Dawn*, November 24, 2018, https://www.dawn.com/news/1447232.

peaceful intentions haven't been helped by the events of 2018, when the Chinese consulate in Karachi was targeted by suicide bombers despatched by the Balochistan Liberation Army. A Pakistan army division has since been deployed to protect CPEC projects, and Beijing has actively engaged Baloch militant groups and tribal leaders, issued formal invitations, and even paid for delegations to meet with senior Chinese leaders in Beijing.[124] Tensions are meanwhile festering in war-damaged Afghanistan, where plans to extend the Belt and Road Initiative and to extract oil in the Amu Darya basin, the Taliban regime's first major foreign investment deal, are not exactly straightforward.[125]

The disparate cases of Sudan, Myanmar, Pakistan, Afghanistan, and the International Space Station have a much wider significance. They highlight a major conundrum lurking within the young empire's attachment to a *yīn-yáng* understanding of peace and war. For the sake of its survival and flourishing, the galaxy empire must guard against jealousies and rivalries. It has to be permanently on alert and prepared to face down opponents at home and abroad. Against its enemies, and in support of its friends, it can rely, as it presently does in various conflict zones in Africa, on a patchwork of local military, private security firms, and mercenaries to protect the interests of Chinese diplomats, corporations, and workers. But when that peace strategy fails, as evidently it did in Sudan, and as it shows signs of doing in outer space as well as in Myanmar, Pakistan, and other settings back on Earth, the empire may be tempted to intervene, to use violence to rebuff violence, or to advance its interests forcefully. The trouble

---

124. Adnan Aamir, 'Pakistan's Belt and Road Hub Gwadar Hit by Protest Clampdown', *Nikkei Asia*, January 2, 2023; David F. Gordon, Haoyu Tong, and Tabatha Anderson, 'Beyond the Myths—Towards a Realistic Assessment of China's Belt and Road Initiative: The Security Dimension'*, International Institute for Strategic Studies*, 2020, pp. 25–26, https://ispmyanmarchinadesk.com/wp-content/uploads/2020/12/BRI-Report-Two-Beyond-the-Myths-Towards-a-Realistic-Assessment-of-Chinas-Belt-and-Road-Initiative.pdf.
125. Sudha Ramachandran, 'Can the Belt and Road Initiative Succeed in Afghanistan?', *China Brief* 23.9 (May 19, 2023), https://jamestown.org/program/can-the-belt-and-road-initiative-succeed-in-afghanistan/.

is that the threatened or actual use of violence, for instance by the PLA in failed states and badly governed settings beyond China's borders, is extremely risky. There are not only the well-known dangers of mission creep. Military intervention would almost certainly incite opposition at home and breed resentment and resistance abroad. Unending wars of attrition and sinking into bottomless quagmires are costly and dangerous for any empire, as leaders of the United States are learning. Countering rivals and winning over opponents without firing shots are clearly preferable options, especially in the era of nuclear and biochemical and Star Wars weapons. *Pacification is a positive functional requirement of stability at home and doing business, diplomacy, and institution building abroad.* Violence in all its forms—from surprise attacks on Chinese facilities by suicide bombers and armed gangs through to threats of aggression and direct attacks by the US military—is anathema to the spreading power and influence of the galaxy empire.

It isn't clear even to the rulers whether their empire's defining reliance upon militarized peace strategies is working, or whether it will enjoy long-run sustainability. The trends so far discussed suggest that quite probably the young galaxy empire is no exception to the old rule that empires never escape the dirty business of militarily defending their homelands and outer zones. Whether the distinctive *yīn-yáng* commitment to militarized peace will be torn apart, with one element, war, triumphing at the expense of the other, isn't yet knowable. The energy-charged, constantly changing *yīn-yáng* relationship may implode, degenerating into a one-sided dynamic marked by war rather than peace and war. To cite the well-known Chinese aphorism: peace and war may be sleeping in the same bed but, under pressure from encroaching realities, peace and war may come to dream different dreams. What is however certain, and very striking, is the way Chinese leaders, diplomats, and academics are repeatedly affirming their commitment to self-restraint and non-violence, their support for what President Hu Jintao first called 'a harmonious world' (at an international summit in Jakarta) and what nowadays they like variously to call 'global peace', 'peaceful understanding', and 'developmental peace' (*fā zhǎn hé píng*).

The peacebuilding efforts are energetic and often impressive. Much diplomatic energy has been expended in *settling disputes—successfully—with China's neighbouring states*. Xi Jinping's government remains committed to signing a Code of Conduct with the ten-member ASEAN pact for the purpose of reducing potential clashes and conflicts in the South China Sea, for instance by promoting maritime cooperation and hosting regular dialogues among diplomats and defence and military officials. In the wake of the collapse of the Soviet Union, China established the Shanghai Cooperation Organisation (SCO) to preempt border disputes and promote peace in the central Asian region. So far, in contrast to festering armed conflicts elsewhere in the former Soviet Union, none of the six founding member states engaged in border disputes.[126] With the inclusion (in 2017) of India and Pakistan as SCO members, it remains to be seen whether the organization can continue to maintain peace and control border conflicts among its member states.

Efforts are also in hand to ensure that China's BRI infrastructure projects are not at risk of failing or being terminated by key BRI client states.[127] In early 2022, at the Boao Forum, Xi Jinping proposed a new 'Global Security Initiative', urging that peace is best achieved through global economic development backed by no-strings-attached strong government geared to the maintenance of political and social stability.[128] In a follow-up move, the Ministry of Foreign Affairs announced the establishment of an international mediation centre in Hong Kong, a space for supporting international parties in conflict to settle their disputes peacefully. President Xi Jinping and German

---

126. Baogang He, 'Regionalism as an Instrument for Global Power Contestation: The Case of China', *Asian Studies Review* 44.1 (2020), pp. 79–96.
127. Helena Legarda, 'China as a Conflict Mediator: Maintaining Stability along the Belt and Road', *Mercator Institute for China Studies*, August 22, 2018, https://merics.org/en/short-analysis/china-conflict-mediator.
128. Abb Pascal, 'China's Emergence as a Peacebuilding Actor' (*Policy Brief* 4/2018, Austrian Study Centre for Peace and Conflict Resolution, 2018), p. 3.

chancellor Olaf Scholz have since issued a public statement opposing the use of nuclear weapons. A special peace delegation has been despatched to Ukraine, to help end the Russia-Ukraine war. In early 2023, mediated by Chinese diplomats, the world was surprised by the announcement that Iran and Saudi Arabia would restore diplomatic and economic ties. PLA troops are meanwhile playing an active role in UN peacekeeping operations. In 2022 alone, China despatched 2,240 soldiers and support staff in seven UN missions. China contributes around 15 per cent of the overall UN peacekeeping budget; it is now the second-largest donor after the United States. In June 2022, Chinese representatives met in Addis Ababa with officials from six East African states for the first China–Horn of Africa Peace Conference. Shortly afterwards (in July 2022) the China-Africa Peace and Security Forum was attended by senior military and defence leaders from nearly fifty African countries.

The galaxy empire commitments to peace aren't always successful, and ground-level dynamics are hampered by the *absence of independent Chinese NGOs* in peacebuilding processes. The failure of Myanmar peace negotiations is a recent case in point. With the future of the China-Myanmar Economic Corridor at stake, Chinese diplomats attempted to mediate and moderate frictions between Bangladesh and Myanmar to solve the grave humanitarian crisis produced by the Tatmadaw military's war on the ethnic Rohingya minority in Myanmar's western Rakhine state.[129] China proposed a ceasefire on the ground, bilateral dialogue between Bangladesh and Myanmar, and economic development and poverty alleviation to address what Beijing considered to be the root cause of the conflict. Prefabricated houses for the displaced people of Rakhine state were handed to the Myanmar authorities and efforts were made to broker the repatriation of Rohingya refugees from Bangladesh. On the sidelines of the UN General Assembly, China, Bangladesh, and Myanmar devised a

---

129. Jason G. Tower, 'Conflict Dynamics and the Belt and Road Initiative', *Brot für die Welt*, Analysis Paper No. 97 (2020), p. 23, available at https://www.brot-fuer-die-welt.de/fileadmin/mediapool/blogs/Kruckow_Caroline/Analyse97-en-v08-Web.pdf.

'tripartite working mechanism' to implement the plans. With the advent of the coronavirus pestilence and (in February 2021) a military coup d'état in Myanmar, all these peacebuilding efforts were stillborn. Meanwhile, the biggest prize of all, peace with the United States, the galaxy empire's chief rival, is still not on the horizon.

Despite the recent record of mixed successes, Chinese scholars and diplomats remain upbeat. The *empire's diplomats* are especially active on all fronts, at all points within its galactic spaces. The Marxist-jargon-spouting Chinese envoys of yesteryear, many of whom knew by heart the famous dictum of Zhou Enlai that diplomats are the People's Liberation Army in civilian clothing—are no more. They have been replaced by sophisticated ambassadors who typically speak the local language, actively participate in social media, and display a good command of the complex issues of the milieux in which they are operating. *Scholars* pitch in with reassurances of China's commitment to global peacebuilding. During the past six decades, claims Fudan University's Su Changhe, China has gradually built a unique model of handling domestic and foreign affairs. The principle of 'cooperation' instead of 'checks and balances' is the core spirit of the *China model*. At home, he says, this spirit of cooperation is manifested in various institutional practices, ranging from political consultation, multiparty cooperation, and the combination of legislative and executive powers to efforts to synchronize and harmonize domestic politics and international politics. In contrast to the checks-and-balances model of the Western political order, the China model, he continues, provides a new and refined ethical and political vision of a future peaceful world order.[130] Zheng Bijian, former vice-president of Central Party School, concurs. China's rise should not be seen as anything but peaceful because, unlike most traditional European empires, China does not build colonies overseas, he says. Zheng argues that China has never been interested in exporting its Communist

---

130. Su Changhe, 'The China Model and World Order', *Wàijiāo pínglùn [Foreign affairs review]* 4 (2009), pp. 21–31 (in Chinese).

Revolution to the world, and that China's contributions to economic globalization has created an interest-based international community that prefers peace to war.[131] Still other scholars explain that China is committed to the theory and practice of what they call *developmental peace*.[132] Their reasoning is strangely reminiscent of a line of thinking traceable back to eighteenth-century European beliefs in the *doux commerce* effect, the precept that 'wherever the ways of man are gentle, there is commerce; and wherever there is commerce, there the ways of men are gentle' (Montesquieu).[133] According to the proponents of developmental peace, non-violence is both a functional requirement and product of investment, trade, and economic growth. Since 128 of the 190 countries in the world now have China as their main trading partner, peaceful cooperation, they say, is within reach of the world.

The chief trouble with this conviction that the empire can bring (armed) peace to the whole world is its silence about the *rising tensions with the United States* in Taiwan and other hot-spot zones. The diplomats of both empires are already acknowledging that these frictions are the most dangerous devil in global affairs. There are moves to thaw near-frozen contacts. High-level 'candid' talks are staged. Sticking points are summarized. Proposals for bilateral agreements are tabled. Leaders deliver big speeches. The US secretary of state is told by Chinese diplomats that 'the root cause of the current downturn in China-U.S. relations lies in the U.S. side's erroneous understanding of China, which has resulted in misguided policies toward China'. The reply is that further Chinese provocations 'would have

---

131. Zheng Bijian, *China's Peaceful Rise: Speeches of Zheng Bijian, 1997–2005* (Lanham, MD, 2005).
132. Yin He, 'Developmental Peace: Chinese Approaches to U.N. Peacekeeping and Peacebuilding', *Journal of International Studies* 38.4 (2017), pp. 10–32 (in Chinese); Xinyu Yuan, 'The Chinese Approach to Peacebuilding: Contesting Liberal Peace?', *Third World Quarterly* 43.7 (2022), pp. 1798–1816.
133. The thesis of the civilizing effects of *doux commerce* is famously analysed in Albert Hirschman, *The Passions and the Interests: Political Arguments for Capitalism before Its Triumph* (Princeton, NJ, 1977). See also Ludwig von Mises, *The Political Economy of International Reform and Reconstruction* (Indianapolis, 2000), p. 43: 'Free traders want to make peace durable by eliminating the root causes of conflict'.

serious consequences in our relationship'. Nothing much goes to plan. Brinkmanship rules. Exchange visits are postponed. Calls for the establishment of 'military communication channels' between the two sides remain unanswered. Military tensions fester. There are moments when things lurch toward dangerously intense confrontations. A US spy plane makes an emergency landing on Chinese soil after colliding with an intercepting PLA fighter jet. Spy balloons are shot down. A Chinese J-16 fighter jet cuts in front of a US reconnaissance aircraft hovering above the South China Sea. US destroyers conduct 'freedom of navigation' patrols of the Taiwan Strait. The US Joint Chiefs of Staff send messages to reassure their Chinese counterparts that the United States will not launch surprise nuclear attacks. In the name of 'Indo-Pacific regional security and stability', the *USS Nevada*, a nuclear-powered submarine carrying a score of Trident ballistic missiles and dozens of nuclear warheads, docks at its base in the US Pacific Island territory of Guam.

Whether these frictions will worsen is unpredictable. The future jealously keeps the cards of the future close to her chest, but that's why, finally, some help can fruitfully be sought from an unexpected source: the genre of *science fiction writing*. The resort to fiction may be thought to be unscholarly, but it should be borne in mind that in the heartlands of the galaxy empire the genre of science fiction has of late been flourishing.[134] We've seen how this empire is shaped and self-propelled by *space power aspirations* and technological breakthroughs: an alternative satellite navigation system, advanced rocketry, space science satellites used for measuring Earth's magnetic field, a lunar crew landing for the first time on its dark side, a machine exploring the surface of Mars. Popular fascination with outer space is

---

134. The background developments are analysed in Xia Jia, 'What Makes Chinese Science Fiction Chinese?', *Tor.Com*, July 22, 2014, https://www.tor.com/2014/07/22/what-makes-chinese-science-fiction-chinese/; Mingwei Song, 'After 1989: The New Wave of Chinese Science Fiction', *China Perspectives* 1 (2015), pp. 7–13, https://journals.openedition.org/chinaperspectives/6618; Mikael Huss, 'Hesitant Journey to the West: SF's Changing Fortunes in Mainland China', *Science Fiction Studies* 27, part 1 (March 2000), pp. 92–104

the complement to this growing technological prowess. Fed by a coterie of prominent and less well-known writers whose books sell millions of copies and feature as short videos, television programmes, and blockbuster films—the first was *The Wandering Earth* (2019) based on a short story by Liu Cixin, the world-famous, nine-times winner of China's Galaxy Award—the genre of science fiction has (mostly) managed to slip through the fingers and under the noses of censors to occupy a prominent space in the cultural life of the empire's heartlands, and well beyond, in North America, Europe, and other territories.

The Chinese science fiction of today is not what it used to be. In the late Qing dynasty and the early years of the Republic, the substantial themes of science fiction writing centred on the modernization of China by taking science, technology, and progress into its arms. The earliest works—the distinguished modernist writer Lu Xun first called them 'science novels' or 'science fiction' (*kē xue xiǎo shuō*)—sketched a marvellous fantasy world of flying cars, submarines, spaceships, and colonies on the moon, even laser weapons defending China against imperialists. After the 1949 founding of the People's Republic, science fiction writing, by now usually called 'science fantasy' (*kē huàn xiǎo shuō*), was rebranded as a sub-genre of children's literature based on socialist principles: a means of spreading scientific knowledge to the masses to strengthen their Party-led struggle to build a new communist order. There were stories of smart spaceships, artificial suns melting glaciers to enable the watering of desert farmlands, factories turning seawater into industrial products. Sci-fi novels judged to be dangerous spiritual pollution (*jīng shén wū rǎn*) and seductive nonsense (*xiǎng rù feifei*) were banned. Nowadays, the themes are no less excited, mocking, and wondrous about the human condition and life on our planet, but their tone and substance are more apprehensive about the future. There is plenty of gloomy ambivalence about ecological ruin, the end of humanity, intergalactic rivalries—and allegories about the limits of peace and the looming dangers of war.

The prize-winning novel *Vagabonds* by Hao Jingfang is exemplary of this shift in tone and substance.[135] It can be read as an allegory describing one possible destiny of the galaxy empire, a future that can be called *cold peace*. Set three centuries in the distant future, *Vagabonds* is a surreal tale of war and peace, capitalism and communism, the human colonization of Mars and the splitting of humans into two hostile and competing groups known as Terrans and Martians. The resonance with the rise of the galaxy empire and its tensions with the United States is striking, and no doubt deliberate, but the tales told self-consciously defy the dualist categories of utopia and dystopia. At first, relations between the planets are peaceful. The inhabitants who have colonized Mars accept and deem beneficial their material dependence on the heartlands of the empire on Earth. On both planets, there are preparations for war but also much talk of peace. Then troubles erupt. Fractiousness and friction get the upper hand. Terrans grow nasty. War breaks out. Mars fights back, then declares independence and goes its own way. A chilling war of words and colliding stereotypes engulfs the inhabitants of the whole galaxy. Peace mediators from Mars, trying their best to put an end to the incessant tensions, are gripped by a sense of futility. They come to feel homeless, trapped between two hostile and opposing worlds. Humanity is permanently fractured. More than a few Terrans are sure that Martians live under autocratic rule. Dissent on that planet is forbidden. Faceless conformism of the masses is normal. These Terrans say that the government of Mars is expansionist—intent only on grabbing Earth's resources. From the other side, growing accustomed to constant hectoring and blind prejudice, Martians are sure that Earth is an unsavoury place where greed for riches and arbitrary power are the norm. Earth is a dog-eat-dog capitalist nightmare. The realities of life on both planets are more complicated, *Vagabonds* makes clear, yet the tensions between Earth and Mars endure. Cold peace is the galaxy's fate.

135. Hao Jingfang, *Vagabonds* (Folkestone, 2020).

A more terrifying future is sketched in the rather unknown debut novel by China's leading sci-fi writer, Liu Cixin. *China 2185* can be read as an allegorical warning about the multiple risks and grave dangers confronting militarized peace strategies in a world of global empires turbocharged with nuclear weapons. The novel is defiantly hopeful, but it also shows what might happen if our galaxy slid uncontrollably towards *hot war*.[136]

The central plot begins with a young man code-named M102 sneaking into Beijing's Memorial Hall under cover of darkness to make a holograph of Mao's brain. Experimenting with holographic simulation software, M102 scans the brains of Mao and five other deceased leaders. The six dead brains unexpectedly come back to life inside M102's computer. Millions of people are at first excited by the big news that human beings can indeed achieve immortality with the help of holographic software. Since human brains can live forever inside computers, there's even speculation that superhuman brains with superhuman bodies might be possible. The excitement rapidly wanes. When one of the resuscitated brains begins copying itself, people grow jittery. In quick time, millions of 'electronic pulse people' (*mài chōng rén*) are born within the country's computer networks. These digital minds decide to invade the National Computer Network for the purpose of establishing an internet-based regime led by the six old brains, who proudly announce the birth of the Huaxia Republic.

Unease spreads. The country of two billion people had suffered past troubles—energy crises, military tensions with the Soviet Union and the United States, sabotage of its moon base in the Copernicus crater—but nothing like this had ever happened. The first heavy-handed putsch of the new internet age had begun. Backed militarily by an unnamed, nuclear-tipped foreign power, the Republic's leaders aggressively call for the revival of national traditions, the eradication

---

136. For various reasons to do with the fact that it was written just prior to the 1989 uprisings in Beijing, Shanghai, and other Chinese cities, Liu Cixin's *China 2185* remains unpublished in hard-copy form. An electronic copy is, however, freely available at https://www.513gp.org/book/2761/142749.html (in Chinese).

of spiritual pollution, and crackdowns on dissent. They demand legal recognition as a state within a state, then go on the warpath. Their yearning for total control tempts them to do the unthinkable: to launch 'software nuclear strikes' on the country's infrastructure. Dams, chemical factories, and power plants are targeted. The country's enemies circle. The US Pacific fleet draws near; NATO's gamma laser guns are readied. Triple distress signals—SSSOOOSSS—are sounded. Thermonuclear bombs streak from their silos. With the entire galaxy tottering on the edge of self-destruction, the frightened subjects of the Huaxia Republic, facing annihilation, fight back. There's talk of the need for courage. Paeans to the indomitable human spirit. Loud calls to protect the future generation of young people. Citizen saboteurs plot to shut down the entire electricity grid. Hopes rise that the online rulers will surrender, but the whole country is plunged into darkness. With 'the huge black wings of the god of death flapping overhead', parts of the country are bathed in radioactive ash. Hot war is the hellish new reality.

What are we to make of these science fiction musings about cold peace and hot war? Their plausibility plainly can't be tested empirically, or with any measure of certainty. These allegories have a different significance: they are urgent, timely reminders of the rising dangers of war in a period of intractable tensions between competing powerful empires. As this short book of connected essays has explained, our planet is again passing through times in which 'conflicts of empires and ideologies' are part of 'a broad process of change through which the unsolved problems of the age are groping for their solution' (the words of the influential historian and political economist Karl Polanyi a century ago).[137] Whether militarized peace efforts can prove durable under these turbulent conditions, in other words, whether, in sharp contrast to the Nazi empire, which lasted no longer than a dozen years, the galaxy empire will demonstrate to the world that it

---

137. Karl Polanyi, *Tame Empires: Book Outline and Introduction*, unpublished manuscripts (1938–39), http://hdl.handle.net/10694/718.

is a 'tame empire', is by definition currently unknowable. The galaxy empire may choose to move cautiously, displaying impressive self-restraint as it wears down the stone of its American opponent one drop of water at a time. Militarized cold peace may well be our destiny. But it is still possible that the flawed 'peaking power' thesis will turn out to be true. The young empire may be stillborn, or like an exploding supernova resist its decline or be tempted to counter its foes using hot war methods. Then again, the peaking power thesis might instead apply to the United States. Perhaps the well-known prediction that 'upon the breaking and shivering of a great state and empire, you may be sure to have wars'[138] is confirmed by the never-ending wars in which the American empire is nowadays embroiled. Maybe we are witnessing the accelerating decline of the United States and a besieged, self-absorbed, and stagnant Europe, a tipping point in world history featuring the nudging aside and displacement of 'the West' by a galaxy empire capable of operating as the dominant global force in such matters as banking and finance, the brokering of peace deals, and the public management of environmental problems. If indeed this dynamic was to get the upper hand, then China might enjoy the unenviable distinction of being the world's only remaining global empire. Or perhaps, with the United States and its allies refusing to accept this outcome, the world as we know it will be ruined by the breaking and shivering of war.

There is an ancient saying that when people speak of the future, the gods laugh. For the sake of our galaxy, its living creatures, and planetary habitats, let us hope the gods are not already shedding tears.

---

138. 'Of Vicissitude of Things', in *The Essays of Francis Bacon and Other Works* (Caddington, 2009), essay 58.

Further Reading

Readers wishing to venture beyond the materials already mentioned in this book's footnotes may like to consult the following short selection of relevant publications.

Arensberg, M., Pearson, Harry W., and Polanyi, Karl, eds. *Trade and Market in the Early Empires: Economies in History and Theory*. Glencoe, IL, 1957.
Barkey, Karen. *Empire of Difference: The Ottomans in Comparative Perspective*. Cambridge, 2008.
Bennett, George, ed. *The Concept of Empire: Burke to Attlee, 1774–1947*. London, 1967.
Burbank, Jane, and Frederick Cooper. *Empires in World History: Power and the Politics of Difference*. Princeton, NJ, 2011.
Dong, Fangyi. *Xióng zhǔ yǔ tuò zhǎn* [A ruler of great talent and bold vision and expansion]. Jilin, 2006 (in Chinese).
Duverger, Maurice, ed. *Le concept d'empire*. Paris, 1980.
Ferguson, Niall. *Empire: The Rise and Demise of the British World Order and the Lessons for Global Power*. London, 2002.
French, Howard H. *China's Second Continent: How a Million Migrants Are Building a New Empire in Africa*. New York, 2014.
Getachew, Adom. *Worldmaking after Empire: The Rise and Fall of Self-Determination*. Princeton, NJ, 2019.
Go, Julian. *Patterns of Empire: The British and American Empires, 1688 to the Present*. Cambridge, 2012.
Guo, Jianlong. *Zhōngyāng dì guó de zhéxué mìmǎ* [A philosophical code of China's empire]. Xiamen, 2018 (in Chinese).
Heather, Peter, and John Rapley. *Why Empires Fall. Rome, America and the Future of the West*. New Haven, 2023.
Johnson, Chalmers. *The Sorrows of Empire: Militarism, Secrecy, and the End of the Republic*. London, 2004.

Kaplan, Robert D. *The Loom of Time: Between Empire and Anarchy, from the Mediterranean to China*. New York, 2023.
Koebner, Richard. *Empire*. New York, 1961.
Kundnani, Hans. *Eurowhiteness: Culture, Empire and Race in the European Project*. London, 2023.
Kupchan, Charles A. *The Vulnerability of Empire*. Ithaca, NY, 1994.
Lal, Deepak. *In Praise of Empires*. New York, 2004.
Li, Ji. *At the Frontier of God's Empire: A Missionary Odyssey in Modern China*. Oxford, 2023.
Lieven, Dominic. *Empire: The Russian Empire and Its Rivals*. New Haven, 2000.
Maier, Charles S. *Once within Borders: Territories of Power, Wealth, and Belonging since 1500*. Cambridge, MA, 2016.
May, Ernest R. *Imperial Democracy: The Emergence of America as a Great Power*. New York, 1961.
Mommsen, Wolfgang J. *Theories of Imperialism*. London, 1981.
Morris, Ian, and Walter Scheidel, eds. *The Dynamics of Ancient Empires: State Power from Assyria to Byzantium*. Oxford, 2009.
Motyl, Alexander J. *Imperial Ends: The Decay, Collapse, and Revival of Empires*. New York, 2001.
Mutschler, Fritz-Heiner, and Achim Mittag, eds. *Conceiving the Empire: China and Rome Compared*. Oxford, 2008.
Myers, Ramon Hawley, and Mark R. Peattie, eds. *The Japanese Colonial Empire, 1895–1945*. Princeton, 1984.
Paltiel, Jeremy T. *The Empire's New Clothes: Cultural Particularism and Universal Value in China's Quest for Global Status*. New York, 2007.
Pang, Zhongying. *Quánqiú zhìlǐ de zhōngguó juèsè* [China's role in global governance]. Beijing, 2016 (in Chinese).
Scheidel, Walter, ed. *Rome and China: Comparative Perspectives on Ancient World Empires*. Oxford, 2009.
Sharman, J.C. *Empires of the Weak: The Real Story of European Expansion and the Creation of the New World Order*. Princeton, NJ, 2019.
Singh Mehta, Uday. *Liberalism and Empire: India in British Liberal Thought*. New Delhi, 1999.
Smith, Linda Tuhiwai. *Decolonizing Methodologies: Research and Indigenous Peoples*. London, 2021.
Steinmetz, George. *The Colonial Origins of Modern Social Thought: French Sociology and the Overseas Empire*. Princeton, NJ, 2023.
Stern, Philip J. *Empire, Incorporated: The Corporations that Built British Colonialism*. Cambridge, MA, 2023.
Toh, Han Shih. *Is China an Empire?* Singapore, 2017.

Wang, Ban. *China in the World Culture, Politics, and World Vision.* Durham, NC, 2022.
Wang, Huiyao, and Lu Miao, eds. *China and the World in a Changing Context: Perspectives from Ambassadors to China.* Singapore, 2022.
Zarakol, Ayse. *Before the West: The Rise and Fall of Eastern Order.* Cambridge, 2022.
Zhang, Jianjing. *Zhōngguó jué qǐ: tōng xiàng dà guó zhī lù dè zhōngguó cè* [The Rise of China: China's Strategy on the Road to a Great Power]. Beijing, 2005 (in Chinese).
Zielonka, Jan. *Europe as Empire: The Nature of the Enlarged European Union.* Oxford, 2006.

Index

For the benefit of digital users, indexed terms that span two pages (e.g., 52–53) may, on occasion, appear on only one of those pages.

abusive power, problem of 115–122, 136, 138, 160, 162, 172, 176–78
   See also hubris; monitory democracy; phantom democracy; public accountability
administrative absorption 141
Afghanistan 79, 83, 193
Africa 1, 8, 21, 23, 27–28, 35, 50, 54–55, 76, 78–81, 87–88, 96, 137, 142, 160–161, 177, 193, 196
African Union 79, 83
air power 41–47
Alibaba group 2
All under one heaven principle (*tiān xià*) 5
   See also mandate of heaven (*tiān míng*) 5
Andrić, Ivo 136
Antarctica 21, 77, 138
Ao Shen *No More Bets* (film) 185
Argentina 21, 81, 87
Aristotle 70
ASEAN 77, 83, 195
Asia Pacific region 1–2, 19, 28, 38, 45, 48, 77, 79, 86, 94, 199, 203
Asian Development Bank 17, 92, 140
Asian Infrastructure Investment Bank (AIIB) 69, 92
AUKUS alliance, 179
Australia 18, 21, 30, 46, 87, 92, 150, 179
autocracy 10, 31, 95, 104, 108

Bahamas 94, 145
Balochistan Liberation Army 193
bamboozling 103, 172
   See also public opinion management
Bangladesh 29, 45, 47, 190, 196
Bannon, Stephen K. 150
Barmé, Geremie 106
Beidou 33, 187
Beijing Fund Town 128
Belarus 20, 83
Belt and Road Initiative (BRI) 1, 20–28, 43, 47, 78–81, 109, 144, 146, 175–6, 193, 195
   debt crisis predictions 22
Bentham, Jeremy 138
Biden, Joe 3, 107–108
Big China, Bad China story 149, 178
big power concept 5, 9, 16, 31, 45, 95
billionaires, Chinese 63–64, 122
Boao Forum 103, 195
borderlands 152–160
Bretton Woods institutions 17, 92, 139
BRICS 19, 81–83
British East India Company 75
British empire 42, 45, 50–51, 59, 75–76, 98, 137, 141, 150, 160–162, 176
Bush, George W. 11
Byzantine empire 49

Cambodia 21, 24, 77, 83–84, 105, 187
Canada 2, 18, 30, 49, 150
Caribbean region 28, 50, 144–146
cashed up rich (*tǔháo*) 72
celestials 29–30
Central Commission for Discipline Inspection 130
Central Military Commission 185
Central Security Bureau 108
Chamberlain, Joseph 98
Charles V 102
Chiang Mai Initiative 19, 77

INDEX

Chile 1, 18
China Africa Development Fund 78
China-Arab States Cooperation Forum 19
China Central Television (CCTV) 124, 130
China Development Bank 39, 43, 144, 176
China-European Union Transport Corridor 148
China Export-Import Bank 27, 144–145
China Global Television Network (CGTN) 107, 131
China-Horn of Africa Peace Conference 196
China-Myanmar Economic Corridor 39, 196
China North Industries Group Corporation (NORINCO) 189–190
China-Pakistan Economic Corridor 29, 192
  See also Pakistan
China-Portuguese Speaking Countries Cooperation and Development Fund 78
China Road and Bridge Corporation 143
China Unicom (company) 53
Chinese Academy of Space Technology 32
Chinese People's Political Consultative Conference 113
CIPS (Cross-border Interbank Payment System) 88–89
civilizational state 6
cold peace 178–204
Cold War, old and new 4, 8–9, 17, 76, 103, 149, 151, 189
colonisation, colonialism 14, 42, 116, 142, 144, 153–154, 173
  See also empire; imperialism
Comac C919 189
Compagnie française pour le commerce des Indes orientales 75
Confucianism 5, 25, 60, 91, 102, 104, 121, 167
COSCO (shipping company) 43–44, 58

Covid-19, impact of 42, 64, 72, 78, 84, 125, 132, 165, 172
Croatia 81–82, 143–144
cross border institutions 75–84
cryptocurrencies 92–94

dao, daoist 102, 167
Darwin, John 151
decoupling 2, 187
de-dollarization 85, 187
democracy life meetings 127
  See also phantom democracy; monitory democracy
Democratic Republic of Congo 170, 173
Deng Xiaoping 5, 17, 20, 164
desertification 164, 173–174
developmental peace 198
Didi Chuxing (company) 62
digital abundance 51–54
digital mutinies 134
  See also public scandals; web people
diplomats, role of China's 2–3, 5, 16, 18–19, 28, 47, 81, 86, 95, 102, 104, 136, 140, 161, 172, 175–176, 188, 191, 193, 195–198
distant troubles, at the empire's margins 135–152
dollar, US 39, 81, 85–87, 91, 93–94
  See also de-dollarization
domestic conflicts 131–135
  See also digital mutinies; public scandals
dual circulation economy 61–62
Dutch East India Company 50, 85, 137
Dutch seaborne empire 35, 50, 70, 75, 85, 137

East Asian region 28
ecological civilization 160–178
Egypt 20, 81, 190
Elvin, Mark 166
empire, concept of (*dì guó*) 9–11, 14–16
  communications, functional importance of 47–54
  denial of 9–11
  middle classes 64–75
  rise and fall of empires 96–98
  See also big power concept; emperors; galaxy empire,

imperialism; internal colonialism;
    land and sea empires;
    maritime power
emperors 15–16, 49, 66, 102, 107–114,
    135, 167
Emperor Wu 107, 109
Empresses in the Palace (Chinese
    television film series 2011) 12
Ethiopia 78–79, 81, 84
European Union 1, 137, 139, 143, 146, 148

finance and banking system, financial
    services 85–94, 90
food contamination and waste, 46–47,
    129, 170, 174–175, 187
Food and Agriculture Organization
    (FAO) 17, 78
fools, and war 184
France 2, 66, 92, 138, 144, 152, 158, 188
Fukuyama, Francis 22, 71

G 20 83, 86
galaxy empire, concept of 29–35, passim
    See also big power concept; denial
    of 9–11; emperors; internal
    colonialism; land and sea empires;
    maritime power; rise and fall of
    empires
Gambia 177
Germany 2, 57, 61, 64, 92
Ghana 50, 78
Gibbon, Edward 97
Giddings, Franklin Henry 10
global arms trade 190–191
globalization 20, 183, 198
Global Times (media platform) 101
GONGOs (governmental non-
    governmental organizations) 84
Great Green Wall 169
Great Leap Forward 168
Greece 21, 40, 43, 82, 161
Guam 199
Guangdong province 28, 130
Guangzhou (city) 73
guanxi (connections, favours) 72, 113–
    114, 139, 143
Guyana 50, 144–146

Han dynasty 13, 20, 39, 48, 109, 167, 181

Hao, Jingfang 201
Hegel, G.W.F. 180
Hobson, John A. 91
Hong Kong 2, 8, 12, 39, 46, 55, 62, 77, 87,
    90, 100, 109, 120–122, 134–6, 145, 195
hot war 178–204
Hu Jintao 126, 164, 194
Huawei (company) 41, 54, 62, 79,
    96, 127
hubris 116–117, 138, 160
    See also abusive power; monitory
    democracy; phantom democracy;
    public accountability
Hui people 158
human rights 8, 11, 80–81, 106, 147, 157
Hung, Ho-fung 38, 135
Hungary 21, 48, 82

ideology 71, 96–105, 119, 157
imperialism 10, 12, 14, 32, 48–49, 59, 77,
    91, 104, 116, 163
    See also empire concept of; internal
    colonialism
Inalcik, Halīl 99
India 12, 27, 29, 39, 50, 57, 81, 83, 140,
    157–158, 170, 187–188, 195
Indonesia 2, 24, 57, 77, 92, 158, 170
Innis, Harold 48 –49
internal colonialism 142, 153
International Monetary Fund (IMF) 1,
    17, 81, 86, 89–92, 140
International Space Station 32–33,
    191, 193
Iran 21, 81, 83, 86, 196
Italy 2, 49, 58, 84, 158

Jamaica 21, 144–145
Japan 2, 57, 77, 86, 129, 188
Ji, Xianlin (author) 74
Jiang, Zemin 67, 153, 164
Jing, Wu, *Wolf Warrior 2* (film) 185
Johnson, Boris 3

Kazakhstan 24, 83, 136, 148, 158
Keating, Paul J. (former Australian
    prime minister) 46
Kenya 78, 160, 162, 173, 177
Keynes, J.M. 53
Khmer empire 49

Kissinger, Henry 17, 149, 190
Kocka, Jürgen 70
Kunming-Montréal Global Diversity Framework (GBF) 170–172
Kyrgyzstan 83, 148

land and sea empires 35–41
  See also maritime power
Landry, Pierre 25
Laos 24, 29, 84
Latin America 1, 18, 28, 96
legal mediation committees 127
legal warfare, 183–184
Lenin, Vladimir 59, 91
Li, Keqiang 134, 164
liberal democracy, US-style 11, 59, 71, 119, 149, 151
Libya 137, 182
Lieven, Dominic 16, 102, 151
life expectancy trends, China-US compared 2
Liu, Ji (Confucian intellectual) 121
Liu, Cixin, *China 2185* (novel) 200–202
Liu, Zehua 124
Lu, Xun 112, 136, 200
Luxembourg 90

Ma, Jian 104–105
Macau 62
Mackinder, Halford John 147
Mahan, Alfred Thayer 45
Malawi 142
Maldives 45
management teams 128
McLuhan, Marshall 51
Mao Zedong 7, 17, 22, 35, 73, 107, 109, 119, 127, 168, 177, 202
maritime power 41–47
Marshall Islands 94
Marshall Plan 21, 25
Marx, Karl 63
Marxism 31, 68, 76, 99–100, 104, 106, 197
Meiya Pico (cybersecurity company) 158
Mengzi (scholar) 135
Mexico 10, 21, 29, 38, 152
middle classes 64 –75
military diplomacy 187–188
military-industrial-aerospace complex 188–191

moderately prosperous society, ideal of 67
Mongolia 83, 109, 118, 173, 198
monitory democracy 116, 122–123, 131, 176–177
  See also abusive power; hubris; phantom democracy; public accountability
Montesquieu 115–116
Mu, Ch'ien 12
Münkler, Herfried 152
Myanmar (Burma) 15, 24, 29, 39, 45, 77, 84, 105, 158, 190–193, 196–197

Namibia 76, 160
Napoleon 4, 106
National Development and Reform Commission 24, 177
National People's Congress 64, 110, 153, 164
NATO 9, 40, 81–3, 137, 183, 191
nationalism 13–14, 42, 65, 99–100
Nazi empire 161, 203
Nehru, Jawaharlal 7
Nepal 83–84
network hearings 130–131
New Zealand 2
Nigeria 21, 76, 101, 142
Nixon, Richard 17, 35
nomenklatura 69
  See also guanxi
North Korea 104
Norway 80, 140

OECD 90
Orwell, George 156, 161–162
Ottoman empire, 38, 49–50, 65, 85, 98–99, 111

pacification 194–197
Papua New Guinea 21
Paulson, Hank 187
peaking power thesis 3, 178–180, 204
People's Daily 130
People's Liberation Army (PLA) 46, 96, 181, 183, 187, 194, 196, 199
phantom democracy 25, 122–131, 138–139, 151, 153
  See also abusive power; hubris; monitory democracy; public accountability

plantation colonies 144
Poland 82
Polanyi, Karl 76, 203
poligarchs, poligarchy 25, 60, 62–63, 122, 136
Politburo 25, 111, 120, 127
political consultation work 112, 197
Portuguese empire 35, 78, 85, 98
public accountability, 25, 138
  See also abusive power; digital mutinies; hubris; monitory democracy; phantom democracy; public scandals
public opinion guidance 125–130, 156, 186
  See also bamboozling
public opinion warfare 185
public scandals 4, 133–134

Qing empire 12–13, 30, 35, 65–67, 82, 124, 132, 153, 161, 176 200
Quadrilateral Security Dialogue (QUAD) 179

rare earth minerals 173
religions, in China 15, 73, 157
renminbi currency (RMB) 20, 85–86, 93
Roosevelt, Franklin D. 10–11
Royal African Company 75
Royal Love in the Palace (Chinese television film series 2018) 12
Rudd, Kevin 150
Rumsfeld, Donald J. 11
Russia 9, 32, 57, 63, 81, 83, 86, 94, 107, 140, 147, 196
  See also Soviet Union
Rwanda 134, 142

Saudi Arabia 81, 87, 91, 190, 196
saving face, custom 172
Schmitt, Carl 36–37, 42, 44
Scholz, Olaf 195–196
Schumpeter, Joseph 59–60
science fiction 199–204
Seeley, John R. 9–10
self-restraint, and power 115, 184, 194
Serbia 40–41, 81, 176–177
Shambaugh, David 19–20
Shanghai 2, 43, 46, 55, 64, 81, 90, 202

Shanghai Cooperation Organization (SCO) 19, 69, 82–87, 140, 148, 188, 195
Shanghai Gold Exchange 87
Sihanoukville 40, 46
Sima, Qian (scholar) 48
Singapore 2, 18, 21, 28, 45, 77, 90, 93, 158, 169, 181
skittishness, of rulers 120
Smith, Adam 163
socialism, one-party 17, 59, 63, 99–100, 104–106, 111, 121–122, 171
social stability maintenance 156
South Africa 21, 54–55, 58, 78, 81, 87, 137
South China Sea 4, 42–43, 45, 109, 184, 195, 199
Southeast Asia 23
  See also Cambodia; Laos; Myanmar; Vietnam
sovereignty, concept of 6–9, 13–14, 16, 18–19, 42, 54, 79, 82, 94–6, 104, 145, 151
Soviet Union, as empire 3–4, 34, 61, 101, 151, 187, 195, 202
  See also Russia
space exploration 32–34
Special Drawing Right 86
Sri Lanka 21, 29, 45, 83, 139, 145
state capitalism 58–64, 69, 75, 77, 94, 105, 122, 168
state-owned enterprises (SOEs) 17, 23, 39–47, 53–55, 58, 61–63, 69, 77, 88, 95, 110, 131, 134, 137, 144, 147–148, 173, 176, 185, 188–190
string of pearls theory 44
Su, Changhe 197
Sudan 181–182, 193
Sun Bin, *Art of Warfare* 182
Sun Tzu, *Art of War* 183
Sun Yat-sen 13–14
Suriname 144–145
Switzerland 87, 140
Syria 189

Tacitus 96
Taiwan 4, 7–8, 39, 45, 62, 100, 109, 137, 198–99
Tajikistan 83, 147
Tanzania 176
Tencent company 53, 55–58, 96

Three Represents, doctrine of 67
Tibet 8, 12, 42, 120, 130, 153–158, 162
Tocqueville, Alexis de 65–66
Tolstoy, Leo 184
totalitarianism 73, 112, 118–119, 151
Turkey 65, 83, 99, 140, 158
Turkmenistan 147

Ukraine 6, 9, 107, 189, 196
UNESCO 17
United Arab Emirates 81
United Nations 17, 19, 42, 69, 78–80, 105, 164, 177, 181
United Nations, China's involvement in peacekeeping operations 45, 79, 181, 196, 198
United Nations Convention on the Law of the Sea 42
United Nations General Assembly 196
United Nations Human Rights Council (UNHRC) 80
United States, as global empire 1–4, 8–11, 17, 20–21, 29–35, 38, 42, 45–6, 49, 57, 64–65, 76, 79–83, 87–92, 96, 98–99, 105, 107, 116–117, 138, 140–142, 146–148, 152, 157, 161, 171, 180–183, 187–199, 201–204
Uyghurs 42, 154–155
Uzbekistan 83, 148, 190

Vietnam 24, 29, 39, 77
Von der Leyen, Ursula 3
Von Richthofen, Ferdinand 4
Vučić, Aleksandar 41

Wang, Yi 187

web people 132
See also digital mutinies; public scandals
Weber, Max 52
WeChat 56–58
Wei, Yuan 35
Wilson, Woodrow 38
Wolf Totem (novel) 166–167
World Trade Organisation (WTO) 18, 140, 171, 179

Xi, Jinping 7, 33, 100, 103, 106–114
Xi Jinping Thought 100, 107, 111
Xinhua (media platform) 26, 33, 101, 107, 157, 164
Xinjiang 8, 12, 27, 35, 42, 109, 120–122, 125, 136, 153–160, 162, 187
Xu, Xuanzi 119

Yan, Xuetong 6
Yang, Jiechi 8
Yang, Liwei, Chinese astronaut 32
yīn-yáng thinking 102, 124–125, 167–168, 180–182, 193–194
Yu, Hua 103, 124
Yu, Keping 12, 16
Yuan dynasty 12, 121

Zambia 78, 136, 177
Zhang, Weiwei 6
Zheng, Bijian 197
Zhou dynasty 13, 168
Zhou Enlai 7
Zhuang Zhou 13
ZTE (company) 53